PRAISE FOR BIZARRE LAWS

'Well assembled and written ... an enjoyable and fascinating book.'

William Roache, OBE
Actor, 'Ken Barlow' in Coronation Street

'Monty Lord's brilliant writing makes this book accessible to everyone.'

The Rt Hon Sir Robert Buckland KBE KC MP
Lord High Chancellor of Great Britain (2019-21)
Secretary of State for Justice (2019-21)
Solicitor General for England and Wales (2014-19)

'Funny and fascinating from beginning to end.'

Chris Daw KC

'An insightful, witty, clever, comprehensive, and sometimes jaw dropping examination of our justice system in the UK.'

Keith Fraser
Chair of the Youth Justice Board for England and Wales
Former Superintendent - West Midlands Police

'A series of fascinating topics, well written and carefully connected.'

Timothy W. Brennand
HM Senior Coroner, Manchester West

'An amazing feat of scholarship, beautifully written, interwoven with humour.'

Professor Jerome Carson
Psychology Department, University of Bolton

'An enjoyable, insightful and informative ... entertaining and an easy read.'

Professor Lennard Funk
Trauma & Orthopaedic Surgeon & author

'Bizarre, funny and sometimes scary!'

Hamza Taouzzale
The Right Worshipful the Lord Mayor of Westminster

BIZARRE LAWS & CURIOUS CUSTOMS OF THE UK

VOL. I.

MONTY LORD

LONDON & MANCHESTER

YOUNG LEGAL EAGLES

A CIP catalogue record for this book is available from the British Library.

ISBN 978-1-7397488-3-8 (paperback)

ISBN 978-1-7397488-4-5 (hardback)

ISBN 978-1-7397488-5-2 (audiobook)

ISBN 978-1-7397488-6-9 (eBook)

ISBN 978-1-7397488-7-6 (large print)

Cover Design: Rhianna Whiteside, Casey-Lee Herbert
& Studio 22 (Runshaw College, Lancashire)

Illustrations by: Priya Ajith

Published in England, United Kingdom, by Young Legal Eagles®
a trademark of Young Legal Eagles Ltd.

www.YoungLegalEagles.com

I dedicate this book to my parents and my friends, past, present and future, for the love and strength they give me.

I also dedicate this book to the many hard-working men and women in the legal system. So many names over the centuries, forgotten or excluded but nonetheless have had such an impact on the lives of so many through the creation, clever interpretation and commonsense reform and application of the laws of this land.

To Frankie, thank-you for sticking around and always supporting me, even when I do weird things like writing this book.

"It is the glory of English Law, that its roots are sunk deep into the soil of national history; that it is the slow product of the age long growth of the national life."

Edward Jenks, FBA

CONTENTS

FOREWORD

Having been a Member of Parliament for over 30 years and a Deputy Speaker for seven, I have participated in huge swathes of Parliamentary procedures and law, affecting the whole of the United Kingdom. Along with other Members of Parliament I have played my part in the passage of a great number of laws which together shape the functioning of British society. My long tenure as an MP has also enabled me to observe up close the reforms and changes to those many obscure laws and traditions which have together shaped the history of our Parliament and indeed the UK as a whole. From simple modernisations such as the introduction of electronic voting in divisions, to such sweeping constitutional changes as devolution and the introduction of a UK Supreme Court, the past thirty years have been transformational. This is the product of our unwritten constitution, and throughout these changes, tradition, convention, and many of our wonderful quirks and customs remain - our nation is without doubt all the better for it.

At such an early age Monty has already managed a huge number of feats the likes of which would be praised in anyone of any age. Perhaps the most impressive of these achievements is in the establishment of his own charity, Young Legal Eagles, through which Monty helps to champion the rights, views and interests of children and young people, providing information on the law, policies or decisions affecting their lives. His work raising awareness of legal rights is certainly a noble cause to be commended and his legal research skills in trawling through the many volumes of Statutes at Large demonstrate a profound understanding of the law for someone of his age. His enjoyment of the law comes across in his writing style, peppered with a typical self-deprecating northern humour.

Monty has taken a light-hearted, retrospective look at some of our most unusual laws and customs passed over the centuries. From touching upon Parliamentary conventions such the Chancellor of the Exchequer's Budget beverage to exploring the obscure British laws surrounding food and drink. Even for the most knowledgeable of legislators there is a huge number of fun facts, quirks and enlightening information to learn in this book. Monty insightfully explores the pillars of British society along with all things the public holds dear, looking into an extensive range of laws within the UK, including many of those that whilst they may have fallen into disuse, are yet to be repealed and remain in British statute.

In this well-written and informative book, Monty Lord unravels the dusty tapestry of our legal system with striking clarity and eloquence, providing an enlightening, sapient legal commentary of some of the most bizarre laws ever passed. He lifts the lid on a selection of our curious customs, holding up a mirror to our beloved British eccentricities.

The Rt. Hon. Nigel Evans MP
Deputy Speaker (The House of Commons)
Second Deputy Chairman of Ways and Means
Shadow Secretary of State for Wales (2001-03)

PREFACE

It was a warm spring afternoon, and I found myself sitting on the train, travelling down to see the Prime Minister at No. 10 Downing Street, London. A gentleman dressed in a sharp suit sat opposite me, occasionally popping his head out from behind the newspaper he was reading in front of his face. An article on the front page of his newspaper attracted my attention. It was about a seldom used ancient law. I pulled out my phone and began to do some research into the matter. It was this moment that sparked my further research. This continued on the journey home, exhausting my phone battery. Half a year later, I finally reconciled myself to the fact that my research for this book is now concluded. I say that as I look at several folders of unused material on my shelf, just prime for a follow-up.

I have always had an interest in the law. I started writing this book at the age of 16. Now 17 and with a burning passion for children's rights and ensuring equal representation through law. This was the topic of my TEDx talk and both speeches at Amnesty International HQ and the United Nations in Geneva.

Have you ever heard a bizarre saying and wondered about its origins or even whether it is true? Things like whether a Welsh person can be shot in Chester or can a woman urinate in a police constable's helmet? Within these pages, you will find the answers to those questions and some other curious customs we have developed over the centuries. This book series in three volumes, seeks to inspire, amuse, shock and educate. Yes, all at the same time.

During my endless hours spent researching for this book in the British Library reading rooms and other locations around the UK, I had to absorb a wealth of information. What started as a small research project expanded to fill an unfathomable amount of my hard drive. At times, researching our ancient laws felt like Alice falling down the rabbit hole. Probably the most challenging aspect of the research process was each time I encountered an ancient manuscript written in Norman French. I can tell you now that Google Translate isn't much help!

Ultimately, I found it a very rewarding process, especially when I came across the occasional golden nugget ... those laws that are so bizarre, even their very existence is questionable.

I wish you well. Enjoy reading, and please drop me a note to let me know how you found the book.

Monty Lord
Lancashire, England (2022)
www.MontyLord.com

INTRO

Our legal system is a veritable Pandora's box of customs, traditions and laws passed over the centuries to protect the people and regulate society.

A quick browse through the archives and ancient manuscripts produces some astonishing finds of laws passed to regulate activity and behaviour at the time, which now seem wholly absurd and anachronistic. In many cases, these laws still live on our statute books. Some are outlandishly bizarre, almost like they were created to amuse and entertain those, like us, who may read them centuries later. It is important to understand that all laws are passed with good reason ... well, what perhaps seemed a good reason at the time.

So, how did some of these bizarre laws ever come into existence?

Æthelberht, King of Kent (560-616AD), can be credited with introducing the first written Anglo-Saxon laws in England. Previously, the law had been unwritten and passed down generations orally, often subject to the vagaries of memory. With the accession of King Alfred the Great (871-899AD), many of our rules became based on those used by the Germanic people of Northern Europe. Local customs and traditions set the standards for people living in individual communities. In these early days, the church and ecclesiastical law played a large part.

In the 12th century, the Crown became more involved in the judicial system. From 1176, the Crown-appointed Royal Judges began to visit the different regions to dispense justice from Westminster. King Henry II divided the country into 'circuits' (areas) for his judges to visit. They were so feared that when they attended a small Cornish village in 1233, the entire community literally fled and hid in the nearby woods. The visiting judges, upon returning to London, would share their knowledge of local customs and, from there, decide upon a common set of laws for the whole country to follow. This became the 'common law'. Towards the end of the 13th century, the visits from the Royal Judges gave way to local courts known as 'the assizes'.

The punishments used to be a lot harsher too. In mediaeval times, trial by ordeal was an acceptable method to determine a person's guilt, until banned by Pope Innocent III in 1215. This saw the accused being subjected to horrific activities often involving fire, water or combat, with their innocence or guilt supposedly being decided by God alone. Trial by jury was offered in the 1220s, but people often refused to submit to a jury. With the passing of the first Statute of Westminster in 1275, those unwilling to submit to the jury system were imprisoned and tortured until they either submitted to trial by jury or died.

From the 13th century onwards, we began to see an increase in the amount of legislation passed by the Kings.

What we now call 'The Law of The Land' is split into two categories: common law and statute law. After the Norman Conquest of 1066, Common law evolved from local customs, which later became recognised and accepted by the visiting judges in the King's Court (*Curia Regis*). It has been developed over the centuries by the decisions and precedents made in the High Courts. Many old common law offences have since been incorporated into various Acts of Parliament, becoming statute law. Interestingly, Parliament may pass statute laws, but it falls to the judges of the High Court to interpret the meaning of these laws in any way they wish.

An Act of Parliament (also called a Statute) is a law made by Parliament. An Act starts its life as a Bill. When approved by both Houses of Parliament (The House of Commons and The House of Lords), it must then receive Royal Assent by the Monarch, after which it becomes part of Statute Law.

Over the years, statute law has redefined offences under common law. With society changing at such an alarming rate, more Acts are passed each year to modify our behaviour and define new societal norms. Regularly, Acts of Parliament are passed to repeal old, irrelevant or outdated laws. Statute law also delegates power to other authorities, such as ministers and local councils, to set local regulations under subordinate legislation, providing for their own penalties. These delegated 'subordinate' regulations come in the form of local bylaws, statutory instruments and codes. They all have a parent Act that provides the authority to make them. The Highway Code is an excellent example of this.

The law books can become filled with stagnant laws derived from the time's social conditions and concerns. Over the years, these have become so outdated that they eventually lose relevance and verge on the absurd. These ancient laws can't litter the law books for eternity, so, over time, new laws are passed, and old ones are repealed.

In 1965, a new independent body, The Law Commission, was set up to review many of the ancient laws in public consultation and to recommend to the government which laws needed to be repealed to tidy up the law books. They review all aspects of law for reform, including criminal, public, commercial, property, and family and trust law. It prunes the statute books of hundreds of outdated regulations and laws. This sounds like a lot, but when you consider that, on average, around 3,000 new pages are added to the law books each year, you get a sense of the enormity of their task. It must feel like painting the Forth Bridge or like the Greek ruler Sisyphus, condemned to roll a heavy boulder up a hill for all eternity.

Scotland has their own Law Commission that performs the same function but reviewing and pruning outdated Scottish laws.

In this Volume I of the Bizarre Laws & Curious Customs of The UK book series, you will find 21 chapters, separated into the various aspects of our British life, each containing some fantastic examples of bizarre laws. Many more outlandish laws, claims, local myths and legends came to light whilst researching this book. They are too numerous to mention and perhaps material for a future book. To keep this book pure and factual, all content has been backed by documentary evidence, with a minimum of three trusted secondary sources. A book filled to the brim with myths, salacious, and other apocryphal statements would undoubtedly sell many more copies. On the very few occasions where something has been unable to be provenanced through multiple trusted sources, this has been indicated in the text with the necessary caveat.

A fellow author told me to explain to my readers how to use this book. Well, frankly, that's entirely up to you. However, I will point out this book is multi-functional: a compendium of wisdom and absurdity; a reference book for law students; a door stop; an insect swatter; a shield to protect your eyes from stray Norman arrows; or an implement to softly repel inquisitive hobgoblins ... the decision is entirely yours!

What you're going to find between the covers of this book will hopefully also give you an insight into a lot of the history of our sceptred isle. Laws are, after all, passed to deal with contemporary issues of the time. The insight it provides us is invaluable.

"Ultimately, law is just common sense with knobs on."
(The Rt Hon Lord Sumption, OBE, FRHistS, FSA)

One last thing ...

Before you delve into the pages of this book, there is one more thing I would like to mention. As this book deals with the topic of law, it has been written within the terms of Section 6 of The Interpretation Act (1978), which seeks to avoid the constant use of the terms '*he*' and '*she*'. Irrespective of what pronoun you use, the gender you were born, or how you presently identify, no offence is intended when the law refers to one specific gender. The law has historically been written using masculine pronouns. Unless expressly stated, masculine and feminine genders are interchangeable within the text. Please bear that in mind. Also, please realise that the nature of this book takes a tongue-in-cheek look at the absurdity of some of our ancient laws. In today's society, many of these may appear bigoted, homophobic, racist, xenophobic and particularly harsh towards certain elements of society.

I would hope that most readers would take a commonsense approach and realise that it's illegal to hang, draw and quarter people, drive along a motorway with a person carrying a red flag walking in front of the car, or even convey a corpse in the back of a taxi. It goes without saying that none of the information contained within this book constitutes legal advice and is provided for general information purposes only. If you insist on using this book to test the law to its limits, I would first consult either a lawyer, a mental health practitioner, an exorcist ... or perhaps all three.

CHAPTER ONE

ALL ROADS LEAD TO ...

The UK consists of many different cities, towns, villages and hamlets, all steeped in their own individual customs and traditions, weaving together the wonderful tapestry of the history of our sceptred isle.

We are a very house-proud nation but step outside your front door, and you will be subjected to the rules of the road and the laws of the pathways. In fact, each time you step foot outside to travel between these individual communities, you will have to negotiate some rather bizarre and archaic laws before you reach your intended destination.

Over the centuries, many laws have been passed to ensure communities can live together peacefully and also to maintain both public safety & hygiene. Many of these laws have focused heavily on the streets of larger conurbations, pathways, rivers, canals, and anywhere else we might travel. From the mischievous child playing knock and run along his street to the ice cream van driving around playing discordant orchestral manoeuvres with its chimes, many of us will be breaking these laws regularly.

In this chapter, we delve into some of the laws passed at a time to protect public safety and prevent discord on our streets. They were undoubtedly as unpopular at the time of passing as they are unknown today. However, as long as these laws exist, we must remember that ignorance is no defence.

"Roads were made for journeys, not destinations."
Confucius

Knock And Run

Knock, Down, Ginger ... Ding, Dong, Ditch ... or as we call it in the UK, Knock and Run.

Even in the UK, this game has different regional names. In the North East, it's known as 'Knocky Nine Doors'. Elsewhere it's 'Knock Down Ginger', 'Chickenelly', 'Knock a Door Run' and even, somewhat menacingly, 'Knock granny out of bed'. It's a prank played mainly by children with origins dating back to the 19th century. Essentially, the knocker would knock on the victim's front door or ring their doorbell and run away before the door could be answered. As amusing as this can be for children, imagine if the victim is an elderly person or someone with severely restrictive mobility issues. Each time they get up to answer the door, they put themselves at risk.

What might seem to many to be a perfectly harmless yet annoying game is, in fact, a criminal offence outlawed in the UK in the mid-19th century. Fortunately, in today's world of camera doorbells and ever-present CCTV, knock and run no longer enjoys the popularity it once did because it's now a lot easier to identify the offender.

A specific offence was created to put a stop to this in London. Section 54(16) of the Metropolitan Police Act (1854) states that it is an offence for "*Every person who shall wilfully and wantonly disturb any inhabitant by pulling or ringing any doorbell or knocking at any door without lawful excuse, or who shall wilfully and unlawfully extinguish the light of any lamp.*" This also includes the offence of extinguishing the light of any lamp. This offence was created in the days of gas-powered street lamps.

At the same time, Knock and Run was also an offence under Section 28 of The Town Police Clauses Act (1847) making it a crime across the whole of the UK and not just in London.

This law was introduced to prevent people from causing annoyance or disturbance to others. The Town Police Clauses Act offence was repealed nationally in 2015, but it remains an offence in London. That said, it would no doubt be covered by other legislation like the catchall Section 5 Public Order Act (1986) for disorderly conduct.

So, would this be an offence for door-to-door salespeople or delivery drivers? No, it wouldn't because they have a 'lawful excuse' to be there and an implied right of access to your front door. You may, however, decide to withdraw that implied right of access by expressly stating this in a sign posted on your pathway.

Illegal to Leave an Occasional Table or Gooseneck Lamp on the Pavement

"*Excuse me, sir, is this your occasional table?*" I'm sure this same line would have been spoken several times by a constable in the Victorian era. From 1847 onwards, it would have been an offence to leave an occasional table or gooseneck lamp on the pavement. In fact, leaving any furniture on the pavement or any other goods, wares, or even a bucket on the pavement would be an offence under The Town Police Clauses Act (1847).

Section 28 of that Act makes it an offence for "*Every Person who places or leaves any Furniture, Goods, Wares, or Merchandize, or any Cask, Tub, Basket, Pail, or Bucket, or places or uses any Standing-place, Stool, Bench, Stall, or Showboard on any Footway, or who places any Blind, Shade, Covering, Awning, or other Projection over or along any such Footway, unless such Blind, Shade, Covering, Awning, or other Projection is Eight Feet in Height at least in every Part thereof from the Ground.*"

This was a very restrictive law considering it didn't just deal with people who abandoned these items on the pavement but also those who merely placed them on the pavement for a few minutes, perhaps whilst going about their business. It must have been challenging to clean the outside windows of houses or fill window boxes with soil.

Fortunately, this law is no longer live on the statute books.

The Orchestral Manoeuvres of an Ice Cream Van

Never mind Star Wars. Have you ever seen ice cream van wars? It's like the mafioso vying to control each other's territory. They seem to have their own dedicated rounds, covering specific streets and woe betide any other cream van driver who strays into their 'hood. These purveyors of flavoured ices, that bring such joy to so many children up and down the UK, like to announce their arrival. The ice cream van chimes ... providing joyous relief for children and leading many an adult to reach for the beta blockers.

Laws were passed to reduce the annoyance of these ice cream van chimes. The Department for Environment, Food & Rural Affairs issued the Code of Practice on noise from ice cream van chimes. Section 62 of the Control of Pollution Act (1974) makes it an offence to operate or permit the operation of any loudspeaker of the 'ice cream van chimes' type in the street outside the hours of 12 noon and 7 pm on the same day. The loudspeaker may also not be operated in a way that annoys people in the vicinity. In addition, the chimes must not be sounded for more than 12 seconds at a time, or more often than once every 2 minutes. They must also not be sounded more often than once every two hours in the same length of the street. Ice cream van chimes must not be sounded within 50 metres of a school (during school hours), hospitals and places of worship (on Sundays and other recognised days of worship).

On top of this, ice cream van drivers must remember that any noise emitted from or caused by a vehicle that is prejudicial to health or a nuisance to others, is also an offence under Section 79 of the Environmental Protection Act (1990).

Illegal to Walk The Streets of Newmarket With a Common Cold

The town of Newmarket in Suffolk is arguably the birthplace of horse racing in the UK. It has been connected with the sport as long ago as 1170AD. It wasn't until the reign of King James I that the sport became popular in that area, after he founded a Royal house at Newmarket in 1605. This transformed the town's fortunes.

Around that time, a bizarre law was passed, effectively making it illegal to blow your nose in the street. The wording of the law prohibited "*a person or persons going about the street with a head cold or distemper.*" Anyone found guilty had to pay a hefty fine. This law has since been repealed.

Interestingly, the law was passed, not to protect the people of Newmarket from infectious diseases but rather, to protect the horses being trained in the town, which were considered of such value to the local commerce.

Seditious Public Meetings

Free speech is something that we all too often take for granted. Many years ago, it didn't exist in the UK. If you look further afield, overseas, even in today's world, there are many countries where free speech doesn't exist. Some countries give the perception that free speech exists when in reality, it doesn't.

In our not-too-distant past, the government felt it necessary to restrict the activities of groups they deemed as subversive. This was around the time of the St. Peter's Field Massacre in Manchester, also known as the Peterloo Massacre. On this occasion, around 60,000 people had gathered to demand reform of parliamentary representation. Their intentions were misunderstood, and when the cavalry was ordered to charge at the crowds, many people were injured, and fifteen people died. It is one of the darkest moments in our recent history.

Fearful of similar activities and large crowds in London, the government passed a series of Acts to suppress such large public meetings over the years. These were the Seditious Meetings Acts of 1795, 1817 and 1819. Immediately after the Peterloo Massacre in Manchester, the third Seditious Meetings Act was passed in 1819. This was far more restrictive than its two predecessors.

The 1819 Act restricted all meetings of more than 50 people that had been called "*for the purpose...of deliberating upon any public grievance, or upon any matter or thing relating to any trade, manufacture, business, or profession, or upon any matter in church or state*" unless the meeting had been arranged by an authorised person. Oddly, it did not apply to meetings, irrespective of the meeting's purpose, where the attendees were all inhabitants of a single parish or township. Although in such cases, a written request was required to be provided to a Justice of the Peace (magistrate) at least six days before the meeting. If the magistrate was unhappy with the purpose of the meeting, they could change the time and place of the meeting at their discretion, and they could do this as many times as they pleased.

The law prohibited the carrying of firearms to such meetings. Flags and banners were also not allowed. It also made it clear that seditious meetings taking place anywhere, such as a room in a building where lectures or debates occurred, would be deemed a disorderly house. In cases where a meeting was unlawful, a proclamation would be read out to the attendees in the name of the King, requiring them to disperse. If they continued to remain, they would be punished with transportation for up to seven years.

A curious set of circumstances occurred in 1855 in Hyde Park in London. This was the location of probably the most famous Speakers' Corner. There are, in fact, several Speakers' Corners in the UK. These are areas open to the public for speaking and debating. Whilst anyone was allowed to speak freely and openly at Speakers' Corner, you were not allowed to use obscenities or blasphemy. It was also an offence to incite a breach of the peace or to insult the monarch. On this occasion in 1855, riots broke out during a protest over the Sunday Trading Bill. This Bill proposed a law to forbid buying and selling on a Sunday. This was the only day that working people had off. This didn't end well. The following year, it had to be pointed out that seditious public meetings could not be prevented at Speakers' Corner or in any of the Royal Parks. This is because the Parks belong to the Crown and are private property. Any dissenters could only be removed from the Royal Parks using trespass laws and only when each of them is provided with a notice of eviction. The police could not order public meetings to disperse from the Royal Parks.

The government suffered another setback in 1866 when it tried to suppress the Reform League's marches and protests. When they arrived at Hyde Park to attend Speakers' Corner, they discovered the park was locked. The protesters caused so much damage, tearing up hundreds of yards of railing and three days of rioting ensued. The following year, a large crowd of 150,000 people disregarded a government ban and marched to Hyde Park. This caused the then Home Secretary to resign immediately. It created quite a quandary for the government. In 1872, they passed the Parks Regulation Act, which set aside an area within each of the Royal Parks to be known as Speakers' Corner.

The Seditious Meetings Act of 1817 was not repealed until the passing of the Public Order Act in 1986.

Free speech was preserved even further after a ruling by Lord Justice Sedley in Redmond-Bate v Director of Public Prosecutions (1999). The judge held that the right to free speech was accorded by Article 10 of the European Convention of Human Rights, which included the right to be offensive. From that moment on, offensive speech was also permitted at Speakers' Corner.

Illegal to Empty Your Toilet Between 6 AM & Midnight

Toilets, or '*the privy*' as it used to be called, weren't the same system we use today. No outflow or sewage pipe was running from the privy, and residents would have to carry their outdoor toilet to empty its contents into the nearby sewers. These would often end up in the River Thames for residents of London.

With the increasing population in the 1800s, it soon became apparent that the number of toilets didn't match the population expansion. This resulted in up to a hundred people sharing the same toilet in inner-city areas of large cities like Manchester and London. Society started to realise that poor sanitary conditions led to increased disease, with raw sewage often finding its way back into the drinking water supply. This became ever more apparent during the cholera pandemic between 1826 and 1837, killing thousands of people. Lawmakers decided something had to be done about public sanitation and, more specifically, the emptying of sewage from the privy.

Section 60(4) of the Metropolitan Police Act (1839) states, "*Every Person who shall empty or begin to empty any Privy between the Hours of Six in the Morning and Twelve at Night*" is guilty of an offence. So, you were still allowed to empty your outdoor toilet, but you had to do it between midnight and 6 o'clock in the morning.

This law was repealed in 1906 by the Removal of Offensive Matter Act.

Illegal to Reserve a Parking Space Outside Your House

Ask any resident living on a street what their neighbourhood annoyances are. I can guarantee someone else parking outside their house is high on their list. The problem is, unless there is a local bylaw or resident parking restrictions in force, it isn't actually an offence to park outside someone else's house. As we saw in another chapter, it's not even an offence to park on someone else's driveway. That said, it can be highly annoying, even more so because we're British. Rather than address the matter face-on, we dwell on it for months and passive-aggressively mumble profane utterances under our breath in the vague hope they'll hear and go away.

Some residents put signs on their walls and fences outside their houses saying that the parking is private. That's all very well, but members of the public need not pay any attention to those signs. Some choose to 'reserve' their parking spaces by placing traffic cones or wheelie bins in the road outside their houses. Please don't be one of these people.

Local councils don't take too kindly to people reserving spaces on the road by coning them off. Unless you park on land you own or within a designated parking space, there is no automatic right to park in front of your house. Anyone can park there. You might not like it, but that is the law. Those who continue to cone-off the area outside their home may be liable for prosecution.

Paragraph 243 of the Highway Code asks that motorists "*do not park in front of an entrance to a property.*" However, since this paragraph uses the term "*do not*", this is not legally binding and only advice.

So, how would you be liable to prosecution? Quite simply, if you cone-off any section of the highway or place anything upon it, for example, wheelie bins, you could be classed as causing a wilful obstruction of the highway. This is an offence under Section 137 of the Highways Act (1980). If you are found guilty of this offence, you could be liable to imprisonment for up to 51 weeks, a fine, or both.

CHAPTER TWO

AN ENGLISHMAN'S HOME ISN'T HIS CASTLE

It's a funny old world. One minute you can be going about your ordinary everyday business; the next, you find yourself in the back of a police van, being carted off to the cells. There are some very bizarre and archaic laws in our land. The Law Commission has managed to repeal many of them. However, many are still clinging on, ready to pop up when you least expect them.

They say an Englishman's home is his castle, but unless you're the Sovereign, I'm sorry to tell you, this statement is simply not true. Not only is your home likely not a castle, but you technically can't stop unwanted visitors. If that doesn't make you feel insecure enough, don't even think about having a neighbourly dispute over trees, overgrown bushes, or an overly smoky barbecue.

Should you subscribe to the nineteenth-century proverb 'An apple a day keeps the doctor away', you better make sure it's not one of your neighbour's apples.

"The house of every one is to him as his Castle and Fortress as well for defence against injury and violence, as for his repose."
Sir. Edward Coke

It is Not an Offence for Someone to Park Their Car on Your Driveway and Leave it There for a Week

Allow me to paint a lovely picture for you. You've just purchased your new home and moved in yesterday. It's your pride and joy. It's in a quiet leafy suburb. You've spent the first night having the obligatory takeaway meal in your new home and go to sleep peacefully. The following morning, you wake up and walk downstairs, still half-asleep, to make a cup of tea, ready to start unpacking the rest of the boxes. As the kettle boils, you stroll to the front of the house and open the curtains, ready to be greeted by the sun's welcoming rays. Instead, you recoil in horror as you see a dirty builder's van parked on your driveway and a large family saloon. These are not your cars. Whose are they? And from where do they come?

This seems to be a growing problem, with many unsuspecting householders finding strange cars parked on their driveways, sometimes for days or weeks. The most likely explanation is that you have an unscrupulous car parking firm operating in the area. This happens more regularly in the vicinity of major airports, where the cost of long-stay parking can be exorbitant. These firms charge members of the public a fee to park their car 'safely'. Quite often, this can be in open fields, dumped on the side of the road or, as is the case here, on a stranger's driveway. In most cases, the car owners will be entirely unaware.

The fact is, this is not a criminal offence. You read that right. It is not an offence to park your car on a stranger's driveway and leave it there for a week or even longer. By that same token, a stranger can park their car on your driveway. Legally, there is very little you can do about this.

The Manchester Evening News featured an interesting article on 16th March 2022 about a concerned householder living near Manchester Airport. He had arrived home to discover a Range Rover parked on his driveway. He had given no prior permission for it to be there. The parked car obstructed his garden access, and he could not get his bins out, ready for collection. He reported the matter to the Greater Manchester Police, who informed him there was nothing they could do because it was not a criminal offence.

Parking on private land is classed as a civil trespass and a nuisance. It is not a criminal offence because it is not parked on the public highway. This is similar to a case reported in June 2018 in which a woman living in Hull arrived home to find someone else's car parked on her driveway. In that instance, Humberside Police could be of no help.

Under these circumstances, you could pursue a civil case against the driver for trespassing on your land. If you win, authorities will then be able to remove the car. You may also pursue a claim for nuisance behaviour because the driver is *"interfering with your use and enjoyment of your property."* However, as we all know, taking action through the civil courts can be a costly affair.

The Road Traffic Act (1991) delegated parking enforcement to local authorities. Even so, the council would not be able to help because your driveway is your private property and not a public highway.

Councils may remove a car from private land if it is believed to be abandoned. Background enquiries would be conducted to establish this. However, if the vehicle on private land is taxed, insured, has a valid MOT certificate and isn't in a dangerous condition, they would be unlikely to remove it.

The only reasonable solution for most of us would be to head over to the DVLA website and download Form V888, which will allow you to request the registered keeper's details of the vehicle parked on your private land. It is perfectly legal for you to do this to trace the registered keeper. However, you must demonstrate a *'reasonable cause'* for doing so. Fortunately, the DVLA website specifically lists 'tracing the registered keeper of a vehicle parked on private land' as a reasonable cause.

In circumstances where the vehicle is blocking your access to the highway, this would be an offence of obstruction of the road under Section 137 of the Highways Act (1980). The police would then have the authority to take action.

On a side note, there have been several other instances of residents around Manchester Airport who became angry with holidaymakers for parking on local roads. Provided the cars are parked legally and not abandoned, there's nothing preventing holidaymakers from parking their vehicles on a public road.

It is for this same reason that you may look through the back windows of your house & see a stranger sunbathing on your lawn. It's a civil trespass.

On a cautionary note, if you are thinking of taking action by leaving abusive messages on the car windscreens, fitting wheel clamps to the offending vehicles or even blocking them in with your own vehicle, don't. This would most likely be an offence. If someone parked on your driveway and you were to block them in, your vehicle may be obstructing the public highway. The owner of the vehicle could then call the police on you. You could end up paying a fine. Just in case you thought about using wheel clamps or getting revenge & blocking the vehicle in, those are also offences.

Apples and Blossom

In May 2022, the media reported on the case of a proud garden owner who was becoming increasingly angry after having to vacuum their garden each day due to the annoyance of the neighbour's blossom tree covering it with blankets of blossom. Believe it or not, tree disputes with neighbours are pretty commonplace.

If you're the victim of a similar circumstance and covered daily with your neighbour's blossoms and leaves, there's not much you can do other than clean it up. That's Mother Nature for you!

But what if your neighbour's tree overhangs your garden and regularly drops fruit and branches, is the fruit yours and are you able to take it? You may be surprised to learn that you may be guilty of theft if you do.

You are permitted to trim the branches or foliage that overhangs your garden at the point where they cross your boundary. But you may not take any fruit from those branches or flowers that sprout from them.

Perhaps rather annoyingly, your neighbours are under no legal obligation to prevent the blossom, leaves or fruit from falling from their trees into your garden. They are not required to clean them up either.

However, if you keep hold of any fruit that falls from their branches, even if it falls onto your garden, in law, this could be considered theft. Bizarrely, this even includes if you collect the fruit and broken branches whilst cleaning your garden and putting them in your bin. This is because it's their property, and you are treating it and disposing of it as though it's your own property.

Section 4 of the Theft Act (1968) clarifies that what is on a person's land belongs to them. It says, "*when he is not in possession of the land and appropriates anything forming part of the land by severing it or causing it to be severed, or after it has been severed.*" So, that refers to the branches, fruit or every leaf that falls from the tree, if it is rooted in your neighbour's garden but blows into yours.

With that in mind, if you collect anything that falls from the branches of your neighbour's tree into your garden, even if it's just to put them in the bin, then you may wish to make some attempt to make it available for your neighbour to recover. That does seem a bit odd.

As for pruning a neighbour's tree, you have a common law right to cut any tree branches that cross the boundary into your land. You must be careful not to cut the tree further than your boundary. Any branches or foliage you cut back must be done at your own expense. You are also not entitled to access your neighbour's land to trim the branches unless you first have their permission. On top of all this advice, you should first ensure there is no tree preservation order on the tree you're about to trim back. If there is, you face a fine if you don't obtain the necessary permission from the local authority.

Even after cutting off the branches, they remain your neighbour's property. As bizarre as it may seem, the right thing to do would be to knock on their door and ask if they want their branches back. This would be the same for any fruit, leaves or blossom that you collect and intend to dispose of in your bin. When you knock on your neighbour's door holding bin bags full of leaves and branches, I wonder what their response will be.

It's not just anything that goes over your fence. It's also things that might grow under your fence. For example, if the roots of your neighbour's tree grow under your fence and into your garden, you are permitted to remove them, at least from your side of the boundary line. If the roots of a neighbour's tree have caused damage to any of your property, they are liable to pay for that damage if it can be shown that they knew or ought to have known that damage would be caused.

Finally, let's consider those colossal towering conifer trees. They can grow wild at times, and if a neighbour doesn't keep them trimmed, they can start to block the light from reaching your windows. The Rights of Light Act (1959) states that if your property has received daylight for the last 20 years, it is entitled to continue receiving that light. So, if a nearby house lets their trees grow too tall or if they build a large fence that restricts your daylight, then you can apply to the courts to restore your daylight.

Interestingly, it is not a criminal offence to plant in your neighbour's garden or any other garden for that matter. There are some exceptions. Public places like the local crown bowling green and Royal Parks all have their own bylaws. Also, you can't grow anything illegal. It is an offence to grow certain species of invasive plants under The Wildlife and Countryside Act (1981). If you decide to grow something for 'medicinal' purposes, you will contravene Section 6 of the Misuse of Drugs Act (1971) and quickly find yourself behind bars.

With all that said, provided you cause no damage in the process, it is not a criminal offence to plant a selection of highly poisonous Water Hemlock, Deadly Nightshade, Foxglove and Monkshood in your neighbour's window boxes for their delectation.

Whilst I said it was not a criminal offence, that doesn't, however, stop an individual from taking action through civil courts for nuisance. This isn't without precedent. In 1945, the Bournemouth Evening Echo newspaper reported on the case of Mrs. Irene Graham of Boscombe. She recalled a German prisoner of war who worked on her garden weekly until his repatriation at the end of the Second World War. She'd described him as a *"nice friendly chap."* Although, she was rather displeased when crocuses came up in the middle of her lawn the following February, spelling the words '*Heil Hitler*'.

Fined for Having an Excessively Smoky Chimney

Barbecues and garden fires aren't the only place that produces excessive smoke. Chimneys are also a producer of smoke. With the recent energy price rises, many homeowners are turning to alternative ways to heat their homes. Some are considering installing a wood-burning stove.

According to a recent European Public Health Alliance report, wood-burning stoves are the single most significant cause of outdoor air pollution, causing approximately 40% of the total air pollution in the UK. This reportedly translates to around £0.9bn a year in health-related damages. Despite this, the report also says that wood-burning stoves produce only 6% of heat in UK homes.

Fortunately, the law recognises this and aims to reduce the amount of pollution caused by their use. Sadly, many sellers won't be informing their purchasers of the laws concerning this, so you must read on to avoid falling foul of the law.

The Clean Air Act (1993) enables local authorities to declare areas of their district to be what's known as a 'Smoke Control Area'. Limits are imposed on households within these Smoke Control Areas regarding how much smoke is permitted to be released from household chimneys. It also prevents the burning of unauthorised fuel.

My advice is to check your local authority website to see whether you reside in a Smoke Control Area. If you do, double-check the fuel types you are permitted to burn. If caught releasing too much smoke by your local authority, you could face a fixed penalty of £300. For those caught burning unauthorised fuel in a Smoke Control Area, the fine increases to £1,000, enough to burn a sizeable hole in your wallet.

Flying Drones Over People's Homes

It's a lovely quiet summer's day. You're sat outside sunbathing and enjoying the British air in the privacy of your garden. Suddenly you hear the distant hum of what sounds like an approaching swarm of bees. With some trepidation, you turn your gaze to the sky and notice a black box hovering above your garden. It's a drone!

Now for a quick lesson on drones. Drones are unmanned aerial vehicles (UAVs), generally controlled by a person on the ground. They are perfectly legal to use and come in a range of sizes, from the large commercially-available drones to the smaller ones. Drones can be flown anywhere in the UK that is not restricted airspace, provided some rules and laws are followed.

The Civil Aviation Authority (CAA) regulates the flying of drones in the UK, which are covered by the Unmanned Aircraft Systems (UAS) Regulations and the 2016 Air Navigation Order.

Whilst the law permits drones to be flown in unrestricted airspace, there are a few prohibitions to restrict drone movements, especially in busy residential areas or where serious harm could be caused if the drone accidentally fell out of the sky.

Drones must not be flown within a 5km radius of any airport. Drones must fly below an altitude of 120 metres. Most larger drones must also be kept a minimum of 50 metres horizontally from any person (except the controller). They are not permitted to be flown over other people, including those in vehicles.

The problem is that the majority of drones you see flying around these days are smaller drones weighing less than 250g. The restrictions are more flexible on these smaller, lighter drones. For example, you can fly them closer to people and even fly them over people lawfully.

So, back to the scenario where you're sitting relaxing in your garden, reading the latest edition of Knitwear Monthly and hearing the distant hum of an approaching drone. You look at the sky and see that it's a small drone weighing less than 250g. The drone hovers for a good 10 minutes over your house, apparently watching you. I'm sure we can all agree that this is very intrusive. Most likely, you would stop what you are doing, utter a few expletives and take cover indoors until the drone has gone away. Is there anything you can do?

Unless you live within 5 km of an airport and provided the drone isn't being operated dangerously, then irrespective of the fact that it appears to be ruining the privacy of your garden, there isn't much you can do about it. You could try to locate the drone pilot. If they're a company or organisation, they may be in breach of data protection regulations by taking photographs or videos in a place where there is a reasonable expectation of privacy, i.e., your garden. Under these circumstances, the General Data Protection Regulations (GDPR) would apply to any images or video recordings made by the drone operator. The good news is that any drone fitted with a camera must be registered with the CAA, even if it weighs less than 250g. The drone operator may be guilty of a public nuisance or a public order offence if the drone is being flown in a disorderly manner.

Bizarrely though, there isn't much you can do. Flying a drone over private property is not even a trespass. The High Court ruling in the case of Bernstein v. Sky Views and General Ltd [1978] found that a property owner does not have unqualified rights over the airspace above their land. As we have seen elsewhere in this chapter, they have some rights, but only to "*such height as was necessary for the ordinary use and enjoyment of his land and the structures upon it.*"

Before you get any wild ideas about shooting down a drone or throwing projectiles at it, as it overflies your garden, think again. At a minimum, you could be found guilty of committing criminal damage. Remember that a drone is essentially an aircraft. So, by shooting at a drone, you could end up being charged with endangering an aircraft, the same as if you shot at an aeroplane. This carries a prison sentence.

Houses In Scotland Can Not Have a Pink Front Door

Eighties R&B singer Shakin' Stevens would have no issue with his 'Green Door' in Edinburgh. However, for some other unlucky householders, their choice of paint colour may get them into a spot of bother. In October 2022, one Edinburgh resident was left pink-faced when she received a letter from the City of Edinburgh Council, insisting that she repaint her front door white or face a fine of up to £20,000.

Miranda Dickson living in the historic Georgian area of the city, received this shocking request from the local council shortly after repainting her front door the colour pink. The council informed Ms. Dickson that her door was not in keeping with the local historical character and ordered her to paint her front door to a more "*suitable*" colour which should be "*dark and muted.*"

Ms. Dickson challenged the decision taken by the council and pointed out that there were dozens of other brightly-coloured doors in her neighbourhood. She pointed out that her door was only pale pink and not ostentatiously bright. She also alluded to the fact that Georgians often used the colour pink.

Confused with this request, she sought clarification from the council on what colour she should choose to paint her front door. The council stated that they were "*unable to advise.*" The council's request seems to have come about after receiving just one complaint from an anonymous resident living near Ms. Dickson.

After Ms. Dickson initially refused to repaint her door, the council issued an enforcement notice against her for failing to apply for planning permission for her door colour.

This is not the first time a resident in Scotland has been ordered by their local council to repaint their pink coloured front door to a different colour. In April 2020, a North Berwick, East Lothian resident received a notice from her local council requiring her to make a retrospective planning application after she painted her front door pink.

On this occasion, the issue only came about due to a single complaint from a local resident who stated that the door's colour was "*too bright*" and not in keeping with other street doors. Fortunately, common sense prevailed after six nearby residents submitted letters of support, and the council decided the pink door could remain.

Illegal to Put Rubbish Into Someone Else's Bin

Imagine walking along the street, eating a sandwich or drinking from a local coffee shop cup. You finish your sandwich or drink and decide (hopefully) to do the community-minded thing and not throw it down as litter. But the local council have made no provision for bins in the street where you are. Not to worry, it's bin day, and all the residents have placed their bins out in the street. Do you throw your rubbish discretely into one of their wheelie bins and quickly walk off?

Before you do that, consider the following. The illegal discarding or depositing of waste materials and rubbish products on land or water is contrary to the Environmental Protection Act (1990). You could be guilty of littering if you dispose of your rubbish in someone else's bin without their permission. The law sees this as antisocial behaviour, as it's classed as fly-tipping. Whilst you think you're doing a good deed by not dropping your litter on the ground and finding a bin to put it in, someone else has paid for the right to use those bins exclusively. This is usually in the form of council tax or to a private contractor if it's a bin belonging to retail premises or an office.

The situation is further exacerbated if the bin is already full and adding your waste to it makes it start to overflow. This could incur the householder additional costs, or the council may even refuse to collect their rubbish. It's known as 'bin stuffing'.

Section 87 of this Act makes it an offence to throw down, drop or otherwise deposit and leave litter in any place open to the air, including private land. The same law also applies to placing your rubbish in bins belonging to offices and shops and, of course, one of those large yellow builder's skips that we seem to find on many streets these days.

Between 2016 and 2017, more than one million instances of fly-tipping were dealt with by the councils in England alone. The estimated clean-up cost for this was more than £58 million. These fly-tipping laws were initially introduced to combat unlawful waste disposal by companies, either by tipping their waste 'on the fly' or incorrectly labelling their hazardous waste.

Even if you're thinking, well, it's not a full bin bag of waste that I'm shoving into my neighbour's bin, it's just a drinking cup. That makes no difference. Of course, the amount and frequency of waste unlawfully disposed of would dictate the severity of the punishment.

We have the added element of each household's different waste recycling bins these days. Many local councils will charge a monthly fee for the collection of garden waste bins. So, if you're dumping your garden waste into someone else's bin that they've paid for, then you can see how this is unfair. Many shops and office premises have to pay for the weight of their rubbish collection. So, any additional rubbish you add to their collection will incur additional costs for them.

Illegal to Remove Items From Someone Else's Bin

There's an old saying ... *"One Man's Trash is Another Man's Treasure."* But can it be your treasure? If it's someone else's rubbish and they've thrown it in the bin, are you legally allowed to take it?

The answer to this question is not entirely clear, but, in most instances, it would not be legal. Technically it is theft if you take something from another person's bin without their permission. However, this is a grey area because it depends on the motivations of the person taking it and whether they intend to treat it as their property.

According to the Theft Act (1968), property continues to belong to a person unless it has been abandoned entirely. When people place their rubbish into a bin, they haven't abandoned it. They have left it there, intending for the council to come and remove it. When the council has removed it, it is no longer the property of the person who put it in the bin. They cease 'owning' it. It then becomes the council's property to dispose of in the usual manner.

The Theft Act (1968) states that a person is guilty of theft if he *"dishonestly appropriates property belonging to another with the intention of permanently depriving the other of it."*

Funnily enough, the test for what is considered 'dishonesty' changed very recently. In the 2017 case of Ivey v Genting Casinos (UK), the Supreme Court stated that the new test for dishonesty is: what was the defendant's actual state of knowledge or belief as to the facts; and was his conduct dishonest by the standards of ordinary decent people? The law also accepts that if a person intends to throw something away and wishes to claim no further ownership of it, this would be considered abandonment. If something is 'abandoned', it has no owner legally, so if anyone else takes it, they would not be guilty of theft.

There have been some interesting cases over the years concerning people taking property which they think has been thrown away. In the 1877 case of R v Edwards and Stacey, a farmer shot and buried three diseased pigs. Later that night, Mr. Edwards and Stacey dug up the pigs and sold them to the local butcher. They were found guilty of theft because even though they were no longer of any value to the farmer and he had buried them, he had not abandoned them. They were, therefore, still his property.

In a far more recent case, that of Rickets v Basildon Magistrates court (2011), a man had removed bags of clothing left outside a charity shop. He was charged with theft. The judge ruled that although the clothing had been discarded and abandoned by their original owners, their ownership was intended to pass to the charity shop.

If you thought that taking something that had been thrown into a bin was not theft, then you're not alone. Many people labour under the misapprehension that property left in a bin or a skip on the side of the street is theirs for the taking. As you can see, this is not the case.

In another case from 2011, Sacha Hall of Essex removed a bag of food from a bin belonging to Tesco supermarkets. Tesco claimed the contents of the bin belonged to them because they sent thousands of pounds of leftover meat to be burned for electricity to minimise food waste. The case was sent to court, and Ms. Hall denied theft after taking some discarded potato waffles, pies and ham from a bin outside Tesco express. A store power cut had spoiled the food, so the store binned it. Ms. Hall stated that a friend had delivered the bag of food to her, which had come from the store bin. Rather than let the food go to waste, she took it to feed her family. Eventually, she admitted to handling stolen goods and was given a conditional discharge.

This would be the same if you were to remove items from a builder's skip left on the side of the road. If in doubt, knock on the front door and ask the person for permission to remove items from the skip. They may even be thankful for it.

Illegal to Put Your Wheelie Bin Out on The Wrong Day

It's midday, and as I look out of my window, I see several neighbours have already dragged their wheelie bins out to the pavement. It's not bin collection until tomorrow lunchtime. People live such busy lives that it's often ideal to move the wheelie bin to the front of the house, ready for collection when you remember and get a chance to do it. Is that wrong? Apparently, yes, it is. As hard as this is to believe, some councils in the UK have classed a bin wheeled out to the pavement when it's not collection day, as fly-tipping.

This must be particularly harsh for households with several different wheelie bins for different waste products. For example, in our house, the grey bin is for general waste; the blue bin is for plastic and glassware; the brown bin is for garden waste; the green boxes are for paper and cardboard. So, what happens if you put the wrong bin out but on the correct day? In other words, let's say today is the day for collecting general waste, the grey bin. Through simple human error, I take out the blue bin. This would be the same scenario, and some local authorities would be inclined to fine the householder for doing such a thing.

Section 46A of the Environmental Protection Act (1990) enables councils to issue a fixed penalty to householders who fail to comply with their local waste collection rules. This is generally done if the rubbish causes or is likely to cause a nuisance in the neighbourhood or has a negative effect or is likely to have one on the local amenities.

Common sense would argue that the spirit of the law is to address circumstances where a resident places multiple bin bags and general waste strewn across the pavement. Not situations where well-meaning members of the public put their rubbish bins out a day early.

In the first instance, councils would issue a fixed penalty notice (FPN) with a fine. Householders who don't pay the fine risk going to court. The government has issued guidance to councils that they can not issue FPNs to householders for leaving bins out for just a few hours before collection. This, however, comes down to the council's interpretation of the word 'few'.

There have been cases in the past where councils fined householders £110 each for putting their bins out too early or wheeling them back too late. In multi-occupancy properties, this can raise a lot of revenue for the town hall coffers. In Leicester, a household of four students had to pay £110 each. In 2016, residents of Stoke-on-Trent were shocked to receive notices threatening them with £80 fines or a day in court if they left their rubbish bins out over the Christmas period.

A Freedom of Information request showed that in 2018, 19 councils issued fines for breaches of these bin rules. My advice is to double-check your bin collection dates.

CHAPTER THREE

ANCIENT JUSTICE

B ritain is known worldwide for having a fair, transparent and tolerant justice system. It hasn't always been that way, with all sorts of blood feuds and unfair trials during mediaeval times.

Our judicial systems have matured over the centuries. We pick up in this chapter from our Anglo-Saxon ancestors with some of their unorthodox methods for dispensing 'like for like' justice. People were valued at a set price, from the forlorn slave and commoner to the King himself.

In this chapter, we'll learn about a time when families who were wronged could hold blood feuds over the relatives and ancestors of the perpetrator. We also see how it was perfectly legal to buy and sell stolen property until as recently as 1994. We look at one of the most significant pieces of legislation ever signed by a King, the Magna Carta and its effects on society, even to this day.

"At his best, man is the noblest of all animals;
separated from law and justice he is the worst."
Aristotle

The English Common Law of Deodands

A Deodand is something that is forfeited because it caused death. It has its foundations in English common law, dating back to the eleventh century.

During Anglo-Saxon times, whenever death or serious damage was caused by a person's property or their animals, these would be classed as banes. In an early form of compensatory damages known as *'noxal surrender'*, the property or animal was handed over to the victim or their surviving relatives. Following the Norman Conquest, many of these earlier Anglo-Saxon customs were either lost or altered in some way. This seems to have happened when England transitioned from the system of noxal surrender to deodand.

The term is derived from the Latin *'deo dandum'*, which means 'to be given to God'. Under this law, an item of personal property (chattel) would be forfeited as a deodand if it was decided that it had caused the death of a person. This chattel could be anything from a horse, a wagon, a haystack or a myriad of other items of personal property, including animals.

When a person had been killed, the coroner's jury would decide whether there was a causal link between the death and the item of property. If they determined that was the case, they would then appraise the value of that item of property, and the owner would be ordered to pay a fine equal to this amount to the relatives of the injured party. This was the deodand. On other occasions, the item of 'guilty' property was forfeited by the Crown. They would then sell this chattel, and the sale proceeds would be distributed amongst religious or charitable causes, quite often in the form of alms for the poor. The Coroner's Rolls often mentioned moving property, for example, horses, oxen, carts and boats. It also referred to static property like stones, trees and tubs. In cases where the property owner could not pay the deodand, his township would be held responsible for paying the fine to the injured party. The common law of deodands was practised throughout the Tudor and Stuart periods, although not as frequently as during the Middle Ages.

A newspaper article from The Windsor and Eton Express, dated 20th October 1837, refers to a Coroner's inquest into the death of labourer James Stevenson. Mr. Stevenson had died after falling from a cart on Chobham Common. In this sad case, Mr. Stevenson suffered from hearing loss. A person began talking loudly to him so that he could better listen to what they were saying. The horse took this raised voice as a cue to move off. At this point, Mr. Stevenson, standing on the back of the cart, lost his balance and fell off, hitting his head on the ground. The attending doctor gave the cause of death as a violent concussion of the brain. The jury returned a verdict of *"Accidental death, with a deodand of one shilling on the horse."*

This bizarre ancient remedy of deodands continued into the mid-nineteenth century. Its demise occurred during the Industrial Revolution when the rapid expansion of the railway network and lack of safety laws saw a dramatic increase in railway-related deaths.

Under common law, compensation could only be paid for physical damage to the claimant or their property. This meant that the relatives of those killed on the railways were not entitled to claim for their loss. As a result, public hostility grew towards the railways. Coroner's juries circumvented this by offering deodands to the victim's relatives to compensate them and punish the railway operators.

In November 1838, a locomotive exploded on the Liverpool to Manchester line, killing the engineer and the fireman. The coroner's jury assessed a deodand of £20. The following year, a much higher deodand was assessed, based on the total value of the locomotive, £1,400. In this case, the locomotive had struck a man and his horse at a street crossing.

This reached a climax on a foggy Christmas Eve in 1841 when a train on the Great Western Railway ran into a landslide, resulting in the death of eight passengers. The Coroner's Inquest jury valued the train at £1,000 and awarded that fine as a deodand. A Board of Trade inspector later exonerated the railway company, quashing this deodand, leaving the relatives with no compensation. This led to the passing of the Fatal Accidents Act (1846), which compensated the victims of railway accidents. That same year, The Deodands Act was passed, finally abolishing this curious common law form of compensation.

Keep It In The Family

When someone coined the phrase 'keep it in the family', I don't think this is quite what they had in mind. An ancient Anglo-Saxon law later abolished by King Canute (1016–1035) dealt with stolen property. If stolen property was found in a house, and an occupant of that house was named the thief, his wife and the whole family, including the infant in the cradle, were all punished equally as though they were guilty.

It wasn't just the humans in the household that would be found guilty. Other Anglo-Saxon laws treated all domestic animals in a house as accessories in crimes of violence. All those animals would then be sentenced to death.

Blood Feud

Following the withdrawal of the Romans from England around 400AD, the individual Anglo-Saxon kingdoms began to flourish, each with its own laws and customs. By today's standards, some of these laws were as horrifically gruesome as they were bizarre.

The Anglo-Saxon Kings allowed the victims of crime to punish the criminals themselves. This system became known as '*Blood feud*' and focused heavily on retaliation as a form of sentencing. For the more serious offences, for example, murder, the notion of imprisoning murderers hadn't even been considered. Instead, the Kings allowed retribution through blood feuds. Where a person had been murdered, the closest next-of-kin was permitted to track down and kill the murderer.

This ancient penal system wasn't a complete bloodbath. There were strict rules to be observed. The severity of the crime committed led to the method of punishment, which, more often than not, was through compensation. There were other rules as well governing blood feuds. If the person murdered was himself a convicted thief, then a blood feud was not permitted. Also, if the person who did the killing did so in defence of his Lord or a close female relative, then the King did not sanction a blood feud.

There were two distinct drawbacks to this method of sentencing. Blood feuds often lead to further violence, lasting several years and perhaps wiping out generations of 'feuding' families. It also presumed that the victim's relative would be happy to use violence themselves. In those instances where the next of kin felt unable or unwilling to track down and kill the murderer, there was no other method of justice available to them.

During the reign of King Alfred the Great (886-899AD), a blood feud could only commence after an attempt was made to obtain compensation for the relatives for the loss of life. This was known as 'Wergild.' Blood feuds were still permitted but only if compensation could not be sought.

The Catholic Church also sought to avoid further violence with blood feuds, influencing the event of death through compensation to the relatives of the victims of the murder. Blood feuds continued until just after the Norman Conquest of 1066.

Wergild

Sometimes, Anglo-Saxons believed, in retribution for killing, it was possible to settle a feud between families without further bloodshed or the need to resort to 'Blood feud'. This alternative form of settlement was based on a system of fines as compensation to the victims of crime or their families. This was known as '*Wergild*'. This literally translated as 'man-price'. This system was based on a monetary value established as compensation to the victim's family for the loss of life.

This system of compensation was unfairly unequal, and the level of fine (Wergild) depended on the victim's social standing. For example, the highest fine was for the killing of the King or a Lord. The Wergild paid for the killing of a nobleman was 300 shillings, whereas the Wergild for the death of a freeman was 100 shillings. The murder of a peasant or a slave was considerably lower. Lower still was the Wergild that had to be paid for killing a Welshman.

In some instances, a portion of the Wergild was paid to the King because he had lost one of his subjects, and an amount also went to the feudal Lord if he lost one of his slaves. Interestingly, the Wergild for a woman was more than for a man and could often be twice as much as that given for a man.

Wergild wasn't just used to compensate for unlawful killings. During the reign of King Alfred, it was also used as a form of compensatory damages to settle cases of physical injury. The law started to regulate how much compensation (Wergild) would be paid for each body part lost or injured. A severed nose was 60 shillings, an eye fetched 50 shillings, an ear cut off was 30 shillings, 20 shillings for a big toe, 9 shillings for a little finger, and the victim of a broken arm would only receive 6 shillings.

The Market Overt Rule

Colchester is believed to be England's oldest historic market town. Market towns were small towns in rural areas, legally entitled to hold a weekly market. This was often granted by charter. The Domesday Book of 1086 lists fifty such markets in England. These grew in popularity over the centuries as a place for local commerce. They were also the place where local thieves could sell their recent gains. A bizarre 800-year-old law essentially legitimised the sale and purchase of stolen goods in a public place.

The Market Overt rule or *marché ouvert* (Norman French for '*open market*') was an unusual English legal principle first introduced in 1189. It was known colloquially as the 'Thieves Charter' because it provided an early form of consumer protection for those who purchased stolen goods. Generally, in law, stolen goods remained the property of the original rightful owner. It doesn't matter how often the property changes hands; this is still the case. This is why it has always been vital to undertake due diligence when you purchase an item and are not confident of its origin. If it is stolen, not only do you forfeit that property and any money that you paid for it, but you can also be found guilty of handling stolen goods under Section 22 of the Theft Act (1968), which carries a prison sentence of up to 14 years.

However, according to the ancient Market Overt rule, if you purchased an item openly sold in a designated marketplace between sunrise and sunset, the property was automatically yours. This was even the case if it was later proven that the property had been stolen, provided you purchased it in good faith and were unaware that the item was stolen. The Market Overt rule came into existence when people generally didn't travel too far from their own town. Most trade, including that in stolen goods, was conducted in their local marketplace. It was assumed that the victim of any theft would diligently check their local marketplace on the next market day to see whether their stolen property had turned up for sale.

Bermondsey Market in south London was one such designated market that became a hotbed for the sale of stolen goods. This ancient law started to become an embarrassment for the government when in the early 1990s, several portraits painted by famous eighteenth-century artists and worth millions, were stolen and turned up for sale on a market stall. Even more embarrassingly, they had been stolen from The Honourable Society of Lincoln's Inn, one of the four Inns of Court to which barristers belong.

Two of the stolen portraits were painted by Thomas Gains-borough, and a third by Sir. Joshua Reynolds. Together they were valued at around $11 million. All three paintings were sold for less than £100 each. Unfortunately, even though it was proven that the paintings had been stolen and were worth a lot more, nothing could be done by the police. They had been sold legitimately under the Market Overt rule. So, their new owner, who had paid less than £100 each, was now a millionaire.

This caused outrage and led to the passing of The Sale of Goods (Amendment) Act (1994), otherwise known by its long title as '*An Act to abolish the rule of law relating to the sale of goods in market overt.*'

Magna Carta

The Magna Carta, one of the most famous documents in the world, arguably forms the basis of English law and certainly the foundations of the criminal justice system.

This Charter set out the laws that every person, including The King, had to follow in 63 clauses. It stated that every person was subject to the law and nobody was above it. Essentially, it was the earliest form of the rule of law. It was considered so important that, at the time, copies were sent out to every county in England to ensure everyone knew of its existence and the laws. In 1965, Lord Denning gave his assessment of the Magna Carta, describing it as *"the greatest constitutional document of all times ... the foundation of the freedom of the individual against the arbitrary authority of the despot."*

Today, only four original copies of the Magna Carta survive. Two are kept in the British Library, one is at Lincoln Castle, and the fourth is on display at Salisbury Cathedral. The Magna Carta enjoyed its 800th anniversary on 15th June 2015. It was even cited as recently as 2020/21 in an attempt to defy the government's Covid-19 measures.

Although commonly called the Magna Carta, its full title is the '*Magna Carta Libertatum*', which in mediaeval Latin stands for the 'Great Charter of Freedoms'.

King John of England granted this early Royal Charter on 15th June 1215 at Runnymede, a water meadow on the banks of the River Thames near Windsor. The King knew that many powerful land barons in England were looking to overthrow him, so this first draft of the Magna Carta in 1215 was more about the King making peace by giving up some of his power to the rebel barons. It restrained the King's authority and provided protection for the church, access to justice, protection from illegal imprisonment (especially for the barons), and prevented the King from exploiting feudal payments. As it happened, neither The King nor the barons adhered to their commitments. This first Charter was annulled by Pope Innocent III just ten weeks later.

Following the death of King John a year later, his 9-year-old son became King Henry III. A revised edition of the Magna Carta was issued that same year, with much of the previous content omitted. Subsequent versions were issued in 1217 and 1225. His son, King Edward I, reissued the Magna Carta in 1297 and entered it into the statute role, confirming it as part of England's statute law.

The Magna Carta remained in this form, untouched, for almost 550 years until Clause 26 was repealed during the reign of King George IV with the passing of the Offences Against the Person Act (1828). This clause dealt with inquests and debts due to the Crown.

During the reign of Queen Victoria, we saw the most significant number of changes to the Magna Carta. This started in 1863 with the Statute Law Revision Act, which repealed 17 clauses. These were considered obsolete and mainly related to mediaeval tolls and other things that had become outdated. A further six clauses were repealed before the end of Queen Victoria's reign.

In 1969, Queen Elizabeth II gave Royal Assent to the Statute Law (Repeals) Act which repealed a further six clauses from the Magna Carta, including the bizarre Clause 23, which entitled townsmen and freemen to build as many bridges over rivers as they like and wherever they want.

This brings us into the 21st century, where much of the original Magna Carta has long since been chipped away, with just three clauses remaining on the statute books in England and Wales. These relate to the freedom of the English church, the *"ancient liberties"* of the City of London, and the right to due legal process.

Clause 1 relates to the liberties of the English Church. It states,

"First, that we have granted to God, and by this present Charter have confirmed for us and our heirs in perpetuity, that the English Church shall be free, and shall have its rights undiminished, and its liberties unimpaired. That we wish this so to be observed, appears from the fact that of our own free will, before the outbreak of the present dispute between us and our barons, we granted and confirmed by Charter the freedom of the Church's elections - a right reckoned to be of the greatest necessity and importance to it - and caused this to be confirmed by Pope Innocent III. This freedom we shall observe ourselves, and desire to be observed in good faith by our heirs in perpetuity. To all free men of our Kingdom we have also

granted, for us and our heirs for ever, all the liberties written out below, to have and to keep for them and their heirs, of us and our heirs."

Clause 13 relates to the ancient privileges of the City of London. It states,

"The City of London shall enjoy all its ancient liberties and free customs, both by land and by water. We also will and grant that all other cities, boroughs, towns, and ports shall enjoy all their liberties and free customs."

(Clause 13 in the 1215 charter; clause 9 in the 1297 statute)

Clauses 39 & 40 relate to the Right to Trial by Jury. It states,

"No free man shall be seized or imprisoned, or stripped of his rights or possessions, or outlawed or exiled, or deprived of his standing in any other way, nor will we proceed with force against him, or send others to do so, except by the lawful judgement of his equals or by the law of the land. To no one will we sell, to no one will we deny or delay right or justice."

(Clauses 39 and 40 in the 1215 charter; clause 29 in the 1297 statute)

Interestingly, Magna Carta was mentioned in the media repeatedly during the 2020/21 lockdown periods due to the Covid pandemic. Many business owners incorrectly interpreted the Magna Carta, using it to assert their rights to continue trading during the lockdown. This was despite the fact that the government has passed the Coronavirus Act (2020) enabling them to require certain businesses to close during these lockdown periods from 5th November 2000 due to the rise in cases of Covid-19.

At the time, social media was abound with stories of people asserting their rights under Article 61 of the Magna Carta. Unfortunately, it wasn't a plausible argument, as Article 61 was repealed shortly after the original 1215 Magna Carta. It didn't even make it into the second iteration issued by King Edward in 1297. Besides this, Article 61 of the original Magna Carta only applied to the twenty-five barons, not the general public. It endowed them with authority to "*assail*" the Sovereign.

This didn't stop several business owners from breaching lockdown laws and continuing to trade. On 5th November 2020, a hairdresser in Oakenshaw, Yorkshire, placed a notice on her shop door stating,

"NOTICE: I DO NOT CONSENT. This business stands under the jurisdiction of common law. As the business owners, we are exercising our rights to earn a living. Under Article 61 of Magna Carta 1215 we have a right to enter into lawful dissent if we feel we are being governed unjustly. Contrary to common belief, our Sovereign and her government are only there to govern us and not rule us. This must be done within the constraint of our common law and the freedoms asserted to us by such law. Nothing can become law in this country if it falls outside of this simple constraint ... I am not under any obligation, nor will I, answer any questions or give you any details. I am a living person and statutory regulations only apply with my consent."

The hairdresser was fined a total of £17,000 by officers from Kirklees Council for breaching the Covid restrictions. After she continued trading, Bradford magistrates issued an injunction forcing her salon to close. She was eventually convicted of ten offences and fined £6,000 with an order to pay £2,200 costs. The original £17,000 fine was subsequently dropped by the council.

CHAPTER FOUR

APPEARANCE

T hese days image is everything. You only need to turn on the TV or open a newspaper or magazine and find celebrities sporting the latest fashionwear and accessories. As a nation, we have become preoccupied with our outward appearance and how those around us perceive us.

The focus is more on how we look than on our words and deeds. It is true that part of communication is visual and how we present ourselves to others. But what's the point if wearing the latest high-fashion accessory or clothing is just to keep up with the Joneses? This has plagued our society for many centuries, as seen in this chapter. Over the years, the Crown and Parliament have introduced laws to restrict our appearance and ensure we don't become overly extravagant.

In this chapter, you will find fantastic stories about facial hair and laws passed to regulate our appearance. We see how a couple of our monarchs had a particular disdain for anyone else sporting great beards. Women didn't evade scrutiny. It wasn't long before those wearing make-up were viewed with suspicion and contempt.

*"As a rule, men worry more about what they
can't see than about what they can."*
Julius Caesar

Illegal to Impersonate a Chelsea Pensioner

At most major civic events in London, we see the Chelsea Pensioners wearing their distinctive scarlet uniforms and tricorne hats.

Between 1692 and 1955, the Royal Hospital Chelsea was responsible for paying all British Army pensions. After the Royal Hospital Chelsea was built, those who gave up their pensions and chose to live in the hospital with its full-board were known as 'In-Pensioners' or Chelsea Pensioners. Those who drew their pensions and decided to live outside the hospital were known as 'Out-Pensioners'.

A myth has existed for several years, saying it's illegal to impersonate a Chelsea Pensioner. Well, yes and no. The myth probably stems from the time when unscrupulous sorts would commit fraud by drawing a pension to which they weren't entitled.

The Chelsea and Kilmainham Hospitals Act was passed in 1826 to tidy up a few issues that occurred over the years. It prohibited fraudulent claims to pensions that belonged to Chelsea Pensioners. So, the physical act of impersonating a Chelsea Pensioner by dressing up in their distinctive uniform and walking around the streets, in itself, is not an offence.

This Act was repealed in 2008 by the Statute Law (Repeals) Act.

Beware of 'Persons With Great Beards' and Those Wearing 'Outrageous Breeches'

Following on from the recent beard tax during the reign of King Henry VIII, the City of London decided to pass its own laws for those who lived and worked within the City. In the Court of Common Council, the aldermen passed a law against *persons with great beards*.

The same Ordinance contained provisions for inhabitants of the City of London wards to be suspicious and keep a vigilant eye for anyone seen wearing *outrageous breeches* and to commit transgressors. Fortunately, this law is no longer enforceable within the City, providing unhindered access to 21st century hipsters within the Square Mile.

Illegal For a Woman to Encourage a Man to Marry Her by Wearing False Hair, High Heels or Make-up

There have been some unusual views on the use of cosmetics over the centuries. In the Bible, Jeremiah (4:30) tells us, *"And when thou art spoiled, what wilt thou do? Though thou clothest thyself with crimson, though thou deckest thee with ornaments of gold, though thou rentest thy face with painting, in vain shalt thou make thyself fair; thy lovers will despise thee, they will seek thy life."*

It has been widely stated that during her reign, Queen Elizabeth I passed a law making it illegal for any woman to encourage a man to marry her by wearing false hair, high heels or make-up. For such an offence, the penalty was decreed to be the same as for witchcraft.

After centuries of military success and cheap foreign imports of goods (this was just as much a problem back then as it is now), society began to change. People would adorn themselves with the 15th and 16th century equivalent of 1970s Glam Rock clothing. High society feared that this over-consumption and over-reliance on cosmetics and other modes of self-decoration would lead to immoral behaviour.

It is said that Queen Elizabeth I passed the following edict, *"Any woman who through the use of false hair, Spanish hair pads, make-up, false hips, steel busks, panniers, high-heeled shoes or other devices, leads a subject of her majesty into marriage, shall be punished with the penalties of witchcraft."*

This edict has been repeated so many times throughout historical text. Yet, I am unable to provenance the edict or find any one particular source from which it might originate. All laws and the majority of edicts, particularly from the time of Queen Elizabeth I, would have been thoroughly documented. We are unable to say, therefore, whether this edict is true. Nevertheless, it did reflect many of society's views from the time. Indeed, around that period in our history, many sumptuary laws were passed to control a person's appearance.

During Queen Elizabeth's reign, author Philip Stubbs published his book 'Anatomy of the Abuses in England in Shakespeare's Youth' in 1583. His views within the book reflected those shared by many at the time. He wrote, ' *whosoever do colour their faces or their hair with any unnatural colour, they begin to prognosticate of what colour they shall be in hell.*"

As history entered the period of Puritan rule, the views of cosmetics became even more hostile towards women. An entry in the House of Commons Journal on 7th June 1650 was made under the heading 'Immodest Dress'. It refers to a Bill introduced by a Puritan MP called '*An Act against the Vice of Painting, and wearing black Patches, and immodest Dresses of Women, be read on Friday Morning next*'. The Bill never received a complete reading and was not passed as law.

Men's ill-feeling towards women's use of cosmetics can be seen in one misogynistic reader's letter to the newspaper The Spectator in 1711. He wrote about men who had married women who didn't "*let their husbands see their faces until they are married*" and were "*injured gentlemen.*" He continued, "*No man was as en-*

amoured as I was of her fair forehead, neck and arms, as well as the bright jet [black] of her hair ... but to my great astonishment I find they were all the effect of art. Her skin is so tarnished with this practice that when she first wakes in the morning, she scarce seems young enough to be the mother of [the woman] I carried to bed the night before. I shall take the liberty to part with her at the first opportunity, unless her father will make her portion [dowry] suitable to her real, not her assumed countenance." This was a particularly unusual point of view from a gentleman, considering at the time, men also wore cosmetics and powdered their wigs.

Another fictitious law that has become a legend, is that of the supposed 1770 Hoops and Heels Act, also referred to as the Matrimonial Act. This Act was supposed to provide legal authority for husbands to divorce their wives if they had been seduced into marriage by the use of perfume, make-up, high heels and other forms of 'deception'.

Amusingly, the alleged wording of this law stated, "*That all women, of whatever age, rank, profession, or degree, whether virgins, maids, all widows, that shall, from and after such act, impose upon, seduce, and betray into matrimony, any of his majesty's male subjects, by the scents, paints, cosmetic washes, artificial teeth, false hair, Spanish wool, iron stays, hoops, high-heeled shoes, etc, shall incur the penalty of the law now in force against witchcraft and like misdemeanours, and that the marriage, upon conviction, shall stand null and void.*"

Unlike the Elizabethan edict, where we can't say whether or not it was true, in this case, we can say with absolute certainty that there never was any such law. The origin of this myth came from a piece of satire from the late 18th century, which poked fun at men. It claimed that men who were so idiotic to be seduced by make-up should be fined £100 for their stupidity.

You Must Pay a Lump Sum For Any Facial Hair

Like cosmetics and clothing, at various times throughout our history, it seems that we have fallen out with facial hair. This is probably similar to how things go out of fashion these days, from hairstyles to designer jackets and even our names. In recent years, there have been public relations surveys to determine public perception of those who have facial hair. The results have been fascinating. One survey found that people trust a clean-shaven person more than someone with a beard or moustache.

In 1447, King Henry VI passed a decree to ban moustaches and required men attending the Royal court to shave their upper lip every two weeks.

Facial hair has featured heavily throughout our literature and artwork for centuries, particularly beards. The beard even features in William Shakespeare's play, King Lear. In Act 3, Scene 7, Gloucester utters the words, "*By the kind gods, 'tis most ignobly done. To pluck me by the beard.*" It is said that a beard tax was imposed on the people by King Henry VIII, forcing every man to pay for the privilege of wearing facial hair. There was a sliding scale of how much a person had to pay depending upon their wealth and social status. The greater a person's beard, the more money they were required to pay for it. Wearing facial hair during Tudor times symbolised a person's wealth and position in society. This all sounds very bizarre, doesn't it? Of course it does ... because it's simply not true.

It doesn't seem so far-fetched in the context of all the other bizarre sumptuary laws passed centuries ago. However, like the supposed edict banning make-up by Queen Elizabeth I, there is no evidence of this 'law' in either national or parliamentary archives. The source of this 'law' comes from the book 'That Thin Old Woman' by the Tudor historian John Stow (1525-1605). He wrote that on 8th May 1535, King Henry VIII made an important proclamation to his court. He wrote, "*The king commanded all about his court to poll their heads, and to give then example, he caused his own head to be polled and from henceforth his beard to be knotted and no more shaven.*" It is thought that this may have been an act of deference to the French monarch, King Francis I, who, after an unfortunate accident where a lump of hot coal was thrown at his head, had to undergo the indignity of having his head shaved.

We know that during the reign of King George I, there was a beard tax, just not in our country. I'm referring to the beard tax imposed in 1698 by Emperor Peter I of Russia. His beard tax lasted until 1772 and was levied on a sliding scale based on a person's wealth.

Before we leave this topic, let's look at a more recent turn of events. In 1907, an official in the New Jersey State Legislature in the USA tried to introduce a levy on men with facial hair. His proposal was also based on a sliding scale dependent upon on the amount of facial hair. He stated that those who grew beards had something to hide. In support of his argument, he offered up the names of several people with infamous crimes who had facial hair. These included Holmes the Trunk Murderer and Palmer the Poisoner. His proposal was to levy the following annual fees for those with facial hair: $1 for those with an 'ordinary beard'; $2 per inch for those with facial hair exceeding six inches; if you happened to be bald, you'd pay an extra $5; those with goatee beards would pay $10; and those with ginger beards were charged an additional 20% on top of anything else. His proposal failed, and this law was never passed.

Women Not Permitted to Wear Make-up

It's safe to say that Oliver Cromwell would not be a fan of The Rocky Horror Show, the 80's New Romantic movement or manbags! Cromwell, otherwise known as the Lord Protector of England between 1649 and 1660, had a disdain for anything he deemed to be not within the teachings of The Bible.

Immediately after King Charles I had been executed, the Long Parliament, led by Cromwell, took over, and the country entered a time of Puritan austerity. There was a move away from anything considered fun like sporting activities, drinking alcohol, theatre and musical entertainment. These activities were considered corrupt and a sure pathway to evil. Instead, the Puritan Parliament wanted the people to devote their time to worship and the teachings of The Bible.

The Puritans believed that women should be strictly as nature had intended. Women were expected to dress in a long dark full-length dress with a white apron and wear their hair neatly tied behind a white headdress. They were expected not to dress in extravagant or colourful clothing or wear make-up. Whilst no specific laws prohibited wearing make-up, Puritan soldiers would nevertheless roam the streets and force any women they came across, to remove make-up.

After several years of sobriety and dreariness, it's no small wonder that by the time the monarchy was restored in 1660 by King Charles II, society would have been rejoicing.

CHAPTER FIVE

ASSAULT &
INJURY

"*Thou shall not kill*" ... the principle embodied in The Old Testament of The Bible (Exodus 20:13). It's the bedrock of our homicide legislation. This, along with common law and various Acts of Statute over the centuries, has taught us to be kind and do no harm to others. However, life can be pretty stressful at times. History is littered with some unconventional examples of where people have been unable to control their irritability or have acted out of paranoia.

In this chapter, we take a brief look at the changing face and levels of tolerance towards domestic abuse and the law preventing evil Bond villains wishing to commit omnicide by exploding a nuclear device in the capital.

In a nutshell, you can't kill a ghost, you can't kill another person, and you can't kill yourself.

"Revenge is an act of passion; vengeance of justice.
Injuries are revenged; crimes are avenged."
Samuel Johnson

Illegal to Kill a Ghostly Apparition

This story unfolds on the streets of Hammersmith on the outskirts of London. From December 1803, the local villagers reported multiple sightings of a ghost covered in a white burial shroud. Unfortunately, due to fear and mass hysteria, rumours became rife that the ghostly apparition was starting to attack people, especially in the vicinity of the Hammersmith church-yard.

The locals believed it was the ghost of a man who had com-mitted suicide, which was his punishment to walk the earth for all eternity. Such was the fear caused by these sightings that it scared the driver of a wagon. The driver ran off in fear for his life, leaving behind his eight horses and 16 passengers. A preg-nant woman allegedly came into contact with the apparition, which caused her to faint. She was later reported to have died. The local community set up a neighbourhood watch group to look for the ghastly spectre.

It transpired that the ghostly apparition wasn't anything of the sort and was, in fact, a local bricklayer called Thomas Mill-wood who wore his white trade clothing late at night. He had previously been mistaken for a ghost due to his clothing. His relatives had even begged him not to wear such clothing late at night. Unfortunately, he ignored their protestations.

Late on the evening of 3rd January 1804, Thomas Millwood left his house wearing his distinctive white linen trousers, a white flannel waistcoat, a white apron and white shoes. On this same night, one slightly inebriated neighbourhood watchman, Francis Smith, took a shotgun with him. It defies logic how the belief came about that this was a supernatural being. Yet, they thought a bullet would adequately resolve the issue.

As it happened, on this fateful night, Smith shot at what he claimed was a ghostly apparition coming towards him in the darkened street. Sadly, it was Thomas Millwood, the bricklayer. Smith went on trial at the Old Bailey for murder. In his defence, he stated that he genuinely believed Millwood was a ghostly apparition, and that's why he had shot him. The jury accepted this defence and found him guilty of the lesser offence of manslaughter. However, the judge sent them back to deliberate once again and either convict him of murder or acquit him entirely. They found him guilty of murder, and he was sentenced to death. Still, public sympathy later commuted this with a pardon from the Crown to one-year imprisonment.

The questions raised by Smith's defence 'haunted' the legal books for another 180 years, when finally, in 1984, the case of R v Williams came before the Court of Appeal. The judges overturned the conviction in this case, where a person used their mistaken belief as a defence.

Illegal to Cause a Nuclear Explosion

The world changed at 5.29am on 16th July 1945 when the first atomic bomb was detonated as part of the Manhattan Project in a test in New Mexico, USA. Since that time, we've lived through the Cuban Missile Crisis, the Cold War and the insanity of Mutually Assured Destruction. Rolling the clock forward to today, it is believed that Russia has the largest nuclear arsenal in the world, with a nuclear warhead inventory of approximately 5,977. In comparison, the US has 5,428, France has 290, and the UK has 225. Russia and the United States own around 90% of all nuclear warheads.

Believe it or not, it is illegal to cause a nuclear explosion in the UK. The legislators felt it was necessary to create a law to cover such an occurrence in case anyone was daft enough to ponder their options.

The Nuclear Explosions (Prohibition and Inspections) Act (1998) made it such an offence. This was brought in to implement the United Nations Comprehensive Nuclear-Test-Ban Treaty, which bans nuclear weapons test explosions and other nuclear explosions. This Act makes it an offence to cause an explosion in the UK and any other country if you are a British national.

Should you inexplicably decide to cause a nuclear explosion, you have a defence. Firstly, you must knowingly have caused the explosion, so an accidental one should be just fine. Secondly, if the explosion is carried out during an armed conflict, that should be fine as well, but you would require a certificate from the Secretary of State for Defence if you're launching an armed conflict.

A magistrate has powers to authorise the entry and search of your house if they are satisfied there are reasonable grounds for suspecting that you are about to cause a nuclear explosion. If you forget this legislation exists, don't worry because Parts 6-8 of The Anti-terrorism, Crime and Security Act (2001) also make it a criminal offence to set off a nuclear explosion.

Should the mood take you, please be advised that the local constabulary doesn't take too kindly to mushroom clouds drifting across the local bowling greens.

Unlawful to Lie in Wait to Maim Someone

Mutilating people was apparently all the craze in the 1700s. So, laws had to be explicitly passed to punish anyone by death if they decided to disfigure others facially.

The Coventry Act, also known as the Maiming Act, came into force on 24th June 1671 and was a direct result of an incident where the victim was a member of Parliament, Sir John Coventry.

In this case, the MP Sir John Coventry had made what some considered a derogatory comment about King Charles II during a parliamentary session. Later that night, Sir Thomas Sandys of the Duke of Monmouth's horse guards and a smattering of foot soldiers lay in wait near Coventry's address from 10pm until 2am the following morning. As Sir John made his way back from the local tavern, they pounced on him, threw him to the ground and cut the end of his nose almost entirely off. Just before finishing their endeavours, they were frightened off by passers-by.

The perpetrators were eventually captured and imprisoned. It was believed that had they not been startled, they most likely would have continued to mutilate Coventry, leading to his eventual murder. This caused such an outrage in the House of Commons that they suspended other business and immediately debated a new Bill 'to prevent malicious maiming and wounding', which became known as the Coventry Act. This Bill closed the loophole left by attempted murder not being recognised as a capital felony.

This new, rather long-winded Act of Parliament stated that '*If any Person or Persons ... on Purpose and of Malice fore-thought, and by lying in wait shall unlawfully cut out or disable the Tongue, put out an Eye, slit the Nose, cut off a Nose or Lip, or cut off or disable any Limb or Member of any Subject of his Majesty, with Intention in so doing to maim or disfigure in any the Manners before-mentioned ... shall be, and are hereby declared to be felons, and shall suffer Death, as in Cases of felony, without Benefit of Clergy.'*

This wasn't repealed until 1828 when the new Offences Against The Persons Act came into force. This Act came in handy several years later during the trial of John Woodburne and Arundel Coke in 1772. This trial was over a fight that had broken out, with one of the men being attacked with a sharp implement. The victim didn't die but suffered disfiguring injuries. The problem was that attempted murder didn't carry any capital punishment at the time, so the perpetrators could not be put to death for their horrendous crimes. One of the villains, Coke, was a barrister. In defending himself, he argued that he could not be found guilty because he intended to murder the victim and not just maim him. The court found that in setting out to attack the victim with the sharp implement, they must have known that the victim would have been gruesomely disfigured. So they found both Woodburne and Coke guilty in what is thought to be the first prosecution under the Coventry Act. The perpetrators could then be sentenced to death for their crimes.

It's Okay to Beat Your Wife With a Stick But Not Between the Hours of 10pm & 7am

Whilst it may not have been legal, it was nevertheless considered perfectly acceptable for a man to beat his wife, providing that his stick was no thicker than his thumb. The first documented record in the English language of the term 'rule of thumb' appeared in 1685, but this was more about something being a rough approximation rather than a precise measurement and not a reference to the acceptance of what we now consider domestic violence.

Anecdotally, in 1782 a senior British judge from Devon, Sir Francis Buller, is reputed to have agreed that a man might legally beat his wife. In a ruling, he is alleged to have stated that "*a husband could thrash his wife with impunity provided that he used a stick no bigger than his thumb.*" There is no legal record of this statement being made by the judge. Still, it was widely reported in the sensationalist press at the time, and he was thereafter referred to as 'Judge Thumb'.

To complicate matters further, the system of Coverture existed in common law for several centuries and throughout much of the 19th century. This meant that once married, a husband and wife become one legal person in the eyes of the law, with the husband in charge. It was considered that the husband would be legally responsible for his wife's actions and that as a result, he could lawfully chastise her, both physically and verbally, to control her errant behaviour. This meant that husbands could quite easily get away with beating their wives without being prosecuted, provided the 'chastisement' was reasonable and for the purposes of 'correcting' her behaviour.

In the late 18th century, the famous judge Sir William Blackstone wrote his book Commentaries on the Law of England, stating, "*The husband also, by the old law, might give his wife moderate correction. For, as he is to answer for her misbehaviour, the law thought it reasonable to intrust him with this power of restraining her, by domestic chastisement ... But this power of correction was confined within reasonable bounds.*"

Believe it or not, in 1895, the City of London passed a by-law which created a curfew on wife-beating. It prohibited the beating of one's wife between the hours of 10pm and 7am. This bylaw was passed not to reduce incidences of domestic abuse but rather because the noise would keep the neighbours awake and violate London's noise curfew. So, it was considered acceptable to beat her after waking up in the morning because it was daylight hours.

To rub salt into the wound, in a report dated 6th January 1905, The Manchester Evening News, reported on a case from the courts in Salford where a woman was giving evidence against her husband on a charge of assault. She was duly admonished by the Stipendiary Magistrate, a Mr Makinson, who informed her, "*This is the way with you women. You chatter, chatter, chatter until you irritate. You get the man mad, then you get struck and come here. Try to keep your mouth shut and you will get on better.*"

Embarrassingly, as this brings us even closer to the modern-day, in 1984, the then Commissioner of the Metropolitan Police, Sir Kenneth Newman, stated, "*Domestic violence and stray dogs ... rubbish work for police officers.*"

CHAPTER SIX

CARNAL KNOWLEDGE

O ver the centuries, our law books have become cluttered with some rather fruity laws dealing with fornicators and adulterers. With laws covering all natures of sexual depravity, we must have had a considerably sordid past, from sex workers to sexual impropriety with an unmarried person.

In this chapter, you will delve into the past (and perhaps also the future) of Gretna Green in Scotland, a place where a woman could be legally seduced into marriage. We also try to understand why persons of ill-repute in Chester may be touched by members of one family, as embodied in law. Whether you're a Russian tourist, a visiting alien or just Mr. Smith and Mrs. Jones out for a day at the local hotel for a minor indiscretion, you must still comply with the law. If legal history tells us nothing else, don't be a bastard!

"For truth is precious and divine,
too rich a pearl for carnal swine."
Samuel Butler

Hotel Indiscretions with Aliens

It is an offence for anyone aged 16 or over to check-in to a hotel or bed and breakfast using a fake name. There are many reasons why people may choose to book a hotel room under a pseudonym. Perhaps they are a celebrity travelling incognito, or a couple of Russian tourists 'visiting' Salisbury, or maybe it's an office worker partaking in a little sexual immorality during an overnight trip. Regardless of the reason, it is a legal requirement for guests to provide their full name and nationality upon arrival. Providing false details is an offence. This is covered under Section 4(1) of the British Nationality Act (1981). It also makes it a legal requirement for a representative of the premises to collect the full name and nationality of all persons 16 years or older, upon arrival.

Things get a little more complicated for those wishing to have hotel indiscretions with aliens. I am referring to the legal definition of 'alien' as someone who is not a Commonwealth citizen, a British-protected person, or a citizen of the Republic of Ireland. Not the variety frequently encountered by agent Mulder or the Quatermass team. Anyone aged 16 or above in this category must also supply proof of identity and nationality upon arrival. This would usually be a passport. And upon departure, they must also provide their next destination and the full address if it is known.

The 'Criminal Conversation' of Adultery

King Ælfred (871-886) passed a law concerning adultery. It classified varying degrees of the crime, not based on severity but on the social status of the woman's husband as her rightful 'owner'. The laws reflect those passed by King Ine of Wessex (688-726). In these early times, women were seen as a man's property. This is reflected in the penalties that had to be paid. A translation of the penalties owed by men for adultery is, "*If anyone lies with the wife of a twelve-hundred man, he is to pay 120 shillings compensation to the husband; to a six-hundred man, he is to pay 100 shillings compensation; to a ceorl, he is to pay forty shillings compensation.*"

The term 'twelve-hundred man' referred to the man's elite status as a nobleman. It is believed the King himself was valued at around 6,000 shillings. However, anyone lying with his wife would most likely have met a more gruesome death than merely paying a fee for adultery.

This was the legal principle of 'wergild', where the offender would have to pay for their crimes. Without wergild, the default punishment was the biblical concept of an 'eye for an eye'. This saw the bizarre situation where if a man raped your wife, you were permitted, by law, to rape his wife. She would not be entitled to refuse the ordeal.

The laws over adultery during the reign of King Canute (1016-1035) appeared unbalanced between the genders in terms of punishment. He continued the series of fines (wergild) established by his predecessors. However, whereas male adulterers would be fined or punished with religious penitence, female adulterers were ordered to be mutilated in some way. This usually meant her nose, and both ears were cut off. She would also forfeit all her property to her husband.

During the reign of King Henry I (1100-1135), the *Leges Henrici Primi* (a legal treatise which recorded the mediaeval customs of England) decreed that the King could punish an unfaithful man. However, an adulterous woman would be punished by the Church. Adultery was dealt with far more severely with castration and blinding.

During the reign of King Henry II (1154-1189), adultery was again met with stiff punishments. Some women had their noses and ears cut off, whilst others could be whipped with knives by their community. It wasn't uncommon for women to be ordered to be pushed off a high cliff or cast adrift in the sea in a leaking boat.

Those women punished by ecclesiastical courts could consider themselves lucky. By the late twelfth century, the Church preferred not to impose corporal punishment. Instead, they favoured forms of public penitence like standing before the congregation wearing white sackcloth or sitting on the stool of repentance.

In May 1650, the Puritan Parliament passed the '*Act for suppressing the detestable sins of Incest, Adultery and Fornication*'. It made the offence of adultery a felony, with the penalty of death, without benefit of clergy.

A wronged partner in an adultery case was able to bring a civil case against an adulterer under tort law. This was known as a 'loss of consortium', where an act had occurred that deprived one partner in a marriage of the exclusivity of services (sex) that the other partner in the marriage was expected to provide. This was seen in the 1619 case of Guy v Livesey, where it was established that an adulterer could be prosecuted for depriving the other partner in the marriage (the victim) of exclusive access to the sexual services of his wife.

Another method to prosecute an adulterer through a 'loss of consortium' was to accuse them of 'enticement'. This is where another man enticed a spouse away from the marriage. Again, the victim could claim damages from the adulterer under tort law. Adulterers were considered to have engaged in 'criminal conversation'. Between the seventeenth and eighteenth centuries, claims for damages in criminal conversation cases often reached between £10,000 and £20,000.

This created the curious legal circumstance in which a wronged husband could claim damages from his wife's adulterous lover. This became even more interesting with the passing of the Matrimonial Causes Act in 1857. Now it was no longer just a wronged husband that could claim damages but also a wronged wife if her husband was having an affair with another woman. Although bizarrely, the law stated that if a married woman had an adulterous affair with another woman's husband, whilst the wronged woman (a victim) could sue for damages, if she won, those damages had to be paid by the husband of the other seducing woman. This seemed unfair because he himself would also be a victim of adultery. However, he was legally responsible for his wife's actions and debts. This was changed by Section 3 of the Law Reform (Married Women and Tortfeasors) Act (1935), absolving the accused's husband from any liability to pay for his unfaithful wife's torts.

The right for all injured parties to claim damages for a 'loss of consortium' was abolished under Section 4 of the Law

Reform (Miscellaneous Provisions) Act (1970). The passing of the Matrimonial Causes Act in 1857 also ended the Church's jurisdiction over cases of adultery.

The Detestable Sins of Incest, Adultery and Fornication

Those who read the Bible may be familiar with Leviticus 18:7–11 and 20:11–21, which established the list of prohibited relationships under ecclesiastical law. For example, you can't marry a close relative. That would be classed as incest.

For those who weren't aware, the Puritan Parliament passed an ordinance on 10th May 1650, called '*An Act for suppressing the detestable sins of Incest, Adultery and Fornication*'. This made it an offence of incest to marry or have 'carnal knowledge' of relatives. It was declared an offence to "*Marry, or have the carnal knowledge of the Body of his or her Grandfather or Grandmother, Father or Mother, Brother or Sister, Son or Daughter, or Grandchilde, Fathers Brother or Sister, Mothers*

Brother or Sister, Fathers Wife, Mothers Husband, Sons Wife, Daughters Husband, Wives Mother or Daughter, Husbands Father or Son; all and every such Offences are hereby adjudged and declared Incest." This was a felony, a very serious offence. Any marriages were automatically void in the eyes of the law, and any children resulting from that relationship were classed as illegitimate. The offenders, whether male or female, were sentenced to death without benefit of clergy. The same Act prohibited adultery, which it described as "*any married woman ... be carnally known by any man (other than her husband) (except in case of ravishment).*" This was a felony, and adulterers were also sentenced to death without benefit of clergy.

There were various defences under this Act. For example, a woman would not be guilty of adultery if subjected to "*ravishment.*" That would make her the victim of rape. Men had a defence if they believed that the woman was not married at the time. It also didn't apply to any woman whose husband remained "*beyond the seas*" for at least three years. In cases where a husband intentionally absented himself from his wife for three years, she would not be guilty.

The law didn't just deal with incest and adultery but also fornicators. Fornication occured when a man seduced a virgin, an unmarried woman, or a widow. For each offence, they would be sentenced to 3 months imprisonment. The woman also suffered the same punishment. It punished the keepers of brothels, known as 'common bawds'. For a first offence, they would be whipped, placed in the public pillory and branded with the letter 'B' on their forehead before being sent to the local Prison or the House of Correction for three years. For a second offence, they would receive the death penalty without benefit of clergy.

When King Charles II came to the throne, he passed The Indemnity and Oblivion Act in 1660. This was a general pardon for everyone who had committed crimes during the English Civil War and the Interregnum period. Interestingly, it specifically excluded from the pardon the *'Abominable Vice of Buggery committed with Mankinde or Beast'* along with piracy, poisoners, witches and those who remarried before the death of their former wives or husbands.

Bastards!

Over the years, we've read a lot in the news about the systemic failures of the Child Maintenance Service (CMS) and the Child Support Agency (CSA) before that. It appears there has been a centuries-long legal and administrative battle to obtain certainty of paternity and ensure parental financial involvement in their child's development.

The laws surrounding 'carnal knowledge' are mainly focused on the outcome of that event, never more so than when a child is born. During mediaeval times, an illegitimate child (a bastard) was a *filius nullius* (son of nobody). Provided they could get a certificate from their local Bishop confirming their status as a bastard; they could be released from the protection of their ward. They would then be classed as a freeman rather than a serf.

The ancient Statute of Merton passed by Parliament in 1235, during the reign of King Henry III, defined illegitimacy, stating, *"He is a bastard that is born before the marriage of his parents."* At the time, the decision on illegitimacy was taken by two separate courts. The church court and the secular court, applying common law on property inheritance. It created a strange dichotomy where a child born before its parents married was considered legitimate under church law but illegitimate under secular common law.

It wasn't until 1575 that we saw local parishes taking on the rudimentary functions of the modern-day CMS. The Poor Act was passed that same year which sought to ensure the child's development was paid for by the local parish or the child's parents. Not forgetting, of course, the man in the relationship would be the only breadwinner around this time and still for hundreds of years afterwards. So, this law sought to identify and punish fathers who failed to pay for the support of their children. It ordered that 'bastards' be supported by their putative fathers. This was a time when DNA testing wasn't even a thing, and undoubtedly many men would have been wrongly reputed to be the child's father and forced to pay. If the correct biological father (genitor) was identified, this law enabled the local parish to enforce they pay for their child's maintenance legally. If a man were suspected of being the reputed father, he would be put through the parish Bastardy Examinations to confirm this. If having heard the evidence, the parish believed him to be the child's father, he would be expected to either marry the mother or continue to pay maintenance for the child's upbringing. This was documented in what was known as the parish Bastardy Bonds. If the father of the illegitimate child refused to be bound by the parish Bastardy Bond, a local magistrate could issue a Bastardy Warrant which enabled constables to apprehend him and bring him before a Justice of The Peace. He would then face being imprisoned until the next Quarter Session unless he could pay a security. This remained the basis of bastardy law until it was repealed by the Poor Law Amendment Act (1834).

The Act for the Relief of the Poor was passed in 1601, ensuring that the costs of the child's upbringing would be met. In cases where the mother could not identify the biological father, it then fell to the parish to pay for the cost of keeping the illegitimate child. After this, local parishes experienced an upsurge in the number of Bastardy Examinations to ensure fathers were correctly identified and parishes weren't left footing the bill.

On 7th May 1649, a new law was passed that sadly punished illegitimate children living within the City of London. This was *'An Act for the Relief and Employment of the Poor, and the Punishment of Vagrants, and other disorderly Persons, within the City of London, and the Liberties thereof.'* It ordered that all *"rogues, vagrants, sturdy beggars, idle and disorderly persons"* and *"all such other poor persons and Bastard children"* be forced to work or be *"duly punished by putting in the stocks, or whipping."*

Marriage by Seduction

Following the passing of the Clandestine Marriages Act in 1753, wedding ceremonies had to occur in churches in England and Wales. The age of marrying without parental consent was increased from 16 to 21 years of age. Scotland refused to adopt this Act, and so, many young couples, in the throngs of passion, would cross the border to be married at the nearest point over the border from England. This happened to be Gretna Green.

In Scotland at the time, English couples could seek a quick marriage under Scots law by declaring their wish to be married before witnesses. Unusually, this ceremony was often performed by the local blacksmith, either in his forge or at the local tollhouse. Anyone could officiate, and it wasn't just a blacksmith who could perform the marriage ceremony.

In 1856, the law changed in Scotland, but not very much. It required either the future bride or the bridegroom to reside in Scotland for 21 days before the marriage ceremony. In fact, it wasn't until The Marriage (Scotland) Act in 1939 that marriages had to be officiated by either a minister or a registrar.

With the passing of The Marriage and Civil Partnership (Minimum Age) Act in 2022, the minimum age for marriage and civil partnership is 18 in England and Wales. This law was brought in to protect children from the scourge of forced marriage. I can see Gretna Green again becoming a popular marriage location for those wishing to form a marriage union between the ages of 16 and 18.

Interestingly, until the passing of the Marriage (Scotland) Act in 1939, under Scots law, one of the three methods of irregular marriage available to couples in Scotland, would have appealed to any budding lotharios. This was known as a marriage *per verba de futuro subsequente copula*. During this ancient ritual, couples would be considered married if they first agreed to marry on some future date and then consummated their relationship. The subsequent intercourse made the marriage legally binding.

All 'Whores and Letchers' in the County of Chester

On a Midsummer's Day in 1209 or 1210, the Earl of Chester, Randall Blundeville, found himself suddenly besieged by the Welsh in Rhuddlan Castle in Flintshire. He immediately sent for the Constable of Cheshire, Roger Lacy, requesting him to muster whatever force he could and return to rescue him at the castle. On that same day, a local fair was being held in nearby Chester. Roger Lacy gathered a lawless mob of fiddlers, players, cobblers, and letchers from the fair and quickly marched them over to Rhuddlan Castle. The Welsh saw this mass rabble approaching and promptly fled. The Earl was again free and granted a charter to Roger Lacy and his heirs. This charter peculiarly bestowed upon Roger Lacy and his heirs power over all the fiddlers, letchers, whores, and cobblers, in Chester, in perpetuity. The term 'letcher' was applied at the time to any riotous debauched person.

A few years later, Roger Lacy died at the beginning of King Henry III's reign (1216), and the charter was passed on to his son, John Lacy. He granted by deed to his steward, Hugh Dutton and his heirs, the rule and authority over all the letchers and whores in the county of Chester. The deed read, *"Know all men present and to come, that I John, Constable of Chester, have given and granted, and by this my present charter have confirmed to Hugh de Dutton, and his heirs, the government of all the letchers and whores of all Cheshire, as freely as I hold the government of the Earl, saving my right to me and my heirs."*

In 1499, a *quo warranto* (a writ) against Hugh de Dutton's heir was brought against Lawrence of Dutton, Esq. It required him to prove his claim over all the minstrels of Cheshire and the city of Chester. He was also required to explain why the minstrels must appear before him or his steward at Chester each year on the feast of St. John the Baptist and provide refreshments and payment of four pence and half-penny from each of them. The writ further required him to explain why he claimed every whore exercising her trade in Cheshire and the city of Chester to pay him four pence yearly at that same feast. He must've been able to provide that proof because the charter continued and showed up in later Acts of Statute.

During Queen Elizabeth I's reign (1558-1603), in two of her laws dealing with the punishment of Rogues, Vagabonds, and Sturdy Beggars that we come across elsewhere in this book, John Dutton gets a specific mention. In both laws, it states, "*Provided always, that this act, or anything therein contained, or any authority thereby given, shall not in any wise extend to disinherit, prejudice, or hinder John Dutton, of Dutton, in the County of Chester, esquire, his heirs or assigns for, touching, or concerning any liberty, pre-eminence, authority, jurisdiction, or inheritance, which the said John Dutton now lawfully useth, or hath, or lawfully made, or ought to use, within the county palatine of Chester and the County of the city of Chester, or either of them, by reason of any ancient charters of any kings of this land, or by reason of any prescription, usage, or title whatsoever.*"

In the 43rd year of the Queen's reign, she passed a further law which again mentioned John Dutton but required him once again to prove his claim over the minstrels and whores in Cheshire and Chester. He must have been able to provide proof because in a law passed during the first year of the reign of King James I (1603), John Dutton and this peculiar power and authority over all the whores in Chester appears again.

The final time we see it appearing is in a law passed during the reign of King George II in 1744. In the Vagrant Act, a similar provision is made to the "*heirs or assigns of John Dutton, of Dutton, esquire.*"

If there are any present-day heirs of John Dutton, this law rightfully established by multiple Acts of Parliament ever since 1572, may very well still apply. In this case, they would be entitled to touch and claim all '*whores and letchers*' in the county of Chester.

CHAPTER SEVEN

CURIOUS CUSTOMS

We have some very unusual customs in the City of London, and perhaps none more peculiar than those centuries-old ceremonies of the Tower of London like the Ceremony of The Keys. What happens when ships visit the Port of London? And when is the City of London not actually the City of London?

In this chapter, we peel back more layers of our national history to reveal some of these customs and their origins, like the annual wife-carrying contest and dancing around the maypole.

Don't mention the Morris Dancers!

> *"Customs do not concern themselves with right or wrong or reason. But they have to be obeyed: one reasons all around them until he is tired, but he must not transgress them, it is sternly forbidden."*
> Mark Twain

Until Recently, Part of the City of London Belonged to Cambridgeshire

Ely Place sits just north of Holborn Circus in the City of London. It's a small enclave with a gatehouse guarded by beadles wearing top hats. Walking past the streets, it looks like a quiet cul-de-sac with iron gates, perhaps even part of a Harry Potter set. It hides a historical secret. Whilst it is located physically in the City of London, for centuries, it didn't fall under their jurisdiction. It was considered part of Cambridgeshire until as recently as the 1970s. Neither the Metropolitan Police nor the City of London police could enter without first being invited by the Commissioners of Ely Place. This is because it fell under the policing jurisdiction of the Cambridgeshire Constabulary. Pedestrians are permitted to walk through, but there is a sign warning that they must abide by the rules of the Commissioners of Ely Place.

Since the late 13th century, it had been privately owned by the Bishops of Ely in Cambridgeshire. In 1280, John de Kirkby purchased the land. Six years later, he became Bishop of Ely and built the Ely Palace or Ely House on that land. Upon his death in 1290, he bequeathed Ely Palace to the See of Ely. Since mediaeval times, the Bishops of Ely had a seat in the House of Lords and frequently lived in London. So from this time onwards, Ely Palace became the official London residence of the Bishops of Ely. This enabled them to have a private chapel in the City of London while still maintaining their parliamentary duties.

At the time, the church took measures to ensure that its ecclesiastic buildings were not subject to the laws and taxes of London. To do this, they would establish the residences as enclaves, making them legally part of whichever diocese the bishops belonged to. In this case, that was the Diocese of Ely.

The bishops remained in their official palace until 1772, when both Ely Palace and its land were sold and redeveloped into what is now Ely Place. It was named after the Bishops of Ely, who used to reside there. The land, however, remained under the jurisdiction of Cambridgeshire.

Ely Palace has popped up throughout history and was even referred to in two of Shakespeare's plays. In his play Richard II, he used the famous "*This royal throne of Kings, this sceptre'd isle*" speech. The palace gardens allegedly produced the most succulent strawberries in London. Shakespeare's play Richard III refers to this when Gloster says to Ely, "*My Lord of Ely, when I was last in Holborn, I saw good strawberries in your garden there; I do beseech you, send me some of them.*"

Records show that in 1531, King Henry VIII and Catherine of Aragon dined as guests in the palace's Great Hall. The records are remarkably detailed. They show that over five days, the King and his guests managed to work their way through 24 oxen, 51 cows, 91 pigs, 100 sheep, 168 swans, 444 pigeons, 720 chickens and 4080 larks ... Quite the appetite!

Today, you can still find some historical treasures around Ely Place. If you walk through a narrow passageway leading off Ely Place, you will come across a hidden pub that has existed since 1546. Ye Olde Mitre was constructed under the orders of Bishop Thomas Goodrich of Ely. Due to the strange quirk of Ely Place falling under the jurisdiction of Cambridgeshire and not the City of London, as recently as the 1960s, the pub's licence continued to be issued by the Cambridge authorities.

In 1842, Parliament passed the Ely Place and Ely Mews Improvement Act, which established a group of Commissioners responsible for the security and maintenance of Ely Place. The Metropolis Management Act (1855) provided for the regular nightwatch duties carried out by beadles. Until the late 1960s, the beadles of Ely Place could be heard calling out the hours, and the weather on an hourly basis between 7am and 10pm.

Ceremony of The Keys

In what is believed to be the world's oldest surviving military ceremony, for the last 700 years, a peculiar tradition has taken place at the Tower of London.

In what is officially known as His Majesty's Royal Palace and Fortress of the Tower of London, each night the Yeomen Warders (Beefeaters) perform a ritual known as the Ceremony of the Keys.

Irrespective of the day of the week or how bad the weather might be, each night, at precisely 9:52 PM, the Chief Yeoman Warder of the Tower emerges from the Byward Tower. He is dressed in a long red Tudor watch-cloak and Tudor bonnet and carrying a candle lantern in one hand and the King's Keys in the other.

He walks from the Byward Tower to Traitor's Gate, where he meets the Escort to the Keys, a duty regiment of Foot Guards.

They will escort him during the ceremony. One of the escorts takes the lantern, and they walk purposefully in step toward the outer gate. Any guards or sentries on duty will always salute the King's Keys as they pass. The Chief Yeoman Warder then locks the outer gate. He and the escort walk back to lock the old oak gates of both the Middle and Byward Towers. They then return, making their way along Water Lane towards the Wakefield Tower. Stood in the shadows of the large Bloody Tower archway, a sentry awaits the arrival of the keys. As the escort's footsteps approach through the darkness, the sentry shouts his challenge...

"*Halt!*"   "*Who comes there?*"

The Chief Yeoman Warder replies, "*The Keys.*"

"*Whose Keys?*" replies the sentry.

"*King Charles' Keys*", responds the Chief Warder.

To which the sentry reassures, "*Pass King Charles' Keys. All's well.*"

The Chief Yeoman Warder, accompanied by his escort, then walk through the Bloody Tower archway, entering the fortress and up towards the broadwalk steps where the main Guard stands patiently. They halt at the foot of the broadwalk steps, where the officer in charge gives the order to the Guard to present arms (their rifles) as a mark of respect to the Sovereign.

The Chief Yeoman Warder then takes two paces forward, raises his large Tudor bonnet, and shouts, "*God preserve King*

Charles." With the whole ceremony running to perfect timing, the Guard then replies, "*Amen,*" as the clock chimes 10 PM and the duty drummer sounds The Last Post on his bugle. The Chief Yeoman Warder carries the keys back to the Queen's House for safe keeping until the following day, and the Guard is dismissed for the night.

Aside from changing the monarch's name during each new reign, these are the exact words that have been spoken for centuries without change. The origins of this tradition are unknown. However, it is believed to have begun during the Middle Ages. The ceremony has occurred since December 1340 when a furious King Edward III turned up one night unannounced and walked in both undetected and unchallenged. The King charged the Constable of the Tower, Edward de la Beche, with dereliction of duty and had him imprisoned. He passed a Royal decree stating that the castle should be locked at sunset and unlocked at sunrise.

The Ceremony of the Keys in its current format dates back to the 19th century. Then, the guards known as Yeomen Warders were reformed by the Duke of Wellington, acting in his role as Constable of the Tower.

In 1555, following the failed Protestant plot, Queen Mary I gave a decree with detailed instructions for the security of the Tower keys. The original text from that time details what we now see as the Ceremony of the Keys. It reads,

'*And it is ordered that there shall be a place appointed under Locke and key where in the keys of the gates of the saide Tower shall be laide in the sight of the Constable, the porter and two of the Yeoman Warders, or three of them at the least, and by two or three of them to be taken out when the[y] shall be occupied.*

And the key of that locke or coffer where the keys be, to be kepte
by the porter or, in his absence, by the chief yeoman warder.'

It is interesting to note that the ceremony has never been
cancelled. It has only ever been delayed on one occasion, on
29th December 1940, as a result of an air raid on London
during the Second World War. On this occasion, several incen-
diary bombs landed on the old Victorian guardroom when the
Chief Yeoman Warder and his Escort to the Keys were walking
through the archway of the Bloody Tower. It knocked several
of the Escort off their feet. They stood up, dusted themselves
off and continued with the ceremony.

That night, once the Tower gates had been secured, the Officer
of the Guard hand-wrote a personal letter of apology to His
Majesty King George VI. He apologised that the ceremony
had been delayed a few minutes and offered his resignation.
The King promptly replied by letter, stating that the delay had
been due to enemy action and that the officer should not be
punished. Both of these letters are stored at The Tower.

A Ceremony of the Keys is also held each year during July at
Holyrood Palace in Edinburgh, Scotland when the King visits.
Shortly after the monarch arrives at the Palace forecourt, they
are symbolically offered the keys to the City of Edinburgh
by the Lord Provost. To mark the ceremony, the monarch
returns the keys and says, "*I return these keys, being perfectly*
convinced that they can not be placed in better hands than
those of the Lord Provost and Councillors of my good City of
Edinburgh."

There is a similar Ceremony of the Keys at the opening of
the General Assembly of the Church of Scotland, when the
monarch's representative, the Lord High Commissioner, receives the keys from the Lord Provost.

Further afield, the Ceremony of the Keys also occurs in one of our territories overseas, Gibraltar. This is a re-enactment of the locking of the gates to the old garrison of Gibraltar. During the Great Siege of Gibraltar, which started in 1779, French and Spanish soldiers attempted to capture the garrison. They failed.

Ships Visiting the Port of London Must Deliver a Barrel of Rum to The Constable of The Tower of London

As part of an ancient tradition dating back to a Royal decree made during the time of King Richard II (1377-1399), Royal Navy ships visiting the Port of London must present a barrel of rum to The Constable of The Tower of London. This is known as the Constable's Dues. King Richard II allowed the Constable of the Tower to take a levy from ships that travelled upstream and moored at Tower Wharf, under the protection of The Tower's guns. Generally, this was a portion of its cargo. This cargo would include such things as cockles, mussels, oysters, rushes and kegs of rum or wine. Over the centuries, as taxes became more regulated, this practice fell into abeyance. It is now upheld each year in a ceremonial sense from visiting warships.

Today, the Constable's Dues is in the form of a symbolic barrel of alcohol, usually rum or wine. The ceremony occurs once or twice a year with all the flamboyance expected of a State ceremonial event. In recent years, ship's companies from other navies, including France and Canada, have presented dues to the Constable of the Tower.

This ancient ceremony commences when the ship's company arrives on foot at the Tower. They are then challenged by a member of the Yeoman Guard wielding an axe. The Tower gate is shut in the face of the visiting ship's Captain. Once the captain explains their visit's purpose, they are formally welcomed by the Yeoman Guard. They march through the precincts to Tower Green, flanked by an escort of Yeoman Warders in State Dress and accompanied by a Corps of Drums. The keg of alcohol (Constable's Dues) is presented to the Constable of the Tower, and speeches are made.

There are several other benefits for the Constable of the Tower, dating back to the Middle Ages. These include the entitlement to all flotsam and jetsam found floating on the Thames. They can also keep any livestock that falls from Tower Bridge into the river and take ownership of any swans that pass the Tower. They also received payments for livestock or carts that fell into the Tower moat. They used to receive payment for any State prisoners at the Tower. The last State prisoner to be held in the Tower was Rudolf Hess, the deputy leader of the Nazi Party, who was held prisoner there in May 1941. Interestingly, whilst not State prisoners, the last people to be held in the Tower were the notorious London gangsters, The Kray Twins. They were imprisoned in The Tower for a few days in 1952 for failing to report for national service.

Pearly Kings & Queens

Through a quirky British tradition, our reigning monarch is not the only King or Queen at any one time. However, this is not something our constitutionalists need to spend time debating. They will know I am referring to the Pearly Kings and Queens of London. The Pearly Kings and Queens, or Pearlies as they have become known, have been an iconic image of London for many years and are easily recognised, adorned in clothing and accessories covered with mother-of-pearl buttons. Around thirty Pearly families representing the various districts of London continue the tradition of raising money for charity. To this day, each district of London has a King and his 'Donah' (a colloquialism for 'wife').

Their resplendent attire is handed down through the families with the hereditary title. The suits, dresses, hats and bags are embroidered with symbols, celestial objects, diamonds, flowers, trees of life and fertility designs. Each of these outfits can carry as many as 30,000 mother-of-pearl buttons and weigh 30 kilograms or more. It is said that the use of these buttons originally came from a large shipment of pearl buttons which arrived from Japan in the 1860s. It is alleged that their use became commonplace when one of the costers embroidered buttons around the edge of his wide-bottomed trousers.

The first Pearly King is believed to have been the Victorian street sweeper, Henry Croft. In the 1870s, Mr. Croft covered his suit in mother-of-pearl buttons in a wonderful marketing attempt to draw attention to himself when collecting charity money for the hospitals and local orphanages. He started the Pearly Kings and Queens tradition of supporting charitable organisations.

Many Pearly families trace their heritage back to the coster-monger community. These were the fruit and vegetable street vendors of old London town. Traditionally, 'costers', as the street vendors were known, would elect 'Kings' to protect them from bullies trying to drive them away from their usual market pitches.

The Pearly Kings and Queens don't seem out of place in today's London. They do an enormous amount of work for charity, attending christenings, weddings and funerals. Some even attend in carts adorned with mother-of-pearl buttons and other assorted decorations. At the annual Harvest Festival service at St. Martin-in-the-Fields church in Trafalgar Square, London, the Pearly princesses can be seen providing their offerings in the form of bouquets of vegetables.

Morris Dancing

Grown men, beating sticks and dancing with bells on the knees ... it can only be Morris dancing! Morris dancing is one of our oldest English traditions, dating back centuries. Each year throughout May, villagers all over the length and breadth of rural Britain are treated to what may appear to be a bizarre custom. Men and women wearing white dancing around with bells on their knees, flowers in their hats and hitting sticks or waving handkerchiefs. The dance is usually performed during the May Day festival, Whitsun and Christmas. Although, they can pop up at any time when least expected.

Recent controversies have surrounded the tradition of some Morris groups going blackface, possibly to represent miners or beggars.

Morris dancing is a lively folk dance accompanied by rhythmic music played by an accordion, melodeon or fiddle player. The side of six or eight dancers perform a tightly choreographed routine, often arranged in a line or circle formation, facing inwards.

There are various groups of Morris dancers all around the country and each with its own unique customs. They'll wear different coloured clothing, often seen primarily dressed in white and wearing red braces with baldrics over their shoulders. There are at least six different styles of Morris dancing.

Morris dancing has been around for hundreds of years. It is impossible to say with any degree of certainty when or even why this curious custom began. There are several theories about this.

Some have suggested the dance originated in Spain and North Africa during religious persecution in the 15th century. This might explain the etymology of the name, possibly called 'Moor-ish' or 'Morisk' when first introduced to England. This was in reference to the 'Moors' of that region. Our earliest written records document their name as 'Morys'. It wasn't until the 17th century that we found the modern-day spelling of 'Morris' dancing.

The first written record of Morris dancing in England dates back to 1448. It was found in the archives of one of the oldest Livery companies in the City of London, the Goldsmiths' Company. Their records show that a troupe (or 'side' as they like to be known) of Morris dancers were paid seven shillings. Records from the Great Chronicle of London show that during Christmas 1494, a performance of "*spangled Spanish dancers*" appeared before the court of King Henry VII.

Whilst not mentioned by name, earlier parish records from Bishops Visitations mention dance performances that appear to be very similar to Morris dancing. In 1600, the Shakespearean actor William Kemp performed a Morris dance during his one-hundred-mile journey from London to Norwich as part of the 'Nine Daies Wonder' production.

It is possible that the heavy influence of the Italian culture on the Royal court of Queen Elizabeth I produced a hybrid between English folk dances and that of our 16th century counterparts.

In the 17th century, Cromwell's Puritan Long Parliament attempted to suppress anything seeming remotely of pagan origin. They passed ordinances to ban Whitsun festivals and pretty much all other forms of merriment. Interestingly, as we'll see in another chapter, none of the laws they passed were legally enforceable in any case. Without Royal assent, they couldn't be. However, that didn't stop the Puritans from providing some eye-wateringly harsh punishments for non-compliance. With the restoration of the Crown, King Charles II once again opened the flood gates to all the old festivals, frolics and frivolities. Morris dancing was back!

During the Industrial Revolution, Morris dancing experienced a decline in popularity. To keep the tradition alive, a small number of English folklorists were responsible for reviving the tradition on Boxing Day in 1899.

Between the 1950s and 1960s, there was an explosion of interest in Morris dancing, and we now saw women's sides and mixed sides. The introduction of women Morris dancers caused heated debates until it was pointed out that there is evidence of female Morris dancers from the 16th century.

If it continues for another few centuries, it isn't very comforting to imagine how Morris dancing will evolve.

Answers on a postcard, please, for anyone who can solve the riddle or the purpose of Morris dancing.

Maypole Dancing

Nothing more welcomes in the summer like dancing around a large poll exquisitely adorned with long multicoloured ribbons, with your friends. Each year on the 1st of May, communities around the UK participate in the 600-year-old tradition of dancing around the maypole. Where did this strange tradition come from, and what was its purpose?

The truth is, we don't know for sure, and like many well-known traditions, there are some discrepancies between the various schools of thought. There are suggestions of links between pagan folklore and maypole dancing. During the time of the ancient Celts, they divided their year into four great festivals: *Samhain* signified the arrival of winter; *Imbolc*, which represented the beginning of spring; *Beltane* on the 1st May (May Day), which marked the beginning of summer; and *Lughnasadh* signifying the arrival of the harvest season. Beltane starting on May Day, was celebrated with bonfires and fertility rites. In each community, a tree would be felled, stripped bare and decorated with garlands of flowers.

The maypole would be set up with long coloured ribbons trailing from above, each held by a child dancing. The children then run around the pole, ducking under the ribbons, creating a visual spectacle. A girl from the village would be selected to be the May Queen. At the end of the celebrations, a large funeral pyre was lit, and the May Queen would be sacrificed to the pagan gods.

There was a belief that this maypole represented a sacred tree with spirits. The spirits would bring good luck to the village through the maypole. This often led to neighbouring towns trying to steal each other's poles. Other suggestions include it originating 2000 years ago during Roman rule in Britain. It is believed soldiers danced around decorated trees to thank their Roman goddess of flowers, vegetation and fertility (Flora) for the arrival of spring.

May Day was often a rest day for labourers during the Middle Ages. You can imagine the rowdy behaviour resulting from mass ale drinking, frivolities and merriment when communities got together.

The first documented maypole dance is from the 14th century in Llanidloes, central Wales. This accords with the idea that the tradition first spread from Wales and Scotland into England. In the 15th century, there was mention of a permanent maypole at Cornhill in London in one of Geoffrey Chaucer's poems, 'Chaunce of the Dice'.

The Victorians took the old tradition and tried to clean up the image of the maypole by introducing the concept of children dancing merrily around it to provide a light-hearted community spirit. Communities have been very protective over their maypoles, possibly because of the superstition around it bringing good luck or possibly just because of the community spirit it brings. Over the years, villages have been trying to remove each other's maypoles. One such incident in Leicestershire was reported in The Derby Mercury in May 1772. It referred to *"a body of young fellows from Loughborough, who formed a plot to carry off the maypole, which they executed at night ...*

may be the cause of mischief and bloodshed, for the heroes of Quarndon vow revenge and are forming alliances with their neighbours of Barrow and Sheepshead, and give out they will soon march in a body to retake their favourite maypole."

It hasn't always been merry dancing around the maypole. As a result of the changing religious doctrines of our past Kings and Queens throughout the centuries, the maypole has sometimes been seen as an anti-Christian symbol.

During our short period without a monarch, Cromwell's Long Parliament sought to outlaw maypoles, describing them as *"a Heathenish vanity, generally abused to superstition and wickedness."* In April 1644, Parliament passed 'An Ordinance For The Better Observation of The Lords-Day'. This directed that all maypoles should be taken down and removed and banned the erection of any further maypoles. Any constables or churchwardens who neglected to remove the maypoles were fined at a rate of five shillings per week until the maypoles were removed. There is only one recorded breach of this maypole prohibition, and that was in Henley-in-Arden in 1655. Whilst it can't be proven, there were many more prohibitions. It's more likely that few bothered to report it to the authorities for fear of punishment.

It had only been a few years since King Charles I had been executed, and England was still divided between support for the Royalists and the Parliamentarians. Therefore, the maypole was likely seen as a symbol of resistance to the Long Parliament during this Interregnum period.

In 1660, the monarchy was restored with the arrival of King Charles II. This brought a much-needed period of merriment to England. Once again, dancing and singing on the village greens became commonplace. Maypoles began popping up everywhere!

According to entries from the Oxford diarist Anthony Wood, in May 1660, he wrote, "*a maypole... [was] set up on purpose to vex the Presbyterians and Independents*". His entry went on to detail attempts that had been made to chop it down, but all were futile. It was left to stand as a symbol of the Restoration of the monarchy.

In probably a significant two-finger gesture to Cromwell's memory, the tallest recorded maypole was erected in London's Strand in 1661. It was 143 feet tall (43.5 metres). It remained standing until 1717 when it was removed and used by Isaac Newton as a support for the Huygen brothers' new aerial telescope.

Wife Carrying

The annual event of wife carrying is another one of our more bizarre customs. It occurs each year in The Nower, Dorking in Surrey. It's a strange ritual that sees a man carrying his 'wife' in a competitive race across a hilly 380-metre course around the Surrey town, littered with obstacles of hay and water hazards.

Sounds fun? Yes, if that's your idea of fun. Consider that this tradition has its foundations in a more macabre period of local history. The custom dates back around twelve centuries to 8th June 793AD. In what would have been an otherwise uneventful day, Viking raiders rampaged through Lindisfarne on the northeast coast of England. They destroyed the local monastery and abducted any wives they could find, carrying them off to their awaiting ships. These Viking raids continued for around 300 years.

Almost 900 years later, the practice was revived in 2008, albeit with the full knowledge and consent of the carried 'wife'. These days it's an annual competition, where team members that are being carried no longer have to be 'wives'. They have to weigh over 50 kgs. The quirky rules state that for carried 'wives' who weigh under 50 kgs, the weight must be made up in the equivalent of tins of baked beans, flour, water or other similar items to reach that minimum required. The rules state that the 'wives' can be carried in a number of ways, including the bridal carry, the fireman's lift, the piggyback and even the Estonian Reverse hold, where the 'wife' hangs upside down on the carrier's back with her legs crossed in front of the carrier's face.

The winning prize is £100 and a keg of Pilgrim Ale. The carrier of the heaviest 'wife' also receives a gift of a pound of sausage meat. Runners-up don't go away empty-handed; they receive mini-kegs. The losers forfeit their dignity and receive a ceremonial tin of dog food and a Pot Noodle.

Sadly, in 2018, a woman received serious injuries after her husband dropped her on her head during the competition. Paramedics treated her at the scene, and she was carried away wearing a neck brace on a spinal board. Another competitor who dislocated his shoulder doggedly continued to the finish line.

CHAPTER EIGHT

DEATH &
EXECUTION

W e're all familiar with the name Guy Fawkes and the
Gunpowder Plot. After suffering an excruciating ordeal
on the rack, he was put to death in the only way possible for
those convicted of high treason: hanged, drawn and quartered.
This was a particularly gruesome method of execution, devised
to create as much fear as possible right to the point of death.
Methods of execution often depended upon a person's status
and wealth, and different ways existed to execute women and
men.

Over the centuries, our ancestors have developed some elaborate methods of execution. Executions were a very public
affair, from beheading for commoners to the more mundane
commonplace hangings in the town square. In fact, the London
Underground was built before the end of public hangings, and
many spectators would ride The Tube to attend these gruesome death-fests.

In this chapter, we peer into the grisly world of death and execution. Unsurprisingly, much of this chapter is devoted to King Henry VIII. It seemed to be his favourite pastime. We look at the different methods of execution used for commoners and noblemen. We also see how gender played a significant role in deciding the mode of execution.

"There is no justice in killing in the name of justice."
Archbishop Desmond Tutu

Hanged, Drawn and Quartered

When you think of torture and execution, especially during the reign of King Henry VIII, you imagine confessions being extracted through the rack, followed by being hanged, drawn and quartered. This particular punishment was reserved for anyone who dared to challenge the authority of the King. That was classed as high treason and considered the most serious of all offences. It was deemed to be more serious than murder.

Those found guilty would be held in isolation for a while, usually in the Tower of London, to increase their levels of fear and anxiety. They would often be allowed to see some of the instruments of their torture and execution before death. They would also be forced to watch the execution of other traitors to give them a taste of what's in store for them.

On the day of their execution, they would be stripped to the waist and tied either to the back of a horse or placed on a wooden cart. They would then be taken (drawn) to the executioner's scaffolding and forced to climb it. The King's commission would be read aloud in front of the large crowds waiting to witness this gruesome spectacle; the public would be asked to move back from the scaffold. The prisoner would be allowed to give a final address to the crowd. This is the famous '*Any last words?*' Most of the time, these would be admissions of guilt or some act of repentance, possibly the Lord's prayer. Occasionally, however, some of the traitors took this as a final opportunity to challenge the authority of the King. These final speeches were always closely monitored by the sheriff and chaplain, who sometimes were forced to step in to bring an end to the prisoner's speech. On one such occasion in 1588, the Catholic Priest William Dean gave an address to the crowd which was considered so inappropriate he had to be gagged.

Their arms were bound in front of them, and they were hanged for a short period to cause suffering and the feeling of asphyxiation. Most prisoners would wish they had died at this point, but unfortunately, their suffering was only starting. They were immediately cut down. A large cross would be cut in their stomach, and their bowels would be ripped out and thrown into a bonfire to burn before their eyes. At the same time, his testicles would be cut off. His heart would then be removed. Following death, his head would be decapitated, and his body would be chopped into four pieces (quartered).

Sometimes, the executioner was not as skilled in the art as they should have been, and things didn't always go smoothly. At the execution of Richard Gwyn on 15th October 1584, the executioner did an appalling job of disembowelment. He had to remove the bowel, piece by piece through a small hole in Gwyn's stomach.

Following the quartering, the remains would often be parboiled with salt and cumin seed to preserve the flesh and prevent the birds from pecking at it. The parts would then be displayed in various locations around the realm as a warning to anyone considering high treason. The severed head would be placed on a spike and displayed on London Bridge. This was one of the main routes to enter the City of London.

Following the Restoration of King Charles II, Samuel Pepys witnessed the execution of regicide Major-General Harrison. On 13th October 1660, he wrote in his diary, "*I went out to Charing Cross to see Major-General Harrison, hanged, drawn and quartered; which was done there, he looking as cheerful as any man could do in that condition. He was presently cut down, and his head and heart shown to the people, at which there was great shouts of joy.*"

It's uncertain when the first person was hanged, drawn and quartered. What we do know is that the first documented example of this punishment in its entirety occurred during the reign of King Edward I (1272-1307). This was the execution of the Welsh Prince Dafydd ap Gruffydd, who proclaimed himself Prince of Wales. Following his capture, King Edward proclaimed him "*treacherous*" and imprisoned him. It was decided that Dafydd had committed high treason and must be executed. On 3rd October 1283, it was recorded that he was drawn by horse through the streets of Shrewsbury to his place of execution. He was hanged, then let down and revived. Following this, he was disembowelled and forced to watch as his entrails were burned before his eyes. Once dead, his body was cut into quarters, and the four parts were sent to be stuck on spikes in different parts of the realm. His right arm was displayed in York, his left arm was displayed in Bristol, his right leg went to Northampton, and his left leg was displayed in Hereford. His head was cut off, bound with iron and set on a spear at the Tower of London.

In 1995 Mel Gibson played the Scottish national hero William Wallace in the film Braveheart. Yet, 690 years earlier, the real Scottish knight William Wallace met his end after being convicted of high treason during his trial at Westminster Hall on 23rd August 1305. His fate was equally as gruesome as the Welsh Prince Dafydd's. He was taken outside, stripped naked, and a crown of laurel leaves was placed on his head. He was drawn through the cobbled streets horizontally on the back of a wooden hurdle to his place of execution, Smithfield. En route, the crowds beat him with heavy sticks, punched and whipped him and threw pig swill over him. By the time he had arrived at Smithfield, he was barely alive. He was forced to climb up to the executioner's scaffold, whereupon he was hanged. He was taken down whilst he still had some life left in him. Then his genitals were cut off, and a large deep opening was carved into his stomach. The executioner reached in, pulled out his bowels, and threw them into the bonfire. This would have been the last thing Wallace would have seen before he died, all the while hearing the assembled crowds cheering. His lifeless body was then beheaded and cut into four pieces (quartered). His four body parts would have been displayed in Berwick, Newcastle, Stirling, and Perth as a warning to all other traitors. His head was set upon a spike and placed on London Bridge.

The Treason Act (1351), enacted by King Edward III, declared which offences would be considered treason. The seriousness of the crime dictated the severity of the sentence. High treason was considered more serious than murder as it was an attack on the King's authority. The Act stipulated the statutory penalty for high treason was to be hanged, drawn and quartered.

From the eighteenth century onwards, hanging, drawing and quartering no longer had a place in society. Offenders would still be drawn and then hanged until dead. In some cases, they were still beheaded and quartered, but this occurred after death. The punishment of being hanged, drawn and quartered was not entirely removed from the statute books until Queen Victoria's reign. Section 31 of the Forfeiture Act (1870) finally closed that chapter of bloody history. Beheading remained a viable option for those guilty of high treason under the Treason Act (1814). Interestingly, beheading for high treason was not abolished until 1973, with the passing of the Statute Law (Repeals) Act.

Beheading For Noble Traitors

When we think of public beheadings, we immediately think of King Henry VIII and the untimely demise of his wives, Anne Boleyn and Catherine Howard. A public executioner with an axe usually carried out beheadings. However, there were occasions when a sword was used instead. It was considered a quick and painless way to die, unless your name was Thomas Cromwell.

Beheadings for noble people were carried out on Tower Hill, on the higher ground next to the Tower of London moat. The last person to be executed at Tower Hill was Simon Fraser, 11th Lord Lovat, beheaded for treason on 9th April 1747. Thousands of people would flock from miles around to attend these gruesome public spectacles. The executioner would usually hold the severed head high and shout, "*Behold the head of [name of the executed], a traitor.*" Interestingly, these words were not spoken at the execution of King Charles I.

Whilst it was considered the swiftest and most painless method of execution, it didn't always go according to plan. There are still debates about whether the brain remains functional shortly after death. Eye witness accounts show that after the executioner severed Anne Boleyn's head with a single strike of his sword, her lips continued to move for several seconds in silent prayer. This could just be involuntary muscle movement.

One well-known botched beheading was that of Thomas Cromwell, who was executed on Tower Hill on 28th July 1540. There has been much speculation over the centuries about Cromwell's execution and whether it was botched. However, it's worth mentioning that some sources have indicated that it took up to three blows of the axe by an executioner who is described as ragged, butcherly, ungoodly and a miser. Some accounts report that two executioners had to be involved and were chopping away at Cromwell's neck and head for nearly half an hour.

In another botched execution, Margaret Pole, Countess of Salisbury, suffered her demise on Tower Hill on 27th May 1541. Two written eyewitness reports survive of her execution, one from the French ambassador and the other from the ambassador to the Holy Roman Emperor. One ambassador wrote about the execution by *"a wretched and blundering youth who literally hacked her head and shoulders to pieces in the most pitiful manner."*

Finally, this brings us to the most unusual story of the ignominious end of James Scott, 1st Duke of Monmouth. He was also the eldest illegitimate son of King Charles II. Following the death of King Charles II in February 1685, the Crown passed to King James II. James Scott, being illegitimate, was ineligible as an heir to the throne. He tried to assert his rights to the line of succession, and one of his officers declared him to be the legitimate King. He led the Monmouth Rebellion and landed several ships at Lyme Regis in Dorset in June 1685. In an attempt to usurp King James II, he published a paper called the *'Declaration for the defence and vindication of the protestant religion and of the laws, rights and privileges of England from the invasion made upon them, and for delivering the Kingdom from the usurpation and tyranny of us by the name of James, Duke of York.'* The King had enough and ordered the publishers and distributors of the paper to be arrested. The rebellion failed, and on 8th July, Monmouth was arrested and sentenced for treason. Monmouth, a devout Protestant, offered to convert to Catholicism to avoid execution. The King would not accept this, and on 15th July 1685, Monmouth was led up to Tower Hill, where he was met by the famous executioner Jack Ketch. After inflicting between five and eight blows with his axe, during which it is said Monmouth tried to rise from the executioner's block, Monmouth's head had to be severed from his twitching body with the extra use of a knife. According to legend, following his execution, it was quickly realised that there was no official portrait of the Duke of Monmouth, as was tradition. So, his body was quickly exhumed, his head stitched back on, and his portrait was painted in a few hours before just as quickly being reinterred in the Church of St. Peter ad Vincula in the Tower of London.

Beheading For Commoners

Beheading, as a form of execution, wasn't practised in England until the Norman times. Beheadings for commoners were a very different affair from that of noblemen. Noblemen were often beheaded on Tower Hill with an axeman, placing their heads on the chopping block. The beheading of commoners was often a very botched job.

The first documented person to be beheaded was Walthoef, Earl of Northumberland. He was accused of joining a revolt against William the Conqueror. He was arrested, tried before the King's court and sentenced to death. He was finally beheaded at St. Giles's Hill, Winchester, on 31st May 1076, just two years before the famous White Tower (Tower of London) was completed.

Those sentenced to death by beheading were advised to tip the public executioner in advance. It was hoped this would encourage him to do a swift and efficient job, hopefully despatching the victim in one clean blow. This did not always happen. The notorious public executioner, Jack Ketch, was well known for his botched executions. One such case occurred on 21st July 1683 at Lincoln's Inn Fields, after Lord William Russell had been convicted over his involvement in the Rye House Plot to kill King Charles II. Lord Russell had paid Ketch in advance, hoping he would make the execution swift and painless. Jack Ketch did such a bad job that, after the axe hit the side of Russell's head, Russell looked up at him and said, "*You dog, did I give you ten guineas to use me so inhumanely?*" It took him a further three axe blows to separate the head from the body, during which the amassed crowd jeered Ketch. It is alleged that afterwards, Ketch felt compelled to write a letter of apology to the King. Ketch was sent to prison in 1686 for 'affronting' a Sheriff. His assistant, Paskah Rose, became the public executioner in Ketch's absence. A few months later, Rose himself was convicted and hanged at Tyburn, leading to Ketch's reinstatement.

We often think of the guillotine as a French invention. Before it was introduced to France, an early form of the guillotine was in use in England. It was known as the '*Halifax Gibbet*'. On 30th April 1650, Abraham Wilkinson and Andrew Mitchel were sentenced to beheading at the Halifax Gibbet. The gibbet was described as considerably raised from the ground. They had to climb a flight of stone steps to arrive at the gibbet. The iron axe was fixed on a transverse beam above the prisoner's head. The axe was drawn up using a cord and pulley. A pin inserted near the top held the blade in place, ensuring it didn't drop until the correct time. Every person then took hold of the cord or ceremoniously held out their arm near it. The fourth

Psalm was then played on the bagpipes. A minister offered a final prayer to the prisoner, after which the blade was allowed to fall, chopping off their head. In cases where the offender had been convicted of stealing an animal, the end of the cord was attached to the animal, which was then moved along, pulling out the pin, allowing the blade to drop.

Records from Halifax show that from 1541 until the final beheadings (Wilkinson and Mitchel) using the Halifax Gibbet in 1650, 49 people had been despatched using that Gibbet. That same year, Oliver Cromwell forbade the use of the Halifax Gibbet, and it was dismantled.

There is one amusing story that came out of the Halifax Gibbet. This involved a peculiar custom surrounding the use of the Gibbet. It gave offenders a second chance. If an offender were fast enough to withdraw their head from the Gibbet in time to avoid the falling blade, they would be released if they left the town and never returned. On 29th January 1623, this did happen. The offender, John Lacy, managed to withdraw his head in time and left Halifax. Unfortunately for him, he returned seven years later, wrongly believing that he would have been pardoned in the meantime. He wasn't. He was re-arrested and taken back to the Gibbet. Sadly, the years had not been kind to Lacy. This second time around, he wasn't as fast as he once was. For him, there was no escaping the executioner a second time.

Women Were Drowned or Burned Alive

As recently as the mid-twentieth century, women were still seen as the 'fairer sex'. This wasn't lost on our ancestors either, who considered it too indecent to hang, draw and quarter women. Instead, they were either to be burned alive or drowned.

At the start of this book, I referred to the Interpretations Act (1978), which implies that any reference to the male gender in this book can also be considered to apply to the female gender or, in fact, any gender whatsoever. However, our ancestors never believed an act of high treason could be committed by a woman, so the Interpretations Act would never have applied to the terms of the original Treason Act. It was considered too horrific for the public to watch a woman being disembowelled. As the seventeenth-century Chief Justice of the King's Bench, Sir Edward Coke put it, "*the decency due to the sex forbids the exposing and publicly mutilating their bodies*" Instead, women were dragged to the gallows, hanged and burned.

During the Middle Ages, women who stole were referred to as 'She-thieves' and were usually put to death by drowning. This was considered the most modest method of despatch. The death sentence would be read using the Latin words "*cum fossa et furca*," meaning 'with drowning-pit and gallows'. Apart from the witch trials en masse, where we showed our judicial respect for women who didn't necessarily conform, there are plenty of records of women being drowned for various offences. The sentence of drowning the guilty was finally abolished in England in 1623 during the reign of King James I.

Scotland was hearing nothing of it and continued drowning women. In 1623, eleven Gypsy women were drowned in Nor' Loch, Edinburgh. This was the notorious ducking spot used during the witch trials. They would then be burned at the stake on Castlehill. In 1679, a woman named Janet Grant was convicted of theft in the baronial court of Sir Robert Gordon of Gordonstone in Elginshire. She was found guilty and condemned to be drowned in Loch of Spynie, Moray, Scotland. Drowning women was abolished in Scotland in 1685.

With drowning now off the books, what other method could still be used to execute women? Burning at the stake, of course! Burning was a legally prescribed punishment for women guilty of high and petty treason. Heretics would also find themselves burned at the stake. It was thought that burning would cleanse the soul. This was an important feature for those guilty of heresy and witchcraft. As time passed, further offences, like counterfeiting currency and murdering one's husband, resulted in a public burning.

Burning was favoured in the early centuries because it didn't involve the direct shedding of blood, which was against the teachings of the Roman Catholic church. Burning the accused's body provided no vessel for the afterlife. This was considered the most severe of punishments in the eyes of the church. During the early burnings, prisoners would still be alive to suffer the whole ordeal. Later, they would be hanged or strangled by the executioner and then burned. The crowds of spectators would see the prisoner burn, but there would be no screaming from the lifeless body. In the reign of Queen Mary I, women were stripped naked, and a small bag of gunpowder was placed around their necks. This would eventually explode in the fire, quickening the prisoner's demise as an act of mercy. During the witch trials in Scotland, it fell part of the death sentence for the convicted witches to be strangled and then burned.

There were three distinctly different methods of burning women. One method saw bundles of sticks piled around a central wooden stake. The prisoner would be bound to the stake with iron chains. This was the preferred method, being the most theatrical. It satisfied the crowds of onlookers, watching the slow suffering and hearing the screams and agonising gurgles. It also provided the most suffering as it took a while for the flames to reach the prisoner's head; all the time, the rest of her body was burned. Another method saw the wooden sticks piled high around the central stake. This sped up the burning and death, with the flames quickly consuming the whole body whilst the smoke and hot fumes filled her lungs. The hot air would cause her trachea to swell, leading to asphyxia and death within minutes. The prisoner's suffering would be hidden behind a curtain of flames, but their screams could still be overheard. A third method, seldom used, saw the prisoner bound to the top of a tall ladder and slowly lowered over a burning fire pit.

There are no official records of when the first execution by burning occurred in Britain. However, a record exists of Robert of Reading, a young Christian deacon who was burnt at the stake in Oxford in 1222 for converting to the Jewish faith to marry a Jewish woman.

In 1401, King Henry IV passed a law called '*De heretico comburendo*' (regarding the burning of heretics) to punish heretics with burning at the stake. William Sawtrey was the first to be burned under this new Act. He was a Catholic priest, burned on 26th February 1401 for rejecting Catholic teachings. During the five-year reign of Mary Tudor (1553-1558), there were 274 public burnings for heresy. This was both men and women and rightly entitles Queen Mary to her sobriquet 'Bloody Mary'. Most of these 'criminals' were burned just for following the Protestant faith. Section 6 of Queen Elizabeth I's Act of Supremacy (1558) repealed the earlier 1401 Act.

One famous burning at the stake was the English writer and Protestant, Anne Askew. Sadly for Askew, while she remained a devout Protestant for life, this came at the end of the reign of King Henry VIII. During this turbulent time, there was a struggle in the Royal court between religious traditionalists and reformers. The King was advised to seek an alliance with the King of Spain, Charles V, and halt his own religious reforms. To show that he was doing this, the King made an example of several people harbouring Protestant beliefs. The irony is that it was the King himself who separated the Church of England from papal authority. Despite this, Askew was arrested and placed on the rack at the Tower of London. Records show she was racked "*' till her bones and joints were almost plucked asunder, in such sort as she was carried away in a chair.*" They tried to get her to implicate the King's sixth wife, Katheryn Parr, for harbouring Protestant beliefs. Askew was charged with heresy, tied to the stake and burned alive. She was, some may consider, one of the lucky ones because a barrel of gunpowder was placed near her body to swiftly end her suffering. Witnesses of her execution stated that she had been so badly tortured on the rack that she could not stand unaided. Askew is one of only two women tortured in the Tower of London and burnt at the stake.

A century later, we see the public burning at Smithfield on 10th April 1652 of Prudence Lee. She had been found guilty of murdering her husband. During her execution, she confessed to being jealous of and arguing with her husband and stabbing him with a knife. Witnesses reported that she shrieked five or six times throughout her ordeal. The last heretic to be burned alive was in 1612. Burning alive as a sentence for murder was abolished in 1656, although burning for adultery remained on the statute books. Following this, those condemned to be burned at the stake were first strangled and burned post-mortem.

The last person to be burned at the stake for witchcraft in England is thought to be Alice Molland. She was condemned as one of the Devon witches and burned in Exeter during the Bideford witch trial in 1684.

A year later, in 1685, Elizabeth Gaunt was found guilty of high treason after being convicted for her involvement in the Rye House Plot to assassinate King Charles II and his brother. She was denied strangulation and is the last recorded woman to be burnt alive for high treason.

Catherine Hayes was the last woman in England to be burned alive in 1726. She was found guilty of petty treason by murdering her husband, John Hayes and dismembering his body with the two men with whom she had enjoyed a promiscuous relationship. Before her execution, she had unsuccessfully tried to poison herself. On 9th May, she was tied to a stake at Tyburn with an iron collar around her neck. It is said that the fire was lit too early, and when it started to burn through the rope, this distracted the executioner, who could not strangle her in time. Eyewitnesses reported her many cries and lamentations as she burned alive.

The law also permitted the burning of children aged seven and above at the stake. In one such case, a 16-year-old Mary Troke was burned at the stake in Winchester on 18th March 1738, following her conviction for poisoning her mistress.

Catherine Murphy was the last woman in England to be burned at the stake. She was executed in 1789 for counterfeiting coins in a modified form of hanging. She died of asphyxia, followed by burning. The firewood was not lit for 30 minutes after she had hanged.

Public attitudes towards burning convicts changed in the late eighteenth century. Consequently, Parliament passed The Treason Act (1790). From 5th June that year, a conviction for any coinage offences, which usually led to a sentence of burning at the stake, was substituted for hanging. The 25-year-old Sophia Girton must have thanked her lucky stars, having been convicted at the Old Bailey of coinage offences on 24th April that same year. Her sentence was changed to hanging, but this was later commuted to transportation for life to New South Wales, Australia.

Hanging

Hanging was one of our most popular methods of execution from Saxon times right up to the mid-twentieth century. It certainly was one of the least gruesome methods of punishment. It is believed to have been introduced into England around the fifth century by the Germanic Anglo-Saxon tribes.

When William the Conqueror came to the throne, he favoured the ecclesiastical methods and decreed that hanging should be replaced by blinding and castration. It didn't disappear for too long, having been reintroduced during the reign of King Henry I (1100-1135). It seems to be the predominant mode of execution that has outlasted all others. This was certainly the case by the end of the eighteenth century.

From the early days, hanging used what was known as the 'Short drop' method. The criminal would have the noose placed around their neck, and they would stand on a stool or a ladder. This would then be pulled away quickly by rope, either by the executioner, the waiting crowds or even a horse. Sometimes, the executioner would grow impatient and just kick the stool away, leaving the criminal hanging. This led to very slow and painful strangulation until death. Regularly, friends and family of the prisoner would grab hold of their ankles to pull them down, to speed their strangulation and reduce their suffering.

From the eighteenth century, the mechanics of hanging slowly changed. Sometimes, the criminal would stand over the trapdoor. The trapdoor would quickly open, and they would plummet through it, hanging until their death. If they were lucky, the hanged man would break his neck, but it was more usual for them to dangle whilst being strangled to death. Suggestions at the time considered the position of the noose knot around the prisoner's neck. It was deemed preferable to dislocate their neck when they dropped to speed up the execution. In 1853, the previous 'Short drop' method was replaced with the 'Long drop', which saw the victim fall further, with the help of gravity, which snapped their neck. Death was instantaneous.

During the reign of Henry VIII, most public hangings were conducted at the gallows at Tyburn. Often, the important executions attracted crowds of up to 100,000 people. It became a very theatrical performance. The prisoners would be led up to the gallows, where the hangmen would uncoil a rope, throwing up the free end to an assistant who wrapped it around an upper beam. It would then be attached to a horse which was later whipped to quickly jerk forward, pulling the prisoner off their stand, to be left suspended in the air. They would writhe around in agony, kicking their legs whilst they slowly asphyxiated. This was known as '*dancing the Tyburn jig*'.

Tyburn remained a very popular location for watching public executions in London. The gallows, known as the 'Three-Legged Mare', could hang several criminals at the same time. It was located near where Marble Arch stands today. In 1783, the gallows were moved to their new home outside Newgate Prison. During the early Victorian period, it cost £25 to rent a room with a good view overlooking the Newgate gallows. For distinguished visitors, lavish breakfasts would be served, including the popular treat of the time, devilled kidneys.

In 1770, there were 222 crimes on the statute books, all carrying a death sentence. This was finally reduced to four capital offences with the passing of the Criminal Law Consolidation Acts in 1861.

It is bizarre to think that the London Underground was operating whilst public hangings were still taking place in London. The Metropolitan line, which used to run from Paddington to Farringdon, would have carried many spectators to these gruesome public hangings between when it first opened in January 1863 and the last public hanging on 26th May 1868. During that time, 12 people were executed at Newgate. Farringdon tube station was a 10-minute walk from the gallows. It was undoubtedly a very popular event. You can imagine the bustling crowds with street vendors selling to the thousands of spectators in attendance. In 1864, 20,000 spectators turned up to watch five pirates being hanged. Among them was five-year-old Arthur Conan Doyle, who later went on to write the Sherlock Holmes novels.

On 26th May 1868, the last public execution took place at Newgate. Michael Barrett was hanged for his involvement in a botched jailbreak at the Clerkenwell House of Detention. He planted explosives which subsequently went off and killed twelve bystanders, severely injuring many more. Following Barrett's execution, all hangings were performed behind prison walls, out of view from the public.

In 1908, the Children Act banned the hanging of children under the age of 16. The Children and Young Persons Act (1933) raised this minimum age for hanging to 18 years old. The last woman to be hanged in Britain was Ruth Ellis. She was hanged at HMP Holloway on 13th July 1955 for the murder of her lover, David Blakely. The last people to be hanged in Britain were hanged on the same day, 13th August 1964. One was Peter Allen, hanged at Walton Prison in Liverpool. The other was Gwynne Evans, who was hanged at Strangeways Prison in Manchester. They were both hanged for the murder of van driver John West.

The death penalty for murder ceased to be used in 1965, although it remained on the statute books for murder until 1969. It remained on the statute books until 1998 for treason, espionage and piracy with violence.

CHAPTER NINE

FEATHERED FRIENDS

B irds are our friends. Yet for years, we have sought to do them harm. This was for numerous reasons. For some, our feathered friends could be tasty, whilst some just chose to hunt these defenceless animals for sport.

In this chapter, we learn about the angry swearing parrot that very nearly caused offence to a former Queen. We have national laws and laws specific to the Royal Parks. It is made abundantly clear to us that birds are our friends to be protected, although some may occasionally be eaten ... Just so long as we don't pick on a pelican.

Leave those swans alone!

> *"Look deep into nature, and then you will understand everything better."*
> Albert Einstein

Illegal to Touch a Pelican

It is an offence to touch a pelican within the Royal Parks and surrounding open spaces. You may be interested to know that it would also be illegal for you to ride a pelican. This offence became embodied within the law with the passing of The Royal Parks and Other Open Spaces Regulations (1997). Section 4(24) makes it an offence to *feed or touch any deer or pelican*. It is also an offence to interfere with any plants or flowers within the Royal Parks. This conjures up imagery of Alice in Wonderland in the Queen's rose garden.

You may touch a pelican, ride a deer or even interfere with the King's flowers if you first have written permission from the Secretary of State. It is believed the law stipulates these two animals in particular due to their susceptibility to the bacterial infection *Lyme borreliosis* (Lyme disease), which is spread through ticks.

Illegal to Leave a Dead Parrot in a Public Place

We all share one grim certainty in life; we will someday die. This is shared across the entire animal kingdom. As a nation of animal lovers, when a family loses their pet, it can be such a devastating loss. Often, the dog or cat is treated like a family member. They share our lives, experiences and emotions.

So, what happens when your pet dies?

Many families will choose to hold a private burial in their back garden. As we'll see elsewhere in this book, there are some stringent rules and laws in relation to doing this. So, what else can you do if you can not bury your goldfish or your lovable rogue, the pet cat, in the garden? You can contact your local veterinary surgeon to see whether they will take the body for disposal. The one thing you can not do is leave it in a public place. By this, I don't mean dragging the dead carcass and dumping it on the pavement, although that would be an offence.

There are very strict laws surrounding such things, and you can see why. It's for reasons of public hygiene, especially when historically we have pandemics every century. In between, all sorts of nasty diseases and infections pop up from time to time. Burial outside a pet cemetery or the pet's home is an offence.

Those wishing to bury their pets at home must ensure that they own the plot of land where the pet will be buried. If you're renting your property, you first need to seek permission from the landowner. The burial ground must also be a domestic dwelling, not an active commercial premises like an office. The dwelling where the pet is buried must be the same place where it lived. For example, if you don't have a garden, you can't just dig a hole in the local park, nor can you bury the pet in a friend's property, even if they own it. There are other rules related to proximity to watercourses and depth of the burial plot, but we cover these in another chapter.

Leaving your dead parrot out on the pavement, on a bus seat or a bench in the local park would be an offence of littering. It would also be an offence under The Animal By-Products (Enforcement) (England) Regulations (2013). Failure to comply with these requirements could result in a fine of up to £5,000 and possibly a three-month stay at His Majesty's Pleasure if dealt with in a Magistrates Court. If the matter proceeds to the Crown Court, the penalty can be a fine and possible imprisonment for up to two years.

The Killing of Swans is Illegal

Not just whales, sturgeon, dolphins and porpoises belong to the monarch; His Majesty may also claim a right over all wild, mute swans found in open water. The Crown has held the Royal prerogative over these swans since the twelfth-century.

This isn't all swans, just the mute swans (*Cygnus olor*). The UK is home to 3 types of swans; mute, whooper and Berwick swans. The most common swan in the UK is the mute swan. In reality, the Crown only exercises Royal prerogative over swans on the River Thames and its tributaries and it is not exclusive ownership either. The King shares his right with the Vintners' Company and the Dyers' Company, both City of London livery companies. The first mention of this Royal prerogative over mute swans comes from Gerald of Wales (*Giraldus Cambrensis*), Archdeacon and historian, and a Royal clerk to the King in the late twelfth-century.

It is a popular myth that killing a Swan is an act of treason against the Crown and that the King of England is the only person allowed to eat swan meat. This is not true, and there is no evidence to support these claims either. It is just that, a myth. Killing and eating one of the King's mute swans is undoubtedly unlawful, but it has never been an act of treason. Although, it is said that diners at St. Johns College, Cambridge, were historically granted Royal permission to consume swan meat on their premises.

The King is the Seigneur of the Swans. Each year this mysterious connection between the Crown and mute swans is upheld in a traditional Swan Upping ceremony. The purpose of this ceremony is to mark and record all swans along a stretch of the River Thames and its tributaries. As bizarre as we may think this ancient custom is, the question of who owns swans, who can keep them and who has a right to eat them has been debated since mediaeval times.

Since the twelfth-century, swans have been seen as a status of wealth and nobility. They were the mediaeval equivalent of owning a Bugatti Veyron. Swan meat was seen as a delicacy at Royal feasts and would be served whole and still feathered, often with a lump of smoking incense in its beak. Records show that forty swans were delivered for King Henry III's Royal banquet at Winchester during Christmas 1247.

In 1482-1483, King Edward IV passed the '*Act of Swans*' to address the increase in the number of stolen swans and cygnets, where people unlawfully marked them as their property. This law prevented the unlawful keeping and the marking of Swans by "*Yeomen and Husbandmen, and other persons of little Reputation.*" The Crown authorised any person to seize swans being kept unlawfully. Half of the seizure would go directly to the Crown and the other half to the person seizing the swans. This Act also provided that only those with freehold lands valued at five marks or greater could keep swans. It referenced the system of swan marks developed to show proper ownership.

This allowed the rightful owner to mark the swans with nicks in their beaks. Swans which weren't marked were the property of the Crown. At one time, the Crown kept so many swans along the River Thames that in 1496, it prompted the secretary to the Venetian Ambassador to describe what he saw as *"a truly beautiful thing to behold one or two thousand tame swans upon the River Thames."* In 1570, the '*Order of Swannes*' complemented the 1482 Act by stating, *"if any person do raze out, counterfeit or alter the mark of any swan [they] shall suffer one year's imprisonment."*

On 23rd August 2022, a vellum register from 1566 was placed on auction. The Tudor manuscript listed aristocratic swan owners and the ornate markings attributed to each family for them to mark swan beaks. The book contained more than 600 swan marks used in Norfolk and Suffolk.

In 1592, Sir Edward Coke represented Queen Elizabeth I as her Solicitor General in a case over the ownership of swans in Dorset. The case was brought before the court after the Sheriff of Dorset had been directed to seize 400 swans from the local rivers. Dame Joan Young argued that the swans belonged to her and that they had always been the property of the local abbot of the Abbey of St. Peter at Abbotsbury. When King Henry VIII dissolved the monasteries, the local abbot lost the right to the swans along with his Abbey. The King had then granted the estate to Sir Giles Strangways. Upon Strangways's death, his heir granted rights to the swans to Dame Joan for one year. Queen Elizabeth I was now the monarch, and she wanted her swans. The court held that as the swans were Royal birds, their rights to them could only be granted by *ratione privilegii* (Royal privilege), so their ownership could not legally be transferred to Dame Joan. It held that the swans were *ferae naturae* (of wild nature), and in any case, that which is wild can not be owned as property. This is still recognised in modern-day law.

For example, the Theft Act (1968) states that wild animals can not be owned.

In today's world, if you choose to capture or kill a mute swan, you must be one sick and deranged individual. Secondly, and quite rightly, you should be subjected to punishment. This is provided for by the Wildlife and Countryside Act (1981), as mute swans are now a native species and protected by law. This law makes it an offence to keep or kill them, which is punishable with a £5,000 fine.

In Kent, Cockerels are Not Permitted to Crow Within 182.88 Metres From Any Human Habitation

If you've ever lived on or near a farm, you may have been rudely awoken at first light each morning by the crows from the resident cockerels. If more than one cockerel is kept in an enclosure, they tend to compete with one another, thus raising the volume further.

It is these crows that quite often give rise to neighbourly complaints in rural areas.

The local authority in the agricultural village of Biddenden, in the borough of Ashford, Kent, passed a bylaw prohibiting the keeping of cockerels closer than 200 yards (182.88 metres) to any human habitation.

The Angry Parrots

There are approximately 398 different species of parrots in the world. They can live for up to 60 years. People have been domesticating parrots and keeping them as pets for many years. They have wonderful personalities and often amusingly enjoy mimicking their owners' expressions and repeating a word or two. King George V owned an African grey parrot, Charlotte, who regularly attended the King's Privy Council meetings, perched on His Majesty's shoulder. As the King read through the sensitive material in his red boxes, the parrot on his shoulder would squawk, "*What about it?*"

When the King fell seriously ill, his parrot flew around for hours chattering, "*Where's the Captain?*" A photograph taken in 1930 shows King George V's granddaughter later to become Queen Elizabeth II, chasing after his parrot Charlotte on the gravel driveway.

Parrots have brought us centuries of entertainment, love and fun. Although sometimes they can get a little mischievous. It is this side of their personality and the resulting consequences that we shall look at now. In an amusing but equally absurd case from 1898 in London, we see a mass brawl break out in public caused by nothing more than a small parrot. The facts were reported on at the time in the newspaper, the Falkirk Herald.

Two friends, Arthur Crowe and George Tibbett, were seated at a table having a drink in a Blackfriars pub with a German lady. Another regular to the pub was Mr. Brambani, an Italian ice cream seller. He strolled into the bar to relax and have a drink. The pub's landlord kept a parrot behind the bar, and Brambani had been trying to teach the parrot to speak Italian for some time. The newspaper reported that each time, the parrot replied in English "*with characteristic ineptitude.*" Unperturbed, Brambani continued to try to get the parrot to speak Italian. At that point, the parrot apparently made a foul-mouthed reply. However, the newspaper sparingly printed its reply as "*Oh, you old --*". Whatever this parrot replied was enough to provoke Crowe and Tibbett into a fight. They believed the words had come from Mr. Brambani. They thought Brambani was making a lewd remark about the German lady seated at their table. Despite Mr. Brambani's protestations that the real culprit was the feathered fiend behind the bar, Crowe and Tibbett appeared game for a fight, demanding an apology. It is reported that the parrot excitedly "*kept up a running fire of abusive and scandalous remarks.*"

Brambani, sensing imminent danger, quickly made his escape and ran into his nearby sweet shop. The affronted two men and German woman pursued him and were quickly joined by a small mob. Mr. Brambani's nephew tried to explain what had happened and appealed for calm. Instead, he was pelted with bottles of ginger beer and glasses from the sweet shop counter.

Police Constables Greenway and Hunt arrived on the scene and arrested Crowe and Tibbett. The German lady had already made her escape. They were both jailed for a month. We have no further information on what happened to the parrot. Still, I suspect it remained in the pub due to the entertainment factor it brought.

Sailors arriving at the Port of London imported many parrots into the UK. Surrounded by a motley crew of gruff and foul-mouthed sailors for the duration of their voyage to the UK, it's clear why many parrots of the time picked up their profane vocabulary.

In 1896, we had the curious case of a parrot that did make it into a courtroom. Henry Lovegrove, a solicitor's clerk, had seen a talking parrot in another London pub. He thought it would make the ideal gift for his girlfriend.

He approached the parrot's keeper, ship's steward William Foulger to enquire about the bird and whether it was able to talk. Foulger explained that not only could it speak English but Spanish as well. It could also sing a version of Ta-ra-ra-boom-de-ay. Concerned that the parrot's recent company had been sailors, he enquired whether it was okay to be in the presence of a lady. Foulger reassured him that the bird chose its words carefully and that "*Its language is that of a bishop.*" They agreed on a fair price of

30 shillings for the parrot, who shortly found its way into the home of Lovegrove's girlfriend, Miss. Nelson.

After a short while, Miss. Nelson explained that the parrot had to go. She could not stand being in its presence for a moment longer. In the meantime, Lovegrove had not yet paid Foulger, who decided to take action against him at Shoreditch County Court. During the trial, Miss. Nelson stated, "*The parrot swears more than the troops in Flanders.*" This main issue was that whilst the parrot swore profusely, most people didn't think this was the case. The parrot was originally from Spain and specialised in repeating Spanish swear words. Unfortunately, some years earlier, Miss. Nelson had been a governess in Spain, so she understood the parrot fluently. She described the parrot's language to the court as "*simply sulphurous.*" The judge commented, "*My knowledge of the Spanish tongue is not so profound as Miss Nelson's, nor have I any wish to endure Ta-ra-ra-boom-de-ay again,*" and the case was settled. Mr. Lovegrove kept his cash, and Mr. Foulger was given custody of his parrot. Miss. Nelson was able to retain her sanity.

Parrots have been kept by many pubs and ale houses over the centuries as a friendly and exotic form of entertainment for patrons.

Before we leave the parrots, there is just one more story I would like to share from the early part of 20th century London. A parrot was kept at Ye Olde Cheshire Cheese pub on Fleet Street. It reached the heights of such notoriety that its death on 1st November 1926 was recorded in the Devon and Exeter Gazette newspaper and broadcast on the BBC 2LO radio station. The pub itself dates back to 1538, and the current building has been standing since 1667, so it has seen a fair share of the content we cover in this book.

The newspaper report reads as follows,

"*A Great Bird: The death after a long illness of the Cheshire Cheese parrot has gloomed half of London. The news was broadcast last night from 2LO with due solemnity. So far as a grey and scarlet South African parrot can achieve greatness, that bird did. For 40 years it was the biggest personality in Fleet-street. No really illustrious visitor to this country failed to secure an audience, at which the parrot always took the honours. It was a gifted talker, even by the highest Army stan-dards, and beside such wide-tricks as imitating perfectly all the sounds of a public bar not only swore like a cavalry S.M.* [Sergeant Major] *but obviously knew the right time to do it. I once saw it drop a cigarette box it was perforating. It promptly exclaimed just what most ex-Service men would say if they dropped a half crown down a grid. Once Princess* Mary [later Queen Mary] *insisted on being introduced to Polly. It had to be done, but it aged the manager. If anyone had mentioned the Kaiser the King's daughter would have heard things not mentioned to a drunken cow-puncher.*"

CHAPTER TEN

GRUESOME PUNISHMENTS

W e've all heard about the harsh punishments of the Victorian age. Victorian schools were a particularly hostile environment for any child to find themselves. Those who stepped on the wrong side of the law in Victorian society could find themselves thrown into prison and forced to undergo hard, repetitive and boring labour. Some prisoners found this punishment so harsh they literally dropped dead.

In this chapter, we delve into the murky world of punishments. History shows us a full spectrum of available punishments for different groups of people, from thieving slaves, to beggars and special punishments for 'whores'. We look at why those worse off were often the first to be punished and more harshly.

"Punishment is justice for the unjust."
Saint Augustine

Victorian Classroom Punishments

Life as a child in the Victorian era was not especially pleasant. Many children were forced to work from a very early age. Those were some of the lucky ones. The children with no known parents were forced into workhouses. In an attempt to stop children from being forced to work, for example, as chimney sweeps, Parliament passed several sets of laws setting compulsory school ages. In 1880, the Education Act was passed, making it compulsory for all children between the ages of 5 and 10 to attend school. However, many parents and employers took it upon themselves to keep children away from schools to earn money for the family. In 1893, Parliament passed the Elementary Education (School Attendance) Act to resolve this. This raised the age of compulsory school attendance to 11. In 1899, an amendment to this Act raised the mandatory school attendance age to 12 years old.

It wasn't just the parents and employers who wanted to keep children away from school; Victorian classrooms were sometimes harsh, and many children didn't wish to be there. There was no understanding of mental health issues, learning difficulties, social inclusion or acceptance of individual idiosyncrasies. Instead, every child had to conform to a standard. Those who misbehaved were placed in solitary confinement. They would literally be locked away in a room on their own. In the early nineteenth century, class sizes were enormous, often with more than 100 pupils per class. Records show that one school in Hitchin, Hertfordshire had a class size of over 300 boys in one class.

Life in Victorian schools was harsh, and punishments were unforgiving. Children were frequently caned for the most mundane of transgressions. The canes were made from birch wood. Boys would be caned on the buttocks, while girls were caned across the palms of their hands or on the back of their legs. Children could receive a caning for something as simple as being lazy, lying, poor attendance, insolence, or just leaving a classroom without permission. In Scotland, a leather strap called a tawse was used instead of the cane. A running log of punishments was kept in the school punishments book.

Those children caught fidgeting in lessons, would have their hands tied behind their backs, or their fingers could be placed in small wooden finger stocks. Children unable to answer questions or those considered 'slow' would be forced to wear a pointed Dunce hat with the letter 'D' on it. They would then have to stand in the corner of the classroom for an hour or more. Children caught slouching in lessons would have a rigid wooden backboard shoved down their back to straighten their posture forcefully. Left-handed children caught trying to write with their left hands would quickly find them tied down, and they were forced to continue writing with their right hand. If any of this upset a child and they cried, they would be further punished for crying.

Some of the strict rules that applied in Victorian classrooms were as follows:

1. Students must stand up to answer questions and wait for permission to speak

2. Students must call teachers '*Sir*', '*Miss*' or '*Mrs*'

3. Students must stand when an adult enters the room

4. Students must use the right hand at all times for writing

5. Girls will learn needlework, and boys will learn technical drawing

6. Students must not put their hands up until told they can do so

7. Students must not ask questions

8. Talking and fidgeting will be punished

9. Children who are truant (late), behave badly or do poor work will be caned

Punishment For 'Whores'

Through an ancient Anglo-Saxon law, it was custom in England to subdue harlots, unchaste women and whores (*Meretrices et impudicas mulieres subnervare*). The sentence prescribed in law was to cut the sinews of their legs and thighs or hamstrings. Disfigured and gruesomely disabled for life, they would then be banished from the town and never permitted to return.

How times have changed. These days, society takes a more responsible attitude and understands that many sex workers have found themselves in that line of work through no fault of their own, some through human trafficking, child exploitation and forced dependency on drugs. Prostitution itself is not illegal, but many offences are linked to it. For example, it is an offence to control a prostitute for gain or to keep a brothel.

Punishment For Thieving Slaves

During the reign of King Edmund (921-946), the master-servant relationship was going very strong in England. A servant stealing from his master was considered a highly sinful act. Later, laws would regard this as an act of petty treason.

However, King Edmund's third law details the punishment for light-fingered slaves. It lists scourging (whipping with great suffering), removing the scalp and mutilating the little finger as punishment. This isn't just a 'pick and choose'; the sentence was to suffer all three of those together.

Punishment For Beggars

Over the centuries, the law has not been kind to those less fortunate. A particular group penalised just for their unfortunate circumstances was the poor. This started with the Tudor Poor Laws, designed to provide measures for poor relief but also implemented a system of harsh punishments for the poor.

The Vagabonds Act (1530) stated that *"vagabonds and beggars have a long time increased and daily do increase in great and excessive numbers by the occasion of idleness, mother and root of all vices, whereby had upsurged and sprung up ... continual thefts and murders, and other heinous offences and great enormities."*

Beggars were seen as vagrants. They were stripped, flogged in public and carried around on the back of a cart for all to see. This was a particularly useless punishment, as the beggar would still be in the same unfortunate economic position, without any money and would have to continue to beg just to survive. All it did was humiliate. It wasn't just men that were punished. Female beggars were also stripped to the waist and whipped in public. The whipping order often specified for them to be whipped '*till her body be bloodily*'.

With the increasing number of wars and many soldiers and sailors becoming wounded and disabled through their military service, they would return to England and be unable to find meaningful employment. There was one dispensation. They were allowed to apply to the local justices of the peace for a special licence to beg. In 1596, The Poor Law Act provided for the provision of whipping posts in public places. It also ordered all 'incorrigible rogues' to be committed to Houses of Correction, where they were to be manacled and whipped.

Gradually the mood towards the public flogging of women changed, and it started to decline from the 1770s onwards. It ceased altogether in 1817 and was banned by law in 1820 with the passing of the Whipping Act. Although, male beggars were still publicly whipped until the early 1830s. Public flogging was finally abolished in 1862 with the updated Whipping Act.

A good whipping wasn't the only way that common beggars were punished. Another form of punishment was branding. The Vagrancy Act of 1547 was passed in response to the complex socio-economic environment following the death of King Henry VIII. At the time, the population of England was growing, but there were increasing levels of unemployment. Vagrants became commonplace on the streets. This law stated that any able-bodied person out of work for more than three days should be branded with a hot iron "*in the brest with the marke of V*" and sold into slavery for two years. Fortunately, many local authorities refused to enact this harsh legislation. The slavery provisions were repealed just three years later.

In 1572, during the reign of Queen Elizabeth I, the Vagabond Act was passed, which allowed all unlicensed vagrants to be "*grievously whipped and burned through the gristle of the right ear with a hot iron of the compass of an inch about.*"

Branding, as a form of punishment, was finally abolished in 1829.

Hard Labour

Victorian prisons were known to be harsh. They were places of detention, punishment and deterrence rather than rehabilitation. As if prison life wasn't hard enough, many prisoners were also sentenced to hard labour. Imprisonment with hard labour was first introduced into law when Britain was fighting the American War of Independence. This made transporting prisoners to the colonies in North America an impossibility. So, as a practical measure, many prisoners were being put to good use working along the River Thames. This had to be sanctioned in law in the Criminal Law Act (1776).

Almost a century later, the Prison Act (1865) required that all males aged 16 or over, sentenced to imprisonment with hard labour, had to spend at least three months of their sentence in what was known as Labour Order. The Act stated that prisons had to be "*hard labour, hard fare and hard board.*" Section 19 of the Act listed several recommended hard labour methods, "*Tread Wheel, Shot Drill, Crank, Capstan, Stone-breaking, or such other like.*" After three months, the level of hard labour could reduce in severity.

In 1877, these three months of severe hard labour were reduced to just one month. Hard labour was banned on Sundays, Christmas Day, Good Friday or days appointed for public fasts or thanksgivings.

Since its introduction, several forms of hard labour have been used in prison. Some forms of hard labour have a practical purpose that benefits society or some trade. For example, oakum picking, basket weaving, mat-making, net-making and blacksmithing. Whereas other forms are just purely punitive and used as a deterrent, like the crank, the treadmill or shot drill. Shot drill required prisoners to lean forward without bending their knees and lift heavy objects like a cannonball or block of stone to chest height. They would then move three paces to the right, place it back on the ground and step back three paces. This repetitive cycle would see the prisoner moving a pile of heavy objects from one pile on the left to another on the right and back again.

Picking Oakum was another common form of hard labour in prisons. They would be provided lengths of old rope and required to untwist each strand from the rope, separating them into their individual strands. It had a practical use because the rope could be reused. Unfortunately, the ropes were often covered in tar and picking them apart led to finger blisters and bleeding. The well-known writer Oscar Wilde was one such prisoner required to pick oakum during his stay. Following his conviction for gross indecency, he was sentenced to hard labour in Reading Gaol.

Another prisoner was 15-year-old William Anderson from Lancashire, convicted at the Manchester Petty Sessions for stealing brass fittings from a deserted house. He was sentenced to three months imprisonment with hard labour.

Any form of imprisonment with hard labour was abolished under Section 1(2) of the Criminal Justice Act (1948).

The Crank

The crank machine was a foreboding instrument of Victorian punishments, commonly known as 'The Crank'. A prisoner was forced to turn a crank by hand on the side of this machine. When turned, the crank moved four large paddles through sand or gravel enclosed in a drum. This provided much-unwanted resistance to the turn of the crank. Prisoners sentenced to hard labour often found themselves forced to use the crank machine. Those who chose to misbehave in prison also found themselves forced to turn the crank. It was both monotonous and exhausting work. The prisoner was required to turn the heavy metal crank handle anywhere between 6,000 and 14,400 revolutions in a six-hour period. This was a heart-breaking speed of 1.5 to 3.6 seconds per turn. The number of revolutions turned would be registered on a dial for the prison warder to see. To make the task harder, a prison warder could adjust the tightening screw on the side of the crank machine. This made the task either easier or harder, depending on the level of punishment the prisoner was owed and how much the prison warder disliked them. This is where the colloquial term *'screw'* originates when referring to prison officers.

Victorian punishments like this, undoubtedly served as a deterrent to dissuade prisoners from their immoral ways by causing exhaustion each day. They were a pointless exercise and had no other purpose. They weren't even used to generate electricity. They had no rehabilitative effect whatsoever.

The crank was abolished with the passing of the Prison Act (1898).

Treadmills

The prison treadmill very quickly came to be hated as the worst of all the forms of punishment and hard labour. Also known as treadwheels, they were first introduced into British prisons in 1818. The purpose of the treadmill was to be exhausting labour and a mind-numbing task. It was boring and repetitive. Prisoners were prohibited from talking to each other during this punishing 'exercise'. As far as prison punishments went, this had a strong deterrence effect.

By 1895 there were 39 treadmills in use in English prisons.

The treadmills were long wooden cylinders with metal frames, each containing 24 steps, looking very similar to large paddle wheels. On the outside of the treadmills were wooden steps positioned approximately 7.5 inches (19cm) apart. Each of these treadmills was able to accommodate between 18 and 25 prisoners at any one time. The large wheels turned under the power of the prisoners walking upon its steps. This forced prisoners to move their weight on to the next step above continually. It was essentially like an infinity staircase. Between each prisoner was a wooden partition. So, the prisoners had to climb this long staircase for hours, unable to see or talk to anyone else. All they could do was stare at the wall in front of them. They had to walk for six hours a day, following a quick-change shift pattern of 15 minutes of walking followed by five minutes break. The wheel turned around two revolutions per minute, and every thirty revolutions, a bell rang, indicating time for a shift change. Each prisoner would be forced to walk up to 18,000 feet per day. The distance covered each day depended upon the distance between each step on the wheel. There was no standardised distance, so depending on which prison they were sent to, prisoners could walk thousands of feet more per day than those in other prisons. The punishment was so exhausting that some prisoners simply couldn't handle it.

In 1885, 16-year-old Albert Trendall, after an attempted break-in, received a sentence of six months with hard labour at

Coldbath Fields prison. He couldn't face the prison treadmill one more day and sadly hanged himself from the gas bracket in his cell. In June 1888, 20-year-old Arthur Simmonds received a sentence of 18 months with hard labour at Pentonville prison. His offence was stealing a letter. After serving just three days on the prison treadmill, he could barely walk and was unable to eat food. He was taken to the prison infirmary and died a few days later.

Prisoners would do anything to avoid working on the treadmills. They came up with some of the most creative excuses and fabricated some of the most fictitious illnesses. There are accounts of prisoners swallowing large quantities of salt, which brought about a fever. The prison doctor would not certify any prisoner with a fever as 'fit to work'. Eventually, the prison authorities caught on and banned salt. Following this, the prisoners instead swallowed soap which caused explosive diarrhoea and a low fever.

Treadmills were finally abolished in British prisons in 1898 with the passing of the Prison Act.

Riding The Whirligig

Whilst this torture contraption was solely confined to those in the military, it's too fun not to give it a brief mention in this book.

Before you continue reading, let me ask you to consider whether you have ever been on one of those fairground rides, like the Waltzer, that spins around, where you experience varying levels of g-force, and feel like you're being pushed to the back of your seat? This is essentially what this punishment method is, except you can't just stop the ride and get off after a couple of minutes.

The Whirligig was a six-foot high cylindrical wooden cage suspended in the air, connected through pivots to a post on the ground. The prisoner would be forced inside the cage, after which the central post would spin, turning the cage at very high speeds.

Riders could not help but feel nauseous, repeatedly vomiting and often resulting in musculoskeletal injuries like dislocated bones, torn muscles and even unconsciousness.

This device created such a spectacle that other soldiers crowded around to watch. The purpose of this device was purely to humiliate the unfortunate 'rider' and deter them from their wayward behaviour.

CHAPTER ELEVEN

HIS MAJESTY'S FINEST

C onstables have been around since the sixth-century. It wasn't until the inception of the modern-day police force in 1829 that we started to see consistency in how police constables operated in different counties. That hasn't always been a good thing.

His Majesty's finest, the British police, enforce the laws passed for centuries by Parliament. We are in an eternal love-hate relationship with them. Like them or loathe them, they are the ones who uphold the law and bring transgressors to justice. In the words of Gilbert & Sullivan, "*When constabulary duty's to be done ... A policeman's lot is not a happy one.*" Read just a few pages into this chapter, and you'll soon see why. They have to pay for mass public disturbances, they can't 'spread disaffection' ... and when things get so bad, they're not even allowed to strike.

In this chapter, we'll examine why police officers pretend riots don't happen and how they have employment rights, just not the same as most others. We also delve into the penalties for lying to the police and under what circumstances it is perfectly acceptable to tell a few porkies.

"The mood and temper of the public in regard to the treatment of crime and criminals is one of the most unfailing tests of the civilisation of any country."
Sir. Winston Churchill (20th July 1910)

The Police Have to Pay For All Property Damaged, Destroyed or Stolen During Riots

Each decade we usually get several large outbreaks of widespread disorder on the streets. These can last for several weeks and really stretch both the police and the criminal justice system for months afterwards, dealing with investigations and court cases.

Some notable displays of public disorder have been the 1981 riots in several cities and towns across England. These were caused by rising tensions between black people and the police as well as mass-unemployment. There was the 1990 protests against the Community Charge (Poll Tax riots). A series of major riots during the summer of 2001 saw similar ethnic conflicts across many northern towns and cities. Then there were the mass riots between the 6th and 11th of August 2011, which saw thousands of people rioting in cities and towns across England. These riots saw looting, arson, and mass deployment of police, resulting in the deaths of five people. The causes of the 2011 riots are still being debated. They range from poor community relations with the police, unemployment and poverty, gang culture, criminal opportunism and copycat riots.

When we talk about riots, we imagine widespread disorder with hundreds and thousands of people protesting about something, with shops being damaged or looted and cars set on fire. A riot is defined in law under Section 1 of the Public Order Act (1986). Section 1(1) states a riot is "*Where 12 or more persons who are present together use or threaten unlawful violence for a common purpose and the conduct of them (taken together) is such as would cause a person of reasonable firmness present at the scene to fear for his personal safety, each of the persons using unlawful violence for the common purpose is guilty of riot.*" So, for a riot to occur, in law, it doesn't need thousands of people, only 12 or more. That describes almost every Friday and Saturday night outside pubs and nightclubs in most major UK cities. It also describes occurrences at most major football events.

During these riots, widespread disorder and mass damage were caused to businesses, shops and even people's homes. So, who ends up paying for all of the damage? Is it the individual home and business owner, or is there a general insurance pot that pays out? This question was answered in 1886 with the passing of The Riot (Damages) Act. This Victorian law required local police authorities to pay for any damage, destruction, or thefts occurring during a riot. The police authority had to pay this compensation to victims of these riot-related crimes, irrespective of whether the police force had been negligent.

Many insurance policies covering commercial and domestic properties do not cover loss, damage or destruction caused by rioting due to the expectation that the local police authority will recompense as ordered under this 1886 Act. Those without insurance were able to claim compensation directly from the police. Those with insurance claimed through their insurer who then re-claimed the money from the police authority. However, the former Association of Police Authorities claimed that the police authorities' own insurers no longer provided sufficient cover and that all police compensation for riot claims were to come from their reserves or a special grant made by the Home Office.

For a while, there was a general belief that the police were intentionally not classifying specific episodes of public disorder as a '*riot*', instead choosing to classify them as a '*Violent Disorder*' under Section 2 of the Public Order Act. Perhaps this was for economic reasons. As this would not be a riot, any compensation would not have to be paid from police funds.

As a result of the 2011 riots, there were significant issues with compensation claims being paid on time in accordance with the Riot (Damages) Act of 1886. To modernise the compensation process, the 1886 Act was repealed and replaced with the Riot Compensation Act (2016). This new Act was designed to allow communities to quickly recover from the impact of rioting. You can still claim compensation directly from the local police authority, even if your property is not adequately insured. Those with insurance coverage are still required first to make their claim through their insurance company. However, to qualify for compensation, the victims must demonstrate that the loss or damage sustained resulted from a riot.

It is concerning that the law does not cover consequential loss to a business due to a riot. This means that if a riot persists for several days or even weeks, a business can lose a vast amount of trade. For those businesses with little liquidity, this could be enough to make them insolvent. Sadly, they can not make a claim for this under the Riot Compensation Act (2016).

Interestingly, this is the origin of the phrase '*Reading the Riot Act*'. It refers to the formal reading of the Riot Act (1714). This law was designed to help the authorities swiftly quell public disturbances and unrest. It required that a group of twelve or more people who were assembled and disturbing the peace, be read a specific warning from an official. If the group did not disperse within one hour of the reading of the warning, they could be arrested and punished.

Illegal for Police Officers to Spread Disaffection

Police officers don't exactly exude the persona of being a congenial bunch. I'm sure many readers will have experienced the poor attitudes and unprofessionalism of some of His Majesty's finest. That is not to say that all police officers are unprofessional; far from it. Many do care about victims of crime and do a good job but harbour deep-seated frustrations with the system, their supervision and working practices.

As with all organisations, there are a few bad apples. Visit the websites of most of the police forces, and you can see the listings of police misconduct hearings and even attend them in-person. The news has broken recently about poor recruitment vetting practices across the UK's police forces. Sometimes, all it takes is for that one bad apple to upset the whole apple cart. This can be anything from a police officer discussing with colleagues about ways to make a new rule or working practice unworkable. From interviews with former police officers, it appears there were many attempts to sabotage performance indicators and the introduction of fixed penalty notices for disorder, for offences like urinating or swearing in public.

In an attempt to keep the apple cart upright, legislation was passed to make it an offence for police officers to try to do this sort of thing. In fact, it is now a criminal offence for police officers to do anything that would cause other officers to fall out with each other or not be able to carry out their duties effectively.

Section 91 of the Police Act (1996) creates this offence of 'Causing disaffection'. It states, "*Any person who causes, or attempts to cause, or does any act calculated to cause, disaffection amongst the members of any police force, or induces or attempts to induce, or does any act calculated to induce, any member of a police force to withhold his services, shall be guilty of an offence.*" From the wording of this Act, you can see that this could even include things like where a police officer tells a fellow officer not to take action against an individual, perhaps because they are a personal friend.

Aside from whatever misconduct proceedings their professional standards department may take against them, the punishment for this offence is imprisonment for up to six months and/or a fine. If that matter goes to trial at a Crown Court, the police officer could be imprisoned for up to two years.

It Is Illegal For Police &
Prison Officers To Strike

From time to time, members of the public will moan or whinge about police officers, traffic wardens, politicians and estate agents. However, several polls into the most hated and least trusted professions have revealed some interesting answers. There is always one omission from the top 10 of those polls, which you would expect to see, police officers.

As much as we might moan about police officers, there is no hatred towards them or general acrimonious relations between the public and the police. In the UK, it is said that we operate 'policing by public consent.' Yet, if you speak to many police officers on the street, they are just like you and me. They are representative of our society. That is not to say that there aren't, as in all organisations, a few officers with malicious intent and a downright lackadaisical approach to policing. These few officers alone, with their poor attitudes and arrogance, cause friction between the general public and the police.

A lot of the time, when you phone the police to report a crime, it seems very little is done about it. There are undoubtedly lazy police officers and deceitful police officers who, frankly, can't be bothered to investigate crimes properly. However, on many occasions, where it appears to the public that the police are failing to take action, this is not down to the individual officer but the system, policing procedures and lack of funding. Like any organisation or public service, it can be expected that levels of efficiency deteriorate with reduced funding.

For decades, many police officers have felt underpaid for their work and the dangers to which they are sometimes exposed. In almost any other profession, where employees feel undervalued and underpaid, they would undertake industrial action. However, this is not an option available to the police. It is illegal for police officers to strike.

The last time the police in the UK went on strike was in June 1919. This was a culmination of a series of strikes which started in 1918 when almost every Constable and Sergeant refused to go on duty. At the time, they demanded a significant pay increase, a widow's pension and recognition of their trade union, The National Union of Police and Prison Officers. The then Prime Minister, David Lloyd George, conceded to their request for a pay rise. However, within months, Parliament introduced the Police Act (1919), which banned police officers from belonging to any trade union. It established the Police Federation of England and Wales as the representative body for police officers below the rank of Superintendent. The Police Federation is not a union but has the statutory responsibility to represent its members in all matters affecting their welfare and efficiency. Since the introduction of this Act, police officers have been banned from going on strike. It is now a criminal offence for police to strike.

In 1996, the government introduced the revised Police Act. The third part of this Act preserved the ban on police striking that was first introduced in the Police Act (1919). The rationale remained the same. If police officers were allowed to go on strike, there would be widespread disorder across the UK. Whilst police were not permitted to be members of trade unions, this Act permitted an alternative form of representation for them through the Police Federation of England and Wales.

Section 91 of the Police Act (1996) makes it a criminal offence for anyone to cause disaffection among police officers or to induce any police officer to withhold his services. Section 91(1) states, *"Any person who causes, or attempts to cause, or does any act calculated to cause, disaffection amongst the members of any police force, or induces or attempts to induce, or does any act calculated to induce, any member of a police force to withhold his services, shall be guilty of an offence."* So, it would be a criminal offence to encourage or promote police officers to take strike action, refuse to work overtime or even attempt to 'work to rule' by withdrawing goodwill. As Crown servants, police officers must carry out all lawful orders. They can not refuse to work overtime if they are lawfully ordered.

In 2013, The Police Federation of England and Wales balloted their members for the right to strike but failed to gain enough support to encourage action to change the law. This ban on strikes does not just affect police in England and Wales. North of the border, officers from Police Scotland, are also prohibited from striking. However, after months of failed negotiations, the Scottish Police Federation (SPF) turned down an annual pay increase, describing it as *"derisory."* They announced that from 5pm on 1st July 2022, they would take the *"most overt demonstration of action"* seen in more than a hundred years.

Whilst it is illegal for police officers to go on strike, the officers in Scotland chose not to go on strike but instead chose the action of *"withdrawing goodwill."* This withdrawal of goodwill, while not illegal in Scotland, had a significant impact when police officers refused to work late or take on any additional unpaid responsibilities.

They refused to work outside their contracted hours unless formally ordered, which they would claim as overtime. This included a refusal to turn up early before the start of their shift for briefings. They also refused to charge police equipment like radio sets and data appliances at their homes. Finally, by 15th August, all action was ceased when the union accepted a 5% pay increase.

So far, we have focused on the illegality of police officers striking. However, it isn't only police officers that are banned, by law, from taking such action. Prison officers are also not permitted to strike. In 1994, the government of Prime Minister John Major passed the Criminal Justice and Public Order Act. Section 127 of the Act made it illegal to induce a prison officer to withhold their services or commit a breach of discipline. This brought an effective ban on prison officers striking.

There was a temporary suspension of Section 127 when it was replaced in 2000 by a voluntary agreement between the government of Prime Minister Tony Blair and the Prison Officers Association (POA). This agreement was reached with an assurance that industrial action would be ruled out as a method of solving disputes. However, after several years of soured relations between the POA and the government, things once again reached a head.

In November 2016, thousands of prison officers in England and Wales stopped working, citing safety fears. They began protesting en masse outside the prisons. When asked to describe protests on such a large-scale where employees refuse to work, most people would consider it a form of industrial action, a strike. According to the Prison Officers Association, this was not a strike. They referred to the unannounced action as a gathering of prison workers at "*protest meetings*." They also stated that prison officers had not been '*induced*' to participate in this action.

The government applied for a court order, and the matter ended up in the High Court. Mr. Justice Kerr, after hearing the arguments, granted an injunction to bring an immediate end to the mass walkout by prison officers. He was sympathetic to the arguments presented by the prison officers but stated that several incidents had occurred in prisons whilst up to 80% of staff had taken some sort of action in the majority of prisons. As a result of this, prisoners were being kept in their cells. The POA stated that they would defy any injunction which ordered them to return to work. The government won the High Court action and re-enacted Section 127 of the 1994 Act, once again legally banning prison officers from striking.

The High Court's injunction would be tested once again a couple of years later, when in September 2018, the POA admitted supporting industrial action at HMP Liverpool in February and inducing a national strike by prison officers. The POA argued that the injunction represented a "*disproportionate interference*" with their right to Freedom of Assembly and Association under Article 11 of the Human Rights Act (1998). The two justices hearing the case rejected their arguments finding that the POA "*was and remains bound by the terms of the injunction and ... has breached those terms.*" They pointed out that the exceptional nature of the prison environment meant that the risks and potential consequences of withholding services by prison officers were grave. Consequently, the Prison Officers Association was fined £210,000 for two deliberate breaches of the High Court injunction.

In 2022, the Prison Officers Association once again called for an end to the ban on industrial action, with a representative stating, "*Section 127 limits our bargaining power, the ability to make our employer sit down and truly listen to what we need.*" Whatever happens next, a common-sense approach would determine those police officers and prison officers should not go on strike because this not only imperils the safety of the British public at large but also those within the prison system. However, this has to be balanced with the industrial relations of those two sets of workers with employment rights and the need to restrain them from industrial action. It is an interesting conundrum that will no doubt continue for many decades.

Lying To The Police

As we'll see later in this chapter, with very few exceptions, you have no legal obligation to talk to a police officer. However, during those few occasions when you are required by law to speak to the police, you must not lie. Whilst there is no actual offence of lying to the police, that does not make it illegal. You may commit one or more serious offences depending on the circumstances in which you find yourself speaking to a police officer and choosing to lie.

The whole criminal justice system is based on the foundations of honesty and integrity. Imagine if everyone lied to the police and the courts. There would be guilty people walking free and innocent people being imprisoned. Before the death penalty was abolished, this would have meant innocent people would have been handed the death sentence. This has happened on occasion and continues to happen to this day, which is why laws must exist to prevent lying to the police and the courts and ensure justice is rightly served.

If in doubt, don't say anything at all. Exercise your legal right not to incriminate yourself. Other than the very few occasions we look at later in this chapter, you aren't required to say anything to a police officer, and it is perfectly acceptable, albeit morally questionable, to just walk away.

There are several offences for which lying to the police can end up with you in hot water. We shall examine each of those in detail. The first is what is commonly referred to as the offence of '*Wasting police time*'. This offence generally occurs when a person makes a false report to the police. It carries a maximum penalty of six months imprisonment. Offenders may be given a fixed penalty under the Criminal Justice and Police Act (2001) with a fine. Section 5(2) of the Criminal Law Act (1967) states that a person is guilty of an offence "*Where a person causes any wasteful employment of the police by knowingly making to any person a false report tending to show that an offence has been committed, or to give rise to apprehension for the safety of any persons or property, or tending to show that he has information material to any police inquiry.*" This offence can be committed even if a false report is made to someone other than a police officer, provided that the other person brings it to the attention of the police and it subsequently wastes police time. You also have to knowingly provide a false report for this offence to be committed. This offence can even be committed if you lead the police or any other person to falsely believe that you have information that would assist in investigating a police enquiry.

An example of this could be telling a police officer that you've heard screams and shouting coming from an address. The police officer, after ringing the doorbell for several minutes, is concerned for the safety of the people within. He then uses his powers under Section 17 of the Police and Criminal Evidence Act (1984) to kick the back door in, only to discover there is actually no-one inside the address. He turns around and sees you laughing. You have made a false report leading the police officer to have apprehension for the safety of the people within the property. You can most likely expect a summons in the post and possibly a compensation order for the damage to the address.

Another example would be when a driver has a crash and decides to cover it up by reporting their car as stolen to the police. The police subsequently investigate the alleged theft of the vehicle, but the crime is quickly closed because there are no lines of enquiry. This has wasted police time, and you have committed the offence. There is a significant overlap between this offence and another offence under common law called '*Perverting the Course of Justice*'. This is a much more severe offence with a maximum sentence of life imprisonment. It occurs when a person does an act tending and intended to pervert the course of public justice.

So, let's say the false report you initially made to the police has the consequence of not just wasting a few hours of police time but also leading to a large-scale police investigation involving multiple staff and different departments and resulting in a person being wrongly arrested. In this case, the Crown Prosecution Service (CPS) may decide to charge you with this more serious offence of Perverting the Course of Justice.

Some examples of where this offence has been committed are:

- where a person admits to a crime to let the true offender escape prosecution;

- where a prisoner provides a false identity when they have been arrested;

- making a false allegation of an offence, leading to extensive police resources being used;

- destroying or concealing evidence of a crime;

Police officers themselves, being subject to the law. occasionally also fall foul of it. An interesting case arose in 1986 in the matter of R v Coxhead. In this case, the defendant (Coxhead) was a police sergeant. A young man was brought into the station to be breathalysed. The sergeant recognised him as the son of one of the police inspectors at the same station. The sergeant used his discretion not to administer the breathalyser test and allowed the motorist to go free. The sergeant was prosecuted and convicted for conduct tending and intended to pervert the course of justice.

This offence can also be committed when a spouse or family member agrees to take the points on their driving licence for a road traffic offence. One such instance, which became very famous, is the 2013 case of Chris Huhne, the former Liberal Democrat energy secretary and his ex-wife, Vicky Pryce. This unusual case began on 12th March 2003 when Chris Huhne MP was caught speeding from Stansted Airport to his home in south London. To prevent Huhne from receiving a mandatory driving ban due to the number of points he already had on his driving licence, Pryce stated that it had been her driving at the time. No-one was any wiser until, in June 2010, a newspaper leaked a story about Huhne's long-term affair with his PR adviser. He told his family that he was leaving his wife. A week later, she filed for divorce. In keeping with the old saying 'Hell hath no fury like a woman scorned', in May 2011, Pryce informed a journalist that Huhne had coerced her into taking the penalty points on her driving licence. This did not go quite according to plan. In admitting that she had taken his penalty points, she had also incriminated herself. As a result, both Huhne and Pryce were sentenced to 8 months in prison for perverting the course of justice. They were both released after two months and served the remainder of their sentence electronically tagged. Mr. Huhne resigned his seat in the House of Commons.

This leads us to the next offence related to lying. One of the Ten Commandments from Exodus 20:16 in the Old Testament is *"Thou shalt not bear false witness against thy neighbour."* The Quran also refers to withholding of testimony. This shows us just how equally serious it was considered to give false testimony centuries ago. This is the offence of 'Perjury' under the Perjury Act (1911). Section 1 of this Act states, *"If any person lawfully sworn as a witness or as an interpreter in a judicial proceeding wilfully makes a statement material in that proceeding, which he knows to be false or does not believe to be true, he shall be guilty of perjury."* This means that once lawfully sworn in as a witness in court, if a person knowingly makes a statement which they know is a lie or do not believe it to be true, they commit this offence. The maximum sentence for perjury is seven years imprisonment. You can understand why this offence is so important. If a witness makes a false statement in court, it can lead to an innocent person being found guilty or vice versa.

There is an additional offence of providing *'False written statements tendered in evidence'*. This is an offence under Section 89 of the Criminal Justice Act (1967). It is committed when a person wilfully makes a written statement that they know to be false or do not believe to be true, and that statement is tendered in evidence in criminal proceedings. The maximum sentence for this offence is two years imprisonment.

And finally, there is the offence of *'Obstructing a Police Officer'*. This offence is open to a broad interpretation. It is often used on the streets by police officers to force members of the public to provide their details unnecessarily, some other information or even when asking a member of the public to move out of a specific area. To be clear, refusing to answer a question when asked by a police officer is not an offence of obstructing a police officer. Section 89(2) of the Police Act (1996) states, *"Any person who resists or wilfully obstructs a constable in the execution of his duty, or a person assisting a constable in the execution of his duty, shall be guilty of an offence."*

You can be guilty of this offence if, for example, you warn other drivers of a roadside speed check or even park a van in front of a police speed camera in an attempt to obstruct the view of the speed camera. You could also be guilty of this offence if you warn someone about to commit a crime that they are under police surveillance. This offence is most often committed when people provide misleading information to the police.

However, it is important to understand that any 'obstruction' must be wilful. In other words, you must intend to do it. For example, if you go and stand in front of a police speed enforcement van and obstruct the view of the police officer's camera, you would not be guilty of this offence if you were stood there trying to attract the attention of a police officer within the van to report a serious crime or bring something to their attention. This is because whilst you are still obstructing the police camera and, therefore, the constable in executing his duty, that is not your intention. You intend to attract the attention of the officer to report a matter.

With all this said, I'll remind you again that under most circumstances, there is no legal obligation to talk to a police officer. If you do, it really doesn't pay to lie. There is a whole myriad of offences you can fall foul of if you choose to go down that path.

CHAPTER TWELVE

HOUSES OF PARLIAMENT

The Houses of Parliament are arguably the fountain of democracy for the United Kingdom. The walls of that hallowed place where new laws are passed, are steeped in history. Over the centuries, there have been some incredulous goings-on at the Palace of Westminster. From the seventeenth-century attempt by Guy Fawkes to blow up Parliament along with the King, to a parliamentary predilection for burning books. It is no wonder each newly elected Speaker has to be forcefully dragged to his chair.

Both the House of Commons and the House of Lords have a set of written rules that they have created themselves to manage their day-to-day activities. These are called 'standing orders', and the House of Commons has over 400 of them. They govern everything from when the House is 'sitting' and MPs must be there, to the rules on voting for Acts of Parliament, along with rules on how MPs must behave.

This chapter delves into the private world of parliamentary language, traditions and customs. We trawl the law books back to the Magna Carta and examine the effects on modern-day democracy.

"Parliament must not be told a direct untruth,
but its quite possible to allow them to mislead themselves."
Norman Tebbit

You Can't Die in The Houses of Parliament

Politics isn't everyone's cup of tea. In fact, for some, the mere thought of it bores them to death. But that's okay just as long as they don't die in the Houses of Parliament. Whilst it is not an offence to die in the Houses of Parliament, no-one is allowed to die there. There is a good reason behind this. The Palace of Westminster is a Royal palace, and no person can be declared dead on the estate except for the Royal family. There is a myth that the reason behind this is that anyone who dies in a Royal palace is entitled to a State funeral. This is not the case. If it were, any tourists attending the myriad of Royal palaces around the UK, including Hampton Court and The Tower of London, would also be entitled to a State funeral should they choose to die there.

So, what happens if a visitor on a House of Commons tour suffers the inconvenience of a heart attack and dies in the building? Under these circumstances, their body would be removed from the parliamentary estate and their death certificate is issued at St Thomas' Hospital in Lambeth, just over Westminster Bridge.

Under the Coroners Act (1988), the Coroner of the King's household has jurisdiction over the inquest into deaths in a Royal palace. This law came from the 'Act for Murder and Malicious Bloodshed within the Court' passed by King Henry VIII in 1541.

The key implications arising from an inquest involving the Coroner of the King's household is that if the Coroner empanelled a jury to investigate the death, all jury members had to be empanelled from among the current members of the Royal household.

Whilst State funerals can occur for deaths in Royal palaces; they are not mandatory. They are at the sole discretion of the monarch. This office of the Coroner of the King's household was abolished in 2013. However, the convention still remains that no-one shall die on the parliamentary estate. There have been several deaths on the grounds of the Palace of Westminster, but none of these has received a State funeral.

Sir Walter Raleigh and Guy Fawkes were executed in the Old Palace yard. In 1812, Prime Minister Spencer Perceval died in the lobby of the House of Commons after being shot. The final recorded death at the House of Commons occurred on 9th July 1907. This was the Liberal Party MP Sir Alfred Billson, who collapsed in the 'Aye' lobby whilst casting his vote on sugar duty legislation.

MPs Not Allowed to Carry Nunchucks or Wear Armour in Parliament

The Houses of Parliament are the seat of British democracy. Surrounded by a ring of steel, a perimeter of police officers and estate security, it's no wonder the building feels safe to walk around. There's a good reason for this. According to an ancient law, no-one is permitted to bring weapons of any sort or to wear armour in the Houses of Parliament. This law doesn't just cover MPs; it covers any person on the Parliamentary estate.

The Statute forbidding Bearing of Armour was passed by King Edward II in 1313 during a time of political instability. By this time, the King had reigned for six years and had already upset many of the powerful land barons. Different groups of barons jostled for power and to control the King. To prevent barons from turning up to Parliament dressed in full armour and carrying swords, he decided to pass this law to prevent threats of force inside Parliament. The statute ordered that "*every Man shall come* [to Parliament] *without all Force and Armour.*" Those who refused were to be punished "*according to our Laws and Usages of our Realm.*"

Many didn't adhere to this law, and in June 1318, Thomas, the 2nd Earl of Lancaster, was accused of breaking the law. He was too powerful a force in Parliament for anyone to consider punishing him. This statute has never been repealed, and the law is still in force today. The Crown Prosecution Service has said that it is unaware of anyone being prosecuted under this statute in recent times.

There is one exception to the carrying of weapons. The Serjeant-at-Arms is allowed to carry a sword, as is Black Rod, when entering the Chamber to summon MPs to hear the King's speech.

Parliament is Permitted to Burn Books

Book burnings have been going on for centuries all around the world. They're not just confined to the streets of World War Two Germany. On 20th May 2006, two communal councillors in Italy held a public burning of a copy of The Da Vinci Code in the piazza of the Italian town Ceccano. That same year, Harry Potter books were publicly burned in New Mexico and South Carolina. Book burning has always been seen as a sign of exercising censorship. Sometimes it had the opposite effect and even glorified the author.

The book burnings of old England weren't just about mass censorship. This was also about creating a public spectacle to send out an unequivocal message. They were a further way to legitimise and reinforce the authority of the Crown, Parliament and the Church through this dramatic ritual. This is why in May 1634, the decision was taken that the hangman should carry out public book burnings. This was a further attempt designed to frighten onlookers and reduce the amount of seditious, treasonous or heretic publications.

The burning of books condemned as seditious by the House of Commons and House of Lords was a regular occurrence until the end of the eighteenth century. There have been a few notable examples of book burnings for offensive literary publications. On 29th March 1642, John Bond was sentenced for the forgery of a letter purportedly from the Queen of Holland and addressed to King Charles I. He was ordered to stand in the public pillory at both Westminster Hall door and in Cheapside, wearing paper on his head, upon which was written, "*A contriver of false and scandalous libels.*" His fake letter was then publicly burned in front of him.

The following bizarre example led to the cessation of public book burnings.

This is the case of John Wilkes an MP for Aylesbury and a radical journalist. Over the years, his journalistic activities became a thorn in the side of Parliament. In 1763 he published an article in issue 45 of a satirical pamphlet called 'The North Briton'. In it, he criticised King George III's speech from the opening of Parliament. On the 30th of April, the King issued a general warrant for the arrest of Wilkes and the publishers for seditious libel. In total, 49 people were arrested. Wilkes claimed that as an MP, he was protected by parliamentary privilege. The Lord Chief Justice ruled that parliamentary privilege protected him, so he was released and returned to Parliament. However, the House of Commons took a vote on it and decided that parliamentary privilege afforded no such protection from an offence of seditious libel. On 1st December, both houses of Parliament condemned Wilkes's article in issue 45 of The North Briton. They ordered it to be burned by the public hangman at the Royal Exchange in the City of London.

This public burning took place on the 3rd of December. However, it didn't go quite how Parliament had planned. Records show there was a riotous mob, encouraged by affluent people standing on nearby balconies and in the doorways of shops. They were shouting to the tumultuous crowd *"Well done, boys! bravely done, boys!"* And began hissing, which frightened the sheriff's horses. Eventually, Alderman Hurley, carrying the offending publication, reached the Royal Exchange. As the public hangman lit his torch, the mob seized the paper. The constables were pelted with stones and it was quickly decided to burn a petticoat and a pair of jackboots instead to placate the marauding crowds.

In January 1764, Wilkes was expelled from the House of Commons. The House passed a vote, and from that moment onwards, general warrants were no longer used to arrest persons. The Attorney-General, Sir Fletcher Norton, stated that he would no longer have regard *"to the oaths of so many drunken porters in Covent Garden"* than to the use of general warrants for the apprehension of authors and publishers for printing seditious libel.

The process of book burning has never formally been abolished by Parliament.

Parliament Has Its Own Rule Book

What or who is 'Erskine May'?

It is both a what and who.

Let's start with the 'Who'.

Thomas Erskine May, the 1st Baron of Farnborough was born in 1815. He started work aged 16 as an assistant librarian in the House of Commons library. At the age of 19, he was admitted to the Middle Temple and called to the Bar as a barrister four years later. From 1871 until a week before he died in 1886, he was the Clerk of the House of Commons. He is most notable; perhaps this is why you may have heard his name mentioned, for his book entitled *'A Treatise upon the Law, Privileges, Proceedings and Usage of Parliament'*. This is more popularly known as *'Erskine May: Parliamentary Practice'* or, more simply ', *Erskine May'*.

In turning our attention to the 'What', we now look specifically at his book. This book outlines the main parliamentary procedures and constitutional conventions. It is considered the most authoritative rulebook on how the UK Parliament functions. It was published in 1844 and has since been updated several times. As of 2019, it is in its 25th edition.

It is based upon many of the parliamentary conventions dating back to 1604. Essentially, it has become the rulebook for Parliament. You will often hear The Speaker of the House of Commons refer to Erskine May when making rulings.

Members of Both Houses of Parliament Must Attend When Called

Members of Parliament perform a vital public role. They represent the views of their constituents in Parliament. Regular attendance is important, and they are paid public money to fulfil their valuable function.

In 1514, the Attendance in Parliament Act was passed by King Henry VIII, requiring that no-one who had been *"elected to come or be in Parliament ... Depart from the said parliaments, nor absent himself from the same, till Parliament be fully ended or prorogued ... upon pain of ... Losing all those sums of money which he or they should or ought to have had for his or their wages."*

Imagine if this was still the law today. In all honesty, it is nothing different to the standard employment contract, requiring employees to attend a place of employment and carry out their duties in return for payment. This Act was repealed in 1993.

There is, however, an even older law which requires all Members of both Houses to attend whenever summoned. Any Members who fail to attend are liable to be fined or receive other punishments. This was Statute 2, passed by King Richard II in 1382. It states, *"The King doth will and command, and it is assented in the Parliament by the Prelates, Lords, and Commons, That all and singular Persons and Commonalties which from henceforth shall have the Summons of the Parliament, shall come from henceforth to the Parliaments, in the Manner as they are bound to do, and* [have] *been accustomed within the Realm of England of old Times. And if any Person of the same Realm, which from henceforth shall have the said Summons ... do absent himself, and come not at the said Summons ... he shall be amerced* [fined], *and otherwise punished, according as of old Times have been used to be done within the said Realm in the said Case."* The Members of both Houses may be interested to know that this law is still live, so parliamentarians should take note.

Members of Parliament are not required to attend the House of Commons for regular sittings. However, their political parties may demand their attendance at certain times, enforced through the whips.

The Parliamentary Practice handbook, Erskine May, on page 47, states, "*On ordinary occasions the attendance of Members in Parliament is not enforced by either House ... In the Commons ensuring attendance has become a function of party machinery, and the Whips of the various parties make it their duty to secure adequate representation for all important divisions.*"

House of Lords Peers Could Only Be Tried By Fellow Peers In The House of Lords

Trial by jury is something that we all take for granted these days. It is the bedrock of our modern-day legal system and has been copied in democratic countries worldwide. This fundamental right that no free man can be imprisoned without being found guilty by the judgement of his peers is derived from the famous Magna Carta, signed by King John at Runnymede in 1215. This later became known as 'trial by jury'.

Clause 39 of the Magna Carta states, "*No free man shall be taken, imprisoned, dispossessed, outlawed, exiled or ruined in any way, nor will we go upon him nor send upon him, except by the lawful judgment of his peers or* [and] *by the law of the land.*" The peculiarity of this law comes from the application and interpretation of the term 'peers'. This was interpreted as the fact that a person could not be tried by their inferiors. This meant that peers of the realm sitting in the House of Lords could only be tried by their peers who would typically deliver judgement in the *Curia Regis* (King's Court).

From 1547, if a peer was convicted of a crime, except treason or murder, they could claim the 'privilege of peerage' to escape punishment if it was their first offence. This privilege was used five times until it was abolished in 1841 when James Brudenell, 7th Earl of Cardigan, tried to claim the privilege to avoid punishment for duelling.

For members of the House of Lords, the convention was that they had the right to be tried by their peers at the House, but only if it was sitting. If Parliament were in recess, the hearing would take place in the Lord High Steward's Court, sitting with Law Lords present and under the chairmanship of the Lord High Steward, acting as judge and jury.

In June 1901, John Russell, 2nd Earl Russell, was arrested on a charge of bigamy. It's an unusual case, as bigamy was rarely prosecuted at the time. Following his initial hearing at Bow Street Magistrates Court, he was indicted and committed for trial before his peers in the House of Lords. His trial began on 18th July 1901, with around 200 peers present, including Prime Minister Lord Salisbury. The Lord Chancellor Lord Halsbury, as the presiding judge, acted in the capacity of Lord High Steward. Russell pleaded guilty and defended his conduct. He was sentenced to 3 months imprisonment at Holloway Prison. Ten years later, he petitioned Prime Minister H. H. Asquith for a free pardon. This was duly issued by the Home Secretary, Winston Churchill.

The final trial by peers in the House of Lords occurred in 1935. This was the trial of Lieutenant Colonel Edward Russell, 26th Baron de Clifford, who insisted on his right to be tried by his peers in the House of Lords for the felony of manslaughter.

In this case, a Coroners Court found that the 26-year-old driver Douglas George Hopkins had been killed in an *'accident involving others'* in Surrey. The 'others' was Lord de Clifford. They found that he had been travelling at high speed, in excess of the speed limit, when his vehicle collided head-on with the car driven by Mr. Hopkins. The police had charged Lord de Clifford, and he was initially indicted and committed for trial at the Old Bailey. This case was a felony and quickly moved to the House of Lords so that Lord de Clifford could be tried with 'the lawful judgment of his peers'.

The trial commenced on 12th December before the Lords Spiritual and Temporal, Peers, Bishops and Archbishops and Judges. It was presided over by the Lord Chancellor, Lord Hailsham, in the capacity of Lord High Steward. The Attorney General prosecuted the case. For his defence, Lord de Clifford claimed that Mr. Hopkins's vehicle was travelling at high speed and on the wrong side of the road. This forced Lord de Clifford to switch lanes quickly at the last second to avoid a collision. Unfortunately, Mr. Hopkins also changed lanes at the last second, bringing both vehicles into a head-on collision. Lord de Clifford was found not guilty by his peers. Unfortunately for him, he faced the additional charge of dangerous driving. This was not a felony, and he was not, therefore, able to avail himself of the right for trial by his peers in the House of Lords. The matter was to be heard at the Old Bailey the following January. However, the prosecution abandoned their case.

A year later, the Lords passed a Bill to abolish trial by peers in the House of Lords. The House of Commons ignored it. It wasn't until the passing of the Criminal Justice Act (1948) that this privilege was abolished. Section 30 of the Act was headed '*Abolition of privilege of peerage in criminal proceedings*'.

Mr. Speaker

With 650 Members of Parliament elected in the House of Commons, that's a lot of voices, high-volume and arguments during the many regular debates held daily in the House of Commons Chamber. There is, of course, the rulebook Erskine May for all MPs to follow, but there still needs to be a person who controls the proceedings, a chairperson if you will. This is the role of the Speaker of the House of Commons, more commonly known as Mr. Speaker. Every question, statement or point of order raised by an MP in the House of Commons must be directed through The Speaker This ensures proceedings remain civil and don't spiral out of control into a shouting match of irrational arguments and profanities.

The Speaker ultimately controls the House and decides what amendments are selected, who speaks and in what order. MPs have the right to have their voices heard in the Chamber, and at times that necessitates Mr. Speaker gently reminding the Members of The House where they are. The Speaker has the authority to discipline and pass summary sentences for minor transgressions in the Chamber, for example, where one MP slanders another and refuses to withdraw their comments. The Speaker may then admonish the offending MP by 'naming' them and suspending them from Parliament for the day.

Upon an MP being elected for the office of The Speaker, they have to renounce all affiliation with their former political party and remain non-partisan throughout all future proceedings. The office of The Speaker is an interesting role, almost as old as Parliament itself. The earliest recorded chair of proceedings in a Parliament is the presiding officer Peter de Montfort in 1258. It was the Parliament held in Oxford. The title of Speaker can be traced back to 1376 when Sir Peter de la Mare held it.

The Speaker can not be present for all debates and committees. As such, in his absence, he has three Deputy Speakers elected by the House of Commons, who all act with The Speaker's full authority. The deputies are referred to as *"Mr/Madam Deputy Speaker."*

The Speaker is Dragged to His Chair

Some days you wake up and feel like going back to sleep again. You almost have to be dragged out of bed. Some people actually do get physically dragged to work. In a curious centuries-old custom, when a new Speaker of the House of Commons is elected, the successful MP is ceremoniously dragged by other MPs from his seat to the Speaker's chair. The Speaker feigns reluctance as they are dragged to their chair.

Historically, it was The Speaker's role to communicate between The House of Commons and the Sovereign. There were times when the Sovereign wasn't too happy with the goings-on at The House or with the messages being conveyed, resulting in punishment or death for The Speaker. As you can imagine, an MP would have been reluctant to be elected as The Speaker; hence, why they have to be physically dragged to The Speaker's chair. Over the centuries, several Speakers have been executed for displeasing the Sovereign. It is also thought that being The Speaker of the House of Commons, their office makes them the 'First Commoner' of the land. This brings with it a certain humility and often feelings of unworthiness to fulfil that powerful office.

Sir. Lindsay Hoyle, the latest incumbent as the 158th Speaker of The House, was dragged to The Speaker's Chair in this elaborate ceremony. On 4th November 2019, the then Father of The House, The Rt Hon Kenneth Clarke MP, announced the election results for The Speaker. Sir. Lindsay was ceremoniously dragged to The Speaker's chair by MPs Caroline Flint and The Rt Hon Nigel Evans.

The House of Commons Has a Father and a Mother

The House of Commons is like one large family, complete with its regular internal squabbling and fallings out. But parliamentary blood is thicker than water, and democracy always prevails come what may.

As with many families, there is a father and a mother. These roles are nothing to do with genealogy, Adam and Eve or the age of a person ... and to clarify further, that also doesn't make The Speaker of The House, *The Godfather*. The '*Father of The House*' is the longest continuously serving male MP at that time. It is the same for the '*Mother of The House*', being the longest continuously serving female MP.

Records show that the longest-serving Father of The House was Winston Churchill. Although his service was not continuous. He was first elected on 1st October 1900 and left the House of Commons on 25th September 1964, 63 years and 360 days later. Sadly, he died just four months after leaving. Before that, Francis Knollys, MP for Oxford and Reading, was elected in 1575 and continued in office for 73 years until he died in 1648. However, during his time as an MP, Parliament didn't meet for 27 years.

If there were a title of '*Baby of The House*', that would have to go to the MP for Devon, Christopher Monck, who was elected in 1667 at just 13 years old. He sat as an MP for three years.

If there were such a length of service less than zero, this honour would have to go to the MP for Portsmouth, Edward Legge, who was elected in 1747. Sadly, however, Mr. Legge could not attend the House of Commons as news eventually arrived that he had died in the West Indies 87 days before he was even elected.

The Father and Mother of the House temporarily preside over proceedings in the Chamber during the process when a new Speaker is being elected and ceremoniously dragged to The Speaker's chair.

Illegal For a Lawyer to Sit as an MP in The House of Commons

Centuries ago, many attempts were made to disqualify lawyers from sitting as Members of the House of Commons. Over the years, repeated Acts and ordinances were made to enforce this.

During the reign of King Edward III (1327-77), many lawyers frequented Parliament. They were paid four shillings a day. The King intended members to be '*gladiis cinctos*' (girded with swords), namely, noblemen like Knights of the Shire. He specifically referred to this in a writ of summons, which also prohibited the election of lawyers as Members of Parliament.

The problem was that Knights could receive ten times that amount in their Shire, and most of the time travelling to London was nothing more than an inconvenience to them. This was an ideal situation for lawyers who attended court in London during term times. They could have the best of both worlds, making extra money simultaneously because courts sat during the same terms as Parliament. Hence, they were in London in any case.

It was later declared that lawyers should not receive the wages paid to the Members if elected to sit as Members of Parliament.

A further writ of summons issued in 1404 during the reign of King Henry IV states, *"the King willed that neither you nor any other sheriff (vice-comes) of the kingdom, or any apprentice, nor other man following the law should be chosen."*

It is, of course, no longer illegal for a lawyer to sit as an MP in the House of Commons. How times have changed. Former Prime Minister Margaret Thatcher was a lawyer. Many current and previous Members of Parliament are prominent lawyers. No fewer than fifteen Prime Ministers trained as barristers at the Inns of Court, including Robert Peel, Benjamin Disraeli, William Gladstone and Tony Blair.

Research compiled by BPP University Law School revealed that 119 of the 650 MPs in 2015 had either studied or practised law before standing for election.

The Other Place...

The House of Commons and House of Lords have shared a love-hate relationship since their inception. MPs in the House of Commons may have mistrust and a dislike for those sitting on the opposition benches in the opposing political party, those with extremist views, or even those within their own party. But nothing unites quarrelling MPs like their mutual disdain for the House of Lords. Historically, there was a lot of bad blood between the two Houses. This is no longer the case; these days, there exists nothing but mutual respect between both Houses. They are, after all, the seat of democracy in the

UK. Both houses understand their place in that process and the conventions that exist between them.

With the same air of drama of a thespian refusing to utter the name 'Macbeth' whilst standing in the theatre, it has become convention for MPs sitting in the House of Commons Chamber, when referring to the House of Lords, to use the term, "*The other place.*" Not to be outdone, the House of Lords will similarly refer to their colleagues in the House of Commons also using the term "*The other place.*"

Each Year The Cellars of Parliament Are Searched For Barrels of Gunpowder

Each year on the eve before the State Opening of Parliament, His Majesty's Yeoman of the Guard assiduously search the cellars of the Houses of Parliament, looking for barrels of gunpowder. They quietly walk through the building and the cellars, each guard carrying a storm lantern. The reality is that the police will always first search the parliamentary estate with trained explosive sniffer dogs, and all searched areas outside the building, including drain covers, will be marked with a seal. This is part of an ancient ceremony dating back to the reign of King James I and the nasty incident of the Gunpowder Plot led by Guy Fawkes.

A brief history lesson ... In 1604, Guy Fawkes and a group of Catholics, led by Robert Catesby, decided it would be a good idea to assassinate the Protestant King James I whilst he attended The House of Lords. They planned to kill the King, kidnap his nine-year-old daughter Princess Elizabeth and convert her to Catholicism. The plot was discovered when an anonymous letter was sent to William Parker, 4th Baron Monteagle and the authorities were alerted. A subsequent search of the Parliament cellars found Guy Fawkes stood guarding a pile of wood near 36 barrels of gunpowder. This led to today's annual searching of the cellars on the eve before the State Opening of Parliament.

Following their search of the cellars, the Yeoman of the Guard are each provided with a seemingly disproportionate reward, half a glass of Port.

I Spy Strangers!

The Cambridge dictionary defines a 'stranger' as 'someone not known or not familiar.' Historically, the House of Commons has always had a slightly different definition of a stranger. It was a convention to use the term stranger to refer to anyone who was not a member of either the House of Commons or the House of Lords.

You would have previously heard calls of "*I Spy Strangers!*" in the House of Commons Chamber. This was the request for visiting members of the public (strangers) to leave the gallery so the Chamber could sit in private. These would often be to discuss matters of national security. In 1998, the Modernisation Committee requested that the 'spying of strangers' be dropped and replaced with a term that has a more welcoming tone. It changed to the motion that "*the House sit in private.*"

In 2004, the term 'strangers' was replaced by 'Members of the Public' across the parliamentary estate. Inside, the Chamber wasn't the only place where 'strangers' frequented, so other changes have also been implemented. Whilst it was retained in the names of the Strangers' Dining Room and Strangers' Bar, it was altered in various other parts of the Palace of Westminster. What used to be the Strangers' Cafeteria is now The Terrace Café, and the Strangers' Gallery in the Chamber is now called the Public Gallery.

Chapter Thirteen

ILLICIT TELEVISION

Since the mass panic caused by the early radio broadcast of the War of The Worlds production, leading several people to believe the Earth was genuinely under attack from Martians, television content has been closely protected by law.

Television, or 'TV' as it is more affectionately known, is considered by many as the king of media due to its power to influence the masses. Stick a person on the TV wearing a white lab coat and hang a stethoscope around their neck, and they're instantly perceived to be an expert doctor. While it might bring together a family in one room to watch the gogglebox, it also isolates us from socialising with people outside the household in other forms of entertainment. This was one such fear which led to the Saturday Football Blackout that was started in the 1960s, and still exists today.

As recently as the late twentieth-century, daytime television programmes were illegal, and hypnosis is still unlawful to be aired on television. However, that hasn't stopped people from trying.

In this chapter, we try to make head or tail of why some have referred to television as *'the idiot's lantern'* and why so many laws have been passed to protect us from this flickering screen of enjoyable imagery, which, in the grand scheme of things, as a form of entertainment, is still in its infancy.

"I find television very educating. Every time somebody turns on the set, I go into the other room and read a book."
Groucho Marx

Illegal to Make Fake News Broadcasts

Over the last few years, we've heard a lot about 'fake news' and countries trying to manipulate the electoral processes of other democratic countries by targeting key demographics with fake news on social media. Incidentally, I hear there's an interesting 123-metre spire at Salisbury Cathedral!

Fake news is not a recent concept. In fact, the now-famous Halloween episode of the radio series The Mercury Theatre on the Air, incited mass hysteria. This was 'The War of The Worlds' episode narrated by Orson Welles on 30th October 1938, broadcast over the CBS Radio Network. The police tried to access the radio studio, and the mayor phoned the studio executive to complain, who promptly hung up the phone.

Many members of the public were left convinced the Earth was under attack from a Martian invasion.

The TV has such a power of influence over people. If you see a person wearing a lab coat on TV, there's a natural assumption that they're expert scientists. Why wouldn't they be? After all, they're on television. The significance that television as a medium can influence the public has been recognised by law. The broadcast regulations regulate what can and can not be shown on British television. These laws don't apply to broadcasts aired in other countries or videos featured on online platforms like YouTube. These regulations make it an offence to broadcast fake news. This is to prevent a 'War of The Worlds' scenario where a member of the public flicks through the various TV channels and comes across a fake news broadcast, only to believe it to be genuine.

As always, there are ways around these regulations. For example, in the 2004 BBC series, 'Crisis Command', a drama based on a fictional crisis, the disaster footage is never shown in full-screen. There is always something else happening. The last major fake broadcast in the UK that caused genuine outrage occurred on Halloween night in 1992. This was the BBC show 'Ghostwatch' in which a fictitious malicious spirit of an old man called Mr. Pipes terrorised a family. This was also supposedly played out live on TV. To make matters worse, the highly-respected senior BBC journalist and interviewer Michael Parkinson fronted the show, along with former Blue Peter presenter Sarah Green. Both of them were highly respected and trusted by the viewing audience. The programme was brought to a shocking end, and the broadcast was cut at the moment it appeared that the evil spirit had taken over and was causing harm to the occupants. This broadcast scared many people and graced the front pages of the tabloid newspapers for days afterwards.

To prevent the broadcast of fake news, the regulating body, The Office of Communications (Ofcom), developed a Broadcasting Code with which all broadcasters, both TV and radio, have to comply. This Code is backed by law under the Communications Act (2003) and the Broadcasting Act (1996).

Section 5 of the Code deals with the 'Accuracy' of broadcast content.

5.1 states, *"News, in whatever form, must be reported with due accuracy and presented with due impartiality."*

5.3 states, *"No politician may be used as a newsreader, interviewer or reporter in any news programmes unless, exceptionally, it is editorially justified. In that case, the political allegiance of that person must be made clear to the audience."*

Not Permitted to Show Too Many TV Adverts

Unless you're watching any BBC channels or an online streaming platform, it seems most of the viewing time is occupied by TV adverts. I don't know about you, but it seems there are many more adverts now on TV than there used to be. Believe it or not, there are rules covering the number of TV adverts displayed per hour and how far apart they have to be. These are covered under the Ofcom 'Code on the scheduling of television advertising'.

The current Ofcom rules state that for channels ITV, Channel 4 and Channel 5, the *"total amount of advertising in any one day must not exceed an average of seven minutes per hour of broadcasting."* During prime time viewing periods (7am-9am and 6pm-11pm), the advertising breaks may be up to 8 minutes long. Other commercial channels can broadcast 9 minutes of adverts per hour, plus an additional 3 minutes per hour for any teleshopping adverts.

These hourly durations are not a rolling average. They are a strict limit per hour. So, broadcasters must swap around their scheduling and adverts to accommodate this. What tends to happen is that for the prime time shows on a channel, the programme before it will contain fewer adverts. These will often be bunched up towards the end of the programme to catch some early viewers tuning in to watch the following prime time TV show.

Before 2008, there was a rule that required adverts to be placed during a programme in a way that didn't disrupt the flow of that programme. This has since changed to reflect that the TV adverts can be shown in any way, so long as *"the integrity of the programme is not prejudiced"* and that the adverts are placed *"where natural breaks occur."*

In June 2022, the regulator Ofcom announced it was considering reviewing the broadcasting rules in light of evolving viewing habits and the rise of online streaming services. This is with a view to extending the duration of the advertising breaks on UK television channels and increasing the frequency of the advertising breaks.

Illegal to Hypnotise The Audience on TV

Depending on who you speak to about hypnosis, some will say it works, and others believe it to be a total scam. Some have ideas of hypnosis limited to stage performances where the participants run around nodding and clucking, pretending to be chickens. In contrast, others see its use as an alternative form of therapy. Either way, we have probably come a long way from the days of the Victorian evil hypnotist wearing a top hat and dark cloak, swinging a pocket watch and telling his victim to look into his eyes. The local council must license hypnosis performances on stage. Conducting an unlicensed performance can result in a hefty fine. This goes back to concerns raised over hypnosis in the 1950s, which resulted in the passing of the Hypnotism Act (1952) to regulate *"the demonstration of hypnotic phenomena for purposes of public entertainment."* From that moment on, hypnosis performances were licensed, and hypnosis broadcast over television was banned.

We are all a lot wiser now and understand that we can't be hypnotised by a megalomaniac despot or the Demon headmaster through a televised performance. However, the danger still exists that if elements of hypnosis were broadcast, someone could genuinely believe that it had caused them harm. This is something broadcasters and Ofcom wish to avoid.

The rules were tested to their limit by Channel 4 on 18th September 2009, when they broadcast a programme featuring the illusionist Derren Brown's 'How to Control the Nation'. As part of the programme, Brown played a short film which he claimed would make some television viewers feel stuck to their chairs. Brown did not state this was hypnosis, and he made no claims to be hypnotising the viewers. Over 3 million people viewed the programme. It is alleged that 1 in 4 viewers were affected by this 'subliminal suggestion'. A Channel 4 spokeswoman claimed they had received 50,000 phone calls within three minutes of the broadcast from viewers who stated they were stuck to their chairs. This programme wasn't hypnosis. It was merely what some might believe to have been hypnosis. This could have made them susceptible to the suggestion that they were momentarily fixed to their chairs. It can't have been hypnosis because hypnotism is banned on British TV through the regulations made by the regulating body Ofcom.

Rule 2.9 of the Ofcom regulations deals with Hypnosis. It states, "*When broadcasting material featuring demonstrations of hypnotic techniques, broadcasters must exercise a proper degree of responsibility in order to prevent hypnosis and/or adverse reactions in viewers and listeners. The hypnotist must not broadcast his/her full verbal routine or be shown performing straight to camera.*"

Illegal to Make People Pay to Watch The Olympics

For all sports lovers, there's always a major regular sporting event on television. Every few years, we get to watch the Olympics, the world athletics, the World Cup and the Euros. In between those, there are other major sporting events like the annual Wimbledon tennis finals and the Grand National. Imagine one year sitting in your favourite chair, in front of the goggle box, ready for a few hours of sporting exhilaration. You switch on the TV, only to see a notice on the screen telling you that your favourite sporting event has now become pay-per-view. This became a real prospect in 1996 when the British viewing audience started accessing satellite and cable television channels. Satellite channels cost a lot of money at the time ... and even more now. With the commercial revenues they raised, there became a danger that they could outbid the free-to-air TV channels for major sporting events like the Olympics and Wimbledon. This would prevent those who could not afford the extra cost of subscription television from viewing such events. So, to protect the Great British public from having to pay-to-view some of our favourite pastimes on television, Parliament passed a law which ensured that key sporting events had to be broadcast for free to all television viewers.

The Broadcasting Act (1996) empowers the Secretary of State for Digital, Culture, Media and Sport to designate key sporting and other national events as '*listed events*'. This Act and the subsequent broadcasting code were created when the Internet was in its infancy, and only 4% of UK households had access to the Internet.

Any of those designated as listed events are legally required to be broadcast to the general public for free. That is to say, broadcasters are not permitted to charge for access to watch those programmes.

In January 2020, the Paralympic Games were added to this designated list. Recently, the FIFA Women's World Cup and UEFA Women's European Championship were also added to the list to demonstrate the government's commitment to greater inclusivity and diversity in sports.

The Saturday Football Blackout

Since the advent in the late 1920s of the box that now adorns several rooms, this strange contraption has become a focal point for family life and heavily influenced the public with its moving images and commercial advertisements. No-one could have foreseen the effects of television on society. Even by the standards of the Swinging 60s, many considered it with some degree of suspicion. One such person was the then chairman of Burnley Football Club, Bob Lord. He became a staunch opponent of televised football matches, arguing that live coverage would "*damage and undermine attendances.*" Such was his disdain for televised football that when the first Match of the Day programme was aired in 1964, he banned the BBC cameras from televising matches from Burnley's Turf Moor ground. This ban remained in place for a further five years.

Consequently, in the early 1960s, he hatched a plan and convinced fellow Football League chairmen that televising matches on Saturday afternoons would have a negative impact on the attendance of lower league games. He genuinely believed that if a 3pm match between, for example, Manchester United and Liverpool football clubs were televised, many supporters would rather watch that on television than attend a lower division team match at their stadium. Following this, a gentleman's agreement was reached where a football broadcasting blackout was enforced for all clubs playing Premier League, Football League or FA Cup matches on a Saturday afternoon. The blackout lasted between 2:45pm and 5:15pm. This meant that most Saturday 3pm kick-offs could not be televised in the UK. From that moment on, the TV networks could only show Saturday matches with early or late kick-offs. There has never been a legal ruling on this matter, and so it is not covered in the law. However, this early gentleman's agreement nevertheless exists even to this day.

It also affects foreign football matches that can not be aired during the Saturday blackout period. This occurred in 2013 when viewers had to miss the first 15 minutes of the El Classico match between FC Barcelona and Real Madrid. To accommodate our blackout period, this was rectified in future years with the Spanish La Liga's traditional 6pm kick-off (accommodating our time zone difference), being moved to a 6.15pm slot. There are, of course, exceptions to this blackout rule. For example, the FA Cup final can be televised during this blackout period.

Interestingly, live radio broadcasts are still permitted during the blackout. It is only enforced on televised broadcasts.

In February 2011, the German Advocate General Juliane Kokott from the European Court of Justice pointed out the Draconian nature of this ban or whether it had any place in today's society. She commented, *"It is, in fact, doubtful whether closed periods are capable of encouraging attendance at matches and partic-*

ipation in matches. Both activities have a completely different quality to the following of a live transmission on television."

Illegal to Broadcast Without Subtitles

There are currently 11 million people in the UK with some form of hearing loss. That's one in six people. We are long past the days where the family would sit around listening to the wireless and playing parlour games. In fact, we're even passed the days when the family would sit in the same room enjoying their favourite television programme together. Nowadays, sadly, most family members sit in separate rooms watching television on smaller screens. Research has shown that many television viewers prefer to 'screen stack' whilst watching TV. This is when the viewer watches multiple screens simultaneously, usually a mobile phone, tablet, laptop and TV. So, it is fair to say that our viewing habits have changed considerably since the inception of television.

Fortunately, as television has become more economically accessible to the masses, it has also become essential to cater to the needs of all viewers with disabilities. Broadcasters now offer TV access services and additional facilities to enable the hearing and visually impaired audience to consume TV content. You're probably familiar with subtitles (or 'closed captions' as they're known in other countries). You may not have realised that they have been around for several decades. The British Broadcasting Corporation (BBC) was the first broadcaster in the UK to include subtitles on a television broadcast. This was back in 1979. The BBC now offers subtitles on 100% of its programmes across all its broadcast channels. This closed captioning has now become a legal requirement for all national broadcasters in the UK, including satellite and cable broad-casters.

The regulations governing this are laid down in the Ofcom Broadcasting Code on Access. This sets out the legal require-ments for television broadcasters on the use of subtitles and the provision of both sign language and audio description. The regulations require that all broadcasters from day one provide subtitles on at least 10% of their channel output. This increases to a minimum of 80% of the channel output for the well-es-tablished channels. They're also required to have at least 10% of the broadcast supplied with audio description, and at least 5% must have sign language. Many channels choose to put sign language programmes in their late-night scheduling.

Daytime Television Used to Be Illegal

You can switch on the television at any time of the day or night and find something to watch. It might not necessarily be good, but there's always something to watch. Compare that to the situation just a few decades ago, when if you switched the TV on at 3am, you would be met with a black screen. There were occasions when you switched the TV on during the daytime, only to be met with a selection of pages from Ceefax or Oracle Teletext. In fact, until 1972, daytime television in the UK was illegal! It was previously felt that daytime TV shows would make the British public lazy and lead people astray.

In 1955, broadcasting restrictions meant that the BBC was only permitted to broadcast a maximum of 5 hours per day. That same year, the commercial channel ITV launched, and both channels were permitted to broadcast up to 7 hours per day.

This gradually increased and by 1972, broadcasting restrictions meant that TV channels were only allowed to broadcast 50 hours a week and a maximum of 8 hours in any one day. At the time, television broadcasting fell under the control of the Postmaster General.

Bizarrely, until 1957, there was a ban on television programmes being broadcast between 6pm and 7pm. In what was nicknamed the '*Toddler's Truce*', it was felt this was the optimal time for parents to put their children to bed. From 7pm onwards, this became prime time TV. In 1958, this toddler's truce restriction was lifted but not quite how the public might have liked. It was decided that only religious programmes could be aired during that hour.

The broadcasting restrictions were eased for large-scale sporting and State events and other occasions where families would be together, like Christmas Eve, Christmas Day, Boxing Day, New Year's Eve and New Year's Day.

This all changed on 19th January 1972, when the Minister for Posts and Telecommunications announced in the House of Commons that all previous broadcasting restrictions would be lifted. This wasn't an instant move to fill daytime TV scheduling with content. It occurred very gradually over several years. When the government lifted this restriction, most programmes shown on TV in the mornings were primarily schools-based. The BBC started to fill its afternoon TV schedules almost immediately, but this had to be thinned down within a couple of years due to financial constraints. ITV also began providing afternoon TV with programmes for the younger viewing audience being shown during the mornings of school holidays. By November 1972, ITV had launched a full daytime schedule which began at 9.30am each day. That same year, the BBC launched its flagship daytime television show called Pebble Mill at One. It was a live magazine-style show filled with celebrity interviews and music.

Finally, at 6.30am on 17th January 1983, the BBC launched its first ever breakfast television show on BBC1, Breakfast Time. A couple of weeks later, on 1st February, ITV also launched its first breakfast TV slot, TV-am, which I am reliably informed, heralded the arrival of Roland Rat and Timmy Mallett, with a strong focus on the younger viewers.

Chapter Fourteen

LABOUR LAWS

W orking and trade are the bedrock of our great nation of explorers, pioneers and industrialists. In this chapter, we look at the absurdity over the centuries of some strict labour laws that would most likely see modern trade unionists burning effigies in the streets. You will work! You will not receive any pay rise ... or suffer the indignity of going to prison.

There was a time when you could legally buy cigarettes on a Sunday, but it wasn't lawful to purchase a Bible simultaneously.

After a hard week's labour in the office, you can forget about spending some time relaxing with your family or friends at the local park, doing a museum tour or visiting the cinema. For those who enjoy the occasional luxury of working from home, when you answer the door to the postal worker, don't engage them in idle gossip. You may be risking a trip to the magistrate's court.

"Without labour, nothing prospers."
Sophocles

Very Strict Labour Laws

Following on from the Black Death bubonic plague which swept across Europe, killing half of all Londoners and between 30% to 60% of all Europeans, there was a mass labour shortage across England. The unhealthy situation prevailed where workers realised they could profit immediately from the effects of the recent plague by relocating to towns and cities that had suffered the most significant losses. This caused a high demand for labour in those areas, and workers quickly realised they could demand much higher wages. The towns and cities which decided not to provide these higher wages suffered a higher-than-average number of labourers who were seen as idle and unwilling to work without a pay increase.

It's hard to imagine the devastation the plague will have caused to every household across the country. In 1350, King Edward III introduced one of the first labour laws, the Labourers and Artificers Act. This addressed the growing concerns over a lack of a skilled labour force. The Act also sought to punish, "... *the malice of servants, which were idle, and not willing to serve after the pestilence*" without taking excessive wages.

The Act provided that every able-bodied person below 60 years should be required to continue working and receive no more than the customary wages. Punishment for failing to work was imprisonment. It also fixed wages for the different labourers, artisans and servants. If that didn't sound harsh enough, the Act also made it a crime for any labourer to migrate to a different town or city to look for higher wages. It stated, "*If any of said servants, labourers, or artist, do flee from one county to another because of this ordinance, that the sheriffs of such county where such fugitive persons shall be found shall do them to be taken at the commandment of the justices of the counties from whence they shall flee, and bring them to the chief gaol of the same county.*"

In today's world, where mass union walkouts can penalise the entire nation with rail strikes, postal strikes and public sector workers striking, it's hard to imagine the effects of such legislation on the workforce and families at the time. Nevertheless, these strict labour laws continued over the following centuries.

In 1425, King Henry VI passed a law making it an offence for stonemasons to violate the labour laws and form confederacies of masons. Those convicted were judged to be felons, imprisoned and fined.

An Act Concerning Victuallers and Handycrafts Men (1548) made it an offence for artificers, workmen, or labourers to conspire to set unreasonable prices for their work. The penalty for first-timers committing this offence was twenty days imprisonment with only bread and water for sustenance. The punishment was to be placed in the local pillory for a second offence. For third offences, the penalty was to be placed in the local pillory, have one ear cut off and thereafter be considered "*infamous.*"

In 1562, Queen Elizabeth I passed the 'Act Concerning Diverse Orders for Artificers, Laborers, Servants of Husbandry and Apprentices'. It sought to address the insufficiency of existing laws related to the hiring and wages of servants, artificers, apprentices and other labourers. It required all able-bodied persons able to work as labourers or artificers, not having independent means, to work upon demand. The law fixed the hours of work and provided local magistrates with the power to fix the rate of wages. This Act was not repealed until 1875.

In 1720, King George I passed the 'Journeymen Tailors, London Act' to stop agreements between journeymen tailors "...*for advancing their wages or for lessening their usual hours of work.*" The hours of labour were fixed between 6 AM and 8 PM, with an hours break provided for lunch. This Act came about after the master tailors of London presented a series of petitions to Parliament complaining that the journeymen in their trade had created an early form of a trade union and had gone on strike. That year, there were approximately 15,000 journeymen, all striking for greater pay and shorter working hours. In an early labour law case, the 1721 case of R v Journeymen-Taylors of Cambridge, it was found that the strike action of the journeymen amounted to an unlawful and criminal conspiracy. Punishments for contravening this Act were imprisonment with or without hard labour.

King George III passed the Combination Act (1799) to prevent workmen's unlawful combinations (unions) and prohibit trade unions and any collective bargaining by British workers. This law was hurriedly introduced during a period of paranoia where the then Home Secretary believed that workers might strike during times of conflict to force the government to accede to their demands. It suppressed any combination of two or more masters or workmen attempting to change their wages, the number of hours worked, or the quantity of work done.

Talking to The 'Postman' Could Land You In Prison

It's common knowledge and common sense also that you shouldn't open another person's mail. As much as we grow irritable with the postal strikes and the occasional postal worker seemingly practising origami whilst contorting envelopes into all sorts of unfathomable shapes through the letterbox, the postal service has stood the test of time.

The laws surrounding the Post Office date back to the sixteenth century when in 1516, King Henry VII established the role of Master of the Posts. This role continued until it was finally abolished in 1969. It wasn't until 1635 that King Charles I made the postal service available to all, not just the wealthy. Oddly though, the recipient paid the postage costs, not the sender, from the outset. With the amount of junk mail we all receive these days, most of us would be penniless in months!

King Charles II established the General Post Office with his 'Act for Erecting and Establishing a Post Office' in 1660. The following year, the first postage date stamp was introduced. In the early 1980s, the General Post Office disappeared altogether after a rebrand to the Post Office. You can still see many of the original 'GPO' markings on telegraph poles and grid covers.

The Postal Services Act (2000) was introduced to consolidate many previous postal laws. Section 84 of the Act makes it an offence to open post belonging to another person if you know or suspect it has been incorrectly delivered to you. This includes mail sent to your address meant for a previous householder. Royal Mail advises under such circumstances that the envelope should be marked 'Return to Sender' and placed in any post box.

The 2000 Act also created the offence of intentionally delaying the post without reasonable excuse. So, be warned the next time you engage your postal worker in inane chit-chat about the weather. Amusingly, they felt it was necessary to incorporate Section 87 of the Act, making it an offence to display any writing signs or other visible representations of a post box, in or on your house, in such a way that members of the public may believe it to be a public post box.

So, what happens in the cases where the mail has been delivered through your door, and you innocently open it in a hurry, not reading the address label? Well, you'll be pleased to know that you haven't committed an offence because the law requires some criminal intent in doing so. In this case, it was done innocently and unknowingly, so you can rest easy at night. This happened to me only yesterday when I opened a bank statement addressed to someone else supposedly living at this address. I was on a phone call at the time and hadn't even noticed the name on the envelope. Doing my civic duty, I contacted the well-known high street bank. I was passed through multiple call handlers, none of whom saw the severity of their customer's account data exposed to the public, despite their obligations to correct their error under the Data Protection Act. Eventually, after a lengthy fifty-eight-minute phone call, the matter was resolved by a member of their staff.

After the call, I pondered what must happen with such bank statements when they fall into the hands of unscrupulous individuals. They are presented with a wealth of information, sort code, bank account number, full name with middle names and a simple check of birth registers would undoubtedly reveal the account holder's date of birth. It is clear to see the relevance of the Postal Services Act (2000) in today's society.

Section 53 of the Post Office Act (1908) also made it an offence to intercept and withhold mail from reaching its rightful recipient.

Disappearing Linen From The Chelsea Hospital

We've all witnessed the splendour of Chelsea Pensioners at large events, dressed in their distinctive scarlet uniforms and tricorne hats, wearing their badges of ranks and adorned in service medals. What or who exactly is a Chelsea Pensioner? A Chelsea Pensioner is a former member of the British Army and a resident of the Royal Hospital Chelsea, a retirement home in Chelsea, London. It was founded in 1682 by King Charles II as a retreat for veterans. In 1684, when Ireland was still united with England, we also had The Royal Hospital Kilmainham in Dublin.

The Chelsea and Kilmainham Hospitals Act was passed in 1826 to tidy up a few issues that occurred over the years. There must have been problems with theft or 'disappearing' bed linen and towels from the Hospital because this Act sought to address this problem directly. Section 34 of the Act required the Hospital Commissioners to mark all clothes, linen, stores, and other articles belonging to the Hospital with a stamp indicating they were the property of 'Chelsea Hospital'. It made it an offence for any Pensioner or other person to '*unlawfully pawn, sell, embezzle, secrete, or dispose of* such property. It was also an offence '*if any Pawnbroker or other Person or Persons shall unlawfully take in pawn, buy, exchange, or receive any Clothes, Linen, Stores, or other Goods or Articles*' stamped with the 'Chelsea Hospital' mark. This law was finally repealed in 2008. However, any unscrupulous person thinking they can get around this can think again. Such an act would now be considered an offence of theft under Section 1 of the Theft Act (1968) or Handling Stolen Goods under Section 22 of the Theft Act.

It is a common myth that it is an offence to impersonate a Chelsea Pensioner (a resident of the Chelsea Hospital). Whilst that is morally wrong, it is, nevertheless, not an offence in law. However, they may be guilty of fraud depending on the individual's intention, perhaps to defraud. This claim most likely derives from The Chelsea and Kilmainham Hospitals Act (1826), prohibiting fraudulent claims related to taking un-earned pensions that belonged to Chelsea Pensioners. It was repealed by the Statute Law (Repeals) Act in 2008.

Interestingly, until large swathes of this Act were repealed, the Commissioners of Chelsea Hospital were empowered to take away or refuse pensions for those found guilty of fraud or misconduct. The Commissioners still maintain the power to expel Chelsea Pensioners who are guilty of criminal offences or misconduct.

You Could Buy Cigarettes & Saucy Magazines But Not The Bible on Sundays

Those under 30 years of age may have little idea of the pain that many have gone through each Sunday for centuries whilst battling with the old Sunday trading laws. Before 1994, the Shops Act of 1950 was still in operation, placing some strict trading laws across UK shops each Sunday. It wasn't uncommon to visit your local shop to find it closed. This law preserved the attitudes from the early 20th century, where religious observance and an enforced day of rest with the family were considered a high priority.

There were some bizarre rules for Sunday trading. For example, you could buy cigarettes but not frozen fish fingers. You could purchase newspapers and indecent magazines, but you couldn't buy a Bible. These bizarre trading laws only applied to England and Wales. Northern Ireland maintained their own rules. Whilst north of the border in Scotland, they had no Sunday trading laws at all, and they still don't.

Section 1 of the 1950 Shops Act states, "*Every shop shall be, closed for the serving of customers not later than one o'clock in the afternoon on one week day in every week.*" This legislation has its roots in the Shop Hours Act (1904), which gave councils the power to require a single half-day closing each week. However, this could only come into effect if two-thirds of the local retailers agreed. They rarely did.

In the years since the 1950 Shops Act, there had been many failed attempts through private members' Bills to reform the Sunday trading laws. In 1986, Prime Minister Margaret Thatcher attempted to introduce changes but was defeated by 72 backbenchers from her own party. This was the largest parliamentary defeat during Mrs. Thatcher's whole time in office. Behind the rebellion was a powerful alliance of traditionalists, trade unionists and some well-known high street department stores. They formed the Keep Sunday Special alliance. In the changing economic climate of the 1980s, many shops decided to open on a Sunday, regardless of the law. Changes finally came with the passing of the Sunday Trading Act (1994). However, this was a watered-down version from that initially proposed by Prime Minister John Major's cabinet. It still contained restricted opening hours in an attempt to facilitate church attendance. Restrictions were also placed on larger stores to protect the smaller family-run shops.

These restrictions are still in force today. Larger shops with over 280 square metres of floor space are only permitted to open for six hours between 10 AM and 6 PM on Sundays. Consequently, most large retailers are open on Sundays from 11 AM to 5 PM. Some choose to open at 10 AM and close at 4 PM. They can not open at all on Easter Sunday. Smaller shops, however, are permitted to open at any time.

The idea of restricting shop opening hours to facilitate church attendance seems quite irrational when you look at the figures on paper. Church attendance rates have declined steadily since the mid-19th century. In 1851 a government tally showed around half of Britain's population attended church on a particular Sunday. By 1900, church attendance had dwindled to around 25%. A recent clergy count returned a national church attendance of about 6%.

The employee relations side of Sunday trading laws can be said to protect workers from burnout. Working seven days a week just isn't sustainable. Then again, why restrict working hours specifically on a Sunday? In addition to this, Section 40 of the Employment Rights Act (1996) entitles shop employees to provide a three months written notice opting out of Sunday working at any time, even if they previously agreed to it in their contract of employment. Employees can not be dismissed or maltreated for choosing not to work on Sundays. Sunday now appears to be one of the most popular days of the week for families to go shopping.

It also seems odd to restrict the opening hours of brick-and-mortar shops when consumers can now just order online at any time of the day, including Sundays. The larger retail outlets can circumvent the opening hours restriction with their pocket-sized 'Express' shops on the high street.

So, are these Sunday trading laws confined to the 20th century or were they also a thing of the past? Again, we look at one of the primary reasons for Sunday trading restrictions, and this does come down to religious observance. The further you go back in time, the greater the significance and adherence to religious observance.

In the Old Testament of the Bible, Exodus 20:8-11 states, "*Remember the Sabbath day, to keep it holy. Six days you shall labour, and do all your work, but the seventh day is a Sabbath to the LORD your God. On it you shall not do any work, you, or your son, or your daughter, your male servant, or your female servant, or your livestock, or the sojourner who is within your gates. For in six days the LORD made heaven and earth, the sea, and all that is in them, and rested on the seventh day. Therefore the LORD blessed the Sabbath day and made it holy.*"

In 321 AD, the Roman Emperor Constantine passed the first known law restricting work on Sundays. This was for religious reasons. "*On the venerable Day of the Sun let the magistrates and people residing in cities rest, and let all workshops be closed.*" (Codex Justinianus, lib. 3, tit. 12, 3)

In 1781, King George III passed the 'Act for Preventing Certain Abuses and Profanations on the Lord's Day, Called Sunday', otherwise known as the Sunday Observance Act. As well as encouraging Sunday worship, this law aimed to prohibit Sunday trading and restrict public entertainment. The first three sections banned the use of any building or room for public entertainment or debate on Sundays. This Act prevented the public from visiting museums, zoos, public gardens, libraries, concert halls and theatres each Sunday for many years.

One hundred and fifty years later, the Sunday Entertainments Act (1932) was passed, finally making it possible for the public to visit museums, picture galleries, the zoo, public gardens, aquariums, lectures and debates on Sundays. It wasn't until the Sunday Theatre Act (1972) that the Great British public could legally attend theatre shows on Sundays, including pantomimes. Finally, with the passing of the Cinemas Act in 1985, the public was allowed to attend the cinema on Sundays.

On a side note, there was a myth perpetuated for several years that, except for carrots, most goods may not be sold on Sunday. As bizarre and amusing as this may have been, there is no evidential basis for this.

CHAPTER FIFTEEN

LAWLESS COURTS

I t wasn't always the accused that would find themselves in the dock of a court. Often, jury members would be treated with more contempt than the accused. They would find themselves fined or imprisoned alongside the defendant for refusing to agree with the judges.

Through an interpretation of an old law from 1361 written in Norman French, we'll see that magistrates are, even now, legally compelled to bind over every person, even if they're already of good behaviour.

In this chapter, we'll peer into the world of the judicial system, where sometimes courts can themselves be lawless places. There was even a court known as the 'Lawless Court' where people would be summoned to attend through whispers. Those who didn't hear and failed to attend would be punished.

Convicted Criminal: "As God is my judge—I am innocent."

Lord Birkett: "He isn't; I am, and you're not!"

Norman Birkett, 1st Baron Birkett

Magistrates Are Legally Required to Bind Over Every Person of Good Behaviour

The Justices of The Peace Act (1361), which is still in force today, omitted a very important word, *"not."* This Act, passed during the reign of King Edward III, intended to deal with the various problems arising from mass unemployment.

During his reign, the King led the English army to a famous victory at Crécy in France and captured Calais. Unfortunately, things took a turn for the worse, and the French won back most of the territory the English had conquered. The returning soldiers were no longer needed, nor did they have any jobs to return to. This created mass unemployment and what was considered to be laziness. Aside from the fact that a lot of the soldiers probably returned suffering from post-traumatic stress disorder (PTSD), many were deemed to have become *"pillors and robbers."* Those were the words used in the 1361 Act. The Act provides Justices of The Peace (magistrates) with the power to *"restrain...pursue, arrest...and chastise"* any *"offenders, rioters, and all other barators"* and imprison, fine or deal with them using their own discretion. I'm sure we can all agree that acts of pillage and robbery are unacceptable and need to be punished. It's the next part of the Act that contains the peculiarity that still exists today.

The problem is that the Act was written in Norman French and doesn't translate very well.

It states, "*...de prendre de touz ceux qi sont de bone fame ou ils serront trovez suffisant seurete & mainprise de lour bon port devers le Roi & son poeple et les autres duement punir.*" This has, in the past, been translated as, "*to take all them that be of good fame, where they shall be found, sufficient surety and mainprise of their good behaviour towards the King and his people, and the other duly to punish.*" The word 'ne' was omitted. It should say, "*de prendre de touz ceux qi ne sont de bone fame*" (to take all them that be <u>NOT</u> of good fame). Essentially, the Act requires all those brought before magistrates, who are of good behaviour, to be bound over.

Perhaps this might go some way to explaining the curious case of Mrs. Valerie Waters who on 13th November 1976, had been one of several anti-foxhunting demonstrators at a meeting of the Atherstone Hunt. As she was driving away, she was physically attacked and her car was damaged by members of the Hunt. Four of her attackers were charged with the offence of criminal damage as well as conduct likely to lead to a breach of the peace.

In April 1977, the case went to court. All four defendants pleaded guilty. They were fined and bound over by the magistrates. Mrs. Waters was also in court that day, acting as a prosecution witness. Bizarrely, the magistrates decided to also bind her over to be of good behaviour. She refused, stating that she was not on trial. Her refusal to be bound over ended up with her being sentenced to one-month imprisonment at HMP Risley.

As recently as 1978, an amendment Bill was put forward to The Justices of The Peace Act (1361) but this was voted down in Parliament. So the wording of the original 1361 Act still stands to this day.

Juries Could Be Fined or Imprisoned If The Judge Wasn't Happy With Their Decision

The right to trial by jury is something that we take for granted these days. It came about in 1215 at Runnymede when rebellious barons compelled King John to agree to a Charter of liberties, later known as the Magna Carta. Clause 39 of the Magna Carta states, '*No free man shall be seized or imprisoned, or stripped of his rights or possessions, or outlawed or exiled, or deprived of his standing in any way, nor will we proceed with force against him, or send others to do so, except by the lawful judgement of his equals or by the law of the land.*' This is often considered the founding basis of the principle of 'trial by jury'.

These days, doing jury service is seen as a valuable civic duty. You deliberate the verdict with your fellow jurors in the comfort of the jury room, regularly supplied with refreshments, and there are no time pressures. It wasn't always that way. During the 16th century, juries would often be fined or imprisoned if they disagreed with the 'advice' of the judge regarding the verdict. Later on, it was the turn of King James I. His Majesty, along with his Lord Chancellor, Chief Justices and the Chief Baron, decided that if a jury found an accused person guilty, their decision should not be questioned. However, suppose a jury found a person to be not guilty, and the court felt that they were guilty. They decided in that case, the jurors should all be charged in the Court of the Star Chamber '*for their partiality in finding a manifest offender not guilty.*'

In 1667, the Lord Chief Justice Kelynge attracted many complaints for fining and imprisoning jurors, for bringing verdicts contrary to the evidence and advice of the court. The matter was heard against him in the House of Commons after he went too far by dismissing an appeal brought on the basis that he had contravened the Magna Carta. He referred to the Magna Carta as "*Magna Farta.*" Understandably, Parliament was unhappy and ruled that the practice of fining and imprisoning jurors who didn't reach a verdict in agreement with the court's decision, was illegal.

On 14th August 1670, William Penn and William Mead attended their Quaker meeting house in Gracechurch Street, London. They noticed that the authorities had padlocked the doors. They chose to address the crowd of approximately three hundred, preaching to them in the street. This was in contravention of the recently passed Conventicle Act (1664), which forbade gatherings of more than five people for worship in a public place. This law didn't apply to such gatherings for the services of the Church of England. Penn and Mead were arrested for unlawful assembly and preaching. Both men appeared at the Old Bailey in London on 1st September 1670 for a five-day trial.

The indictment included that they had "*unlawfully and tumultuously ... being assembled and congregated together, by reason whereof a great concourse and tumult of people in the street ... in contempt of the said lord the king, and of his law, to the great disturbance of his peace; to the great terror and disturbance of many of his liege people and subjects, to the ill example of all others in the like case offenders, and against the peace of the said lord the king, his crown and dignity.*"

The nine people on the bench hearing the case included the Lord Mayor of London Sam Starling, several aldermen of the City of London, the Lieutenant of the Tower of London John Robinson and the Recorder John Howell.

The proceedings got off to a bad start when Penn and Mead removed their tall Quaker hats in the courtroom. At once, the Lord Mayor ordered one of the officers of the court to put their hats back on. Once this had happened, the Recorder noticed they were wearing their hats in court and asked Penn why he had not removed his hat. Penn replied, *"Because I do not believe that to be any respect."* This incensed the Recorder, who duly fined Penn 40 marks, 13 shillings and 4 pence for showing contempt to the court. Penn stated that their hats had been removed when they entered the courtroom but that they had been put back on by the order from the bench. Therefore it should be the bench that should be fined, not they. When Mead was told that he too had been fined for contempt, he turned towards the jury and commented, *"I desire the Jury, and all people to take notice of this injustice of the Recorder: Who spake to me to pull off my hat? and yet hath he put a fine upon my head. O fear the Lord, and dread his power, and yield to the guidance of his holy spirit, for he is not far from every one of you."*

Shortly afterwards, the officers who arrested Penn and Mead were called to give evidence. They provided evidence that Penn had been seen speaking to people and preaching to them on Gracechurch Street. One officer stated that he had not seen Mead there. The Recorder asked Mead if he was there. Mead replied, quoting the legal principle, "*nemo tenetur accusare seipsum*" (no man is bound to accuse himself) and accused the Recorder of trying to entrap him. The Recorder told him to hold his tongue.

The Recorder then turned his attention to Penn, asking him to enter a plea on his indictment. Penn promptly asked under which law he was being prosecuted. The Recorder, being non-specific, told him it was Common Law. Penn argued that his indictment had no foundation in law, so he could not enter a plea. The Recorder accused him of being a "*saucy fellow*." Penn continued to argue his point until the Recorder ordered him to be placed in a squalid lock-up next to the courtroom. As the Recorder could not provide the appropriate statute, Mead took it upon himself to address the jury, telling them what constituted an unlawful assembly. He was then also ordered to be placed in the squalid lock-up by the Recorder.

When Penn began shouting that their rights were being denied under the conventions set out in the Magna Carta, they were both thrown into the dungeon away from the earshot of the court. In the absence of both defendants, the Recorder then summed up the case for the jury and sent them out to deliberate. After half an hour, four jurors could not reach a verdict. Without a unanimous verdict, the Recorder was unhappy. He singled out one of the jurors, Edward Bushel as a dissenter. The Lieutenant of The Tower, also sitting on the bench, told Bushel, "*You deserve to be indicted more than any man that hath been brought to the bar this day.*" The jury foreman was once again asked their verdict. He replied, "*Guilty of speaking in Gracechurch Street.*" The Recorder told the jury the verdict was not good enough and that they must reach a verdict of 'unlawful assembly'. He sent them back out to deliberate once again.

Half an hour later, the jury returned to the courtroom with a written verdict. It stated, *"We the Jurors, hereafter named, do find William Penn to be guilty of Speaking or Preaching to an Assembly, met together in Gracechurch Street, the 14th of August last 1670, and that William Mead is not guilty of the said Indictment."*

Once again, the Recorder rejected this verdict, and the jury was locked away for the night without meat, drink, fire, and tobacco. The Recorder told them, *"Gentlemen, you shall not be dismissed till we have a verdict that the court will accept; and you shall be locked up, without meat, drink, fire, and tobacco; you shall not think thus to abuse the court; we will have a verdict, by the help of God, or you shall starve for it."*

At this point, one of the jurors asked to be dismissed, stating an indisposition of his body. The court refused this. Notes from the trial also show that the jurors were locked up for the night without any chamber pots. Penn protested, stating it was intolerable that his jury should be menaced in such a way and that they should be free to reach their verdict without being compelled. He pointed out that the Lieutenant of The Tower had implied one of his jurors was worse than a felon. The jury was called back into the courtroom at 7 am and returned the same verdict. The Recorder told the jury, *"Your Verdict is nothing, you play upon the Court; I say you shall go together, and bring in another Verdict, or you shall starve; and I will have you carted about the city, as in Edward III's time."* The Lord Mayor then threatened to have Edward Bushel's nose cut off. The jury was sent out again to return with a different verdict.

When the jury returned to the courtroom for the final time, they stated that the jury foreman had already given their verdict in writing. They were asked again to give their verdict, to which the jury replied that Penn and Mead were both not guilty. The bench, still unable to accept this verdict, insisted that each juror stand up and individually pronounce their verdict. When each answered not guilty, the Recorder rebuked them for not following the "*good and wholesome advice which was given you.*" He duly fined each juror 40 marks, and they were imprisoned until they paid their fines.

Penn then demanded to be set free, stating that it was the judgement of his peers. He insisted it was against the fundamental laws of England and contrary to the 14th and 29th chapters of the Great Charter of England, which say, '*No freeman ought to be amerced but by the oath of good and lawful men of the vicinage.*' The Recorder told Penn that he had been held for his fines for contempt of court, for not having removed his hat at the start of the trial.

Penn, Mead and all the jurors were sent to Newgate prison for non-payment of their fines. Penn and Mead's fines were paid by Penn's father, Admiral Sir William Penn. One of the jurors, Edward Bushel, refused to pay his fine and took out a writ of *habeas corpus*, which was heard at the Court of Common Pleas. A *habeas corpus* is a writ requiring a person to be brought before a judge to investigate the lawfulness of their detention. The presiding judge Sir John Vaughan stated that a jury must be independent, and a judge "*may try to open the eyes of the jurors, but not lead them by the nose.*" He found that the imprisonment of the jury was not legal and contrary to the Magna Carta. This became a landmark ruling in English law, once and for all establishing the jury's independence. It has since become known as Bushel's Case.

Following this, all the Penn and Mead trial jurors were released. Bushel took out a further writ of *habeas corpus* to
free both Penn and Mead. William Penn later released a pamphlet citing numerous precedents since the Magna Carta of
1215. Today, on the wall of the Central Criminal Court (The
Old Bailey) in London, is displayed a plaque commemorating
the brave actions of those jury members in the Bushel Case.
The plaque reads, '*Near this site William Penn and William
Mead were tried in 1674 preaching to an unlawful assembly
in Gracechurch Street. This tablet commemorates the courage
and endurance of the jury Thos, Vere, Edward Bushel and ten
others refused to give a verdict against them, although locked
up without food for two nights and were fined for their final
verdict of Not Guilty. The case of these jurymen was reviewed
on a writ of Habeas Corpus and Chief Justice Vaughan delivered the opinion of the Court which established "The Right of
Juries" to give their verdict according to their convictions.'*

As a side note, King Charles II had previously received a large
sum of money from William Penn's father. On 4th March 1681,
the King settled the debt after Penn's father's death, by granting
William a large area of land south and west of New Jersey in
The Americas. In 1682, William Penn travelled to America and
founded the State of Pennsylvania. Originally Penn had called
the land Sylvania (Latin for 'woods'). The King changed the
name to Pennsylvania in deference to William Penn's father.

In yet another bizarre case of jury intimidation, several years
later, on the 13th May 1688, seven bishops met at Lambeth
Palace and signed a petition against King James II's Declaration
of Indulgence. This granted religious freedom to minorities
like Catholics, Protestant dissenters, Unitarians, Jews and Mus-
lims. The Anglican bishops declared that it was illegal and petitioned to have it withdrawn. The King refused their petition.
Instead, they printed their petition and distributed it on the

streets around London. The King was outraged and charged the seven bishops with seditious libel. They were promptly arrested and locked in the Tower of London to await trial on the 29th June. The King had checked the jury list to ensure that they were all affluent men, more inclined to take the side of the Crown.

When it came time for the jury to deliberate their verdict, the Lord Chief Justice allowed them some wine before they were led away to the jury room. He then swore in the jury Bailiff, saying, *"You shall well and truly keep every person sworn in this jury in some private and convenient room without meat, drink, fire, candle or lodging."*

The jurors were locked into a room with no light. The bishops' solicitor kept a careful watch outside the room to ensure that the court ushers, servants of the Crown, didn't try to enter the room during the night and bribe the jury with food and drink. At 4 am, ushers took basins of water into the jury room so the jurors could wash. Parched with thirst, the jurors drank all the water from the basins.

One of the jurors, Michael Arnold, had a real dilemma. As a local brewer, he supplied beer to the King's palace. He was concerned that if he found the bishops not guilty, then he would lose business from the King. But if he found them guilty, then he was likely to lose business from many others who supported the bishops' cause. By the end of their deliberations, 11 jurors favoured acquitting the bishops, whilst only Mr. Arnold favoured a conviction.

This shortly changed and when the jury returned to the court at 10 am, they gave their unanimous verdict of not guilty. This had implications for the Royal House of Stuart. Six months later,

King James II had fled the country, and the throne had passed to King William III and Queen Mary II.

It wasn't until the Juries Act (1870) that juries were permitted refreshments, fire and light whilst they deliberated, albeit this was at their own expense. The Juries Detention Act (1897) enabled jurors to go home at the end of each day. However, this remained not so for murder cases.

Juries Who Took Too Long to Agree a Verdict Were Carried Around in Carts

Thankfully, a judge is no longer permitted to force a jury to return a verdict. If the jury can't agree on a verdict, then after a while, the jury will be discharged. This is known as a 'hung jury'. There is guidance laid down regarding the approximate times the juries can take to reach verdicts. This can be found in The Juries Act (1974) and judges are always very careful to ensure that the jury never feels under time pressure to reach a verdict. It requires the jury to deliberate for at least two hours before passing a majority verdict. Common practice is to allow two hours 10 minutes, to give the jury time to walk between the courtroom and their jury room.

However, it hasn't always been that way. In past centuries, the judges would travel around, judging cases at various assizes in different towns within their circuit. It was accepted practice that a judge didn't need to wait for the jury's verdict before the end of their circuit sittings. Instead, the jury was detained and carried around by cart from town to town, until they had reached their verdict.

This practice was referred to by the trial judge in the 1670 Penn and Mead case where the sitting Recorder was unhappy with the verdict given by the jury. He kept sending them back to 'deliberate' and return with the verdict that he felt was correct. He threatened the jury, telling them in open court, "*I will have you carted about the City, as in Edward the Third's time.*"

Juries Could Be Kept Locked Away Without Food, Drink, Warmth or Light Until They Reached a Unanimous Verdict

In court trials, after the closing submissions from both the prosecution and defence, the jury will retire to deliberate the verdict. A jury's decision should be based on the evidence before them in court. They will decide what points of law have been proved and whether there is sufficient evidence to convict a person beyond all reasonable doubt, returning a verdict on each count.

A judge will always first seek a unanimous verdict. This is a verdict upon which all of the jury members agree. They can either be guilty or not guilty. These days, members of the jury are treated well, they are provided refreshments and, in most cases, permitted to leave the court at the end of each day. However, this wasn't always the case. In years gone by, they were effectively imprisoned by the courts for the duration of the trial. This was done to prevent any improper influence from an outsider that might affect the verdict.

The requirement for a unanimous verdict by a jury is a curious quirk of early English law, considering that it goes against the principle of democracy, where normally a majority vote would be the most acceptable outcome. Historically, when the accused stood trial, the law of the land required that the winning party had the support of 12 witnesses. This created a situation where the witness testimony had to be unanimous. In the reign of King Henry II (1154-1189), a precedent was established where twelve local knights settled all disputes over land ownership. These became the early juries to decide facts and judge individual cases.

By 1367, it had evolved even further and in one of these earlier cases, we see the requirement for a jury to reach a unanimous verdict. In this instance, the justices required a unanimous verdict from the jury within a few hours. One of the jurors refused to agree to the majority verdict and commented that he would rather die in prison than consent to the verdict. The justices imprisoned this juror as a nonconformist and chose to take the majority verdict from the eleven remaining jurors.

This was the start of many cases where nonconformist jury members would find themselves imprisoned for failing to reach a unanimous verdict. When this harsh practice was eventually abandoned, it became common practice for the jury to be confined until it had reached a unanimous agreement, irrespective of how long this took.

As we've seen elsewhere in this chapter, judges didn't have to wait for the jury to return their unanimous verdict. If the jury were taking too long, the judge would leave and move around the circuit, taking the jury members with him, in a cart, to the next town, where he would proceed to hear other cases. Presumably, the jury members then had to make their way back to their homes, however far away that might have been. Eventually, this practice also stopped and was duly replaced with judges locking the jury away without any food, drink, warmth or light until such a time as they reached a unanimous verdict.

There are some remarkable examples of this occurring throughout our legal history. This was strictly enforced by the judges to ensure a unanimous verdict would be reached in as short a time as possible. An excerpt from the 1752 book 'The Complete Juryman' provides an example of this Draconian practice from Elizabethan days.

"The Jury being withdrawn after Evidence, and remaining a long Time without concluding on their Verdict, the Officers, who attended them, seeing their Delay, searched them, and found that some had Figs and others had Pippins; which being moved to the Court, they were examined on Oath, and two of them confessed that they had eaten Figs before they were agreed on their Verdict, and three confessed that they had Pippins, but had not eat any of them; and that this was unknown to the Parties. Those who had eaten were each of them fined five Pounds, and those who had not eaten the Pippins, were each of them fined forty Shillings; but the Verdict was, upon great consideration, and Conference with the other Judges, held to be good."

In a separate case, from 1650, a juror named John Mucklow was fined twenty shillings for being found with *"sugar-candy and liquorish"* in his possession. It's not hard to imagine the difficulty of having to hold out against the will of other jurors, being starved of food and water or even your favourite sweets. There must have been many such cases where the minds of jurors were unfairly influenced into reaching a unanimous verdict through such a perverse practice.

With the passing of the Juries Act (1870), this practice was abolished by statute. Section 23 of the Act permitted jurors to have fire and refreshments but at their own expense.

As recently as the 1908 case of R v Hartleigh, a jury who said that they were unable to reach a unanimous verdict, were told by the judge that they would be locked up for two hours. By unanimous verdict, they found the prisoner guilty.

The Lawless Court

A curious type of court existed in ancient times and is believed to have continued until the beginning of the twentieth century. This was the 'Lawless Court', also known as the 'Whispering Court'.

This ancient court was previously known as the King's Court of the Manor of King's Hill in Rochford, Essex. Whilst it was a court as we understand it to be, it had one curious fact that differentiated it from all other courts. This is how it earned the title 'lawless'. It met at the lawless hour of midnight.

It is believed the court was first called sometime before 1661 by the Lord of the Manor of King's Hill. One morning, he was awoken by the crowing of a local cockerel. Coincidentally, he noticed that some of his servants were plotting his murder as he awoke. He convicted them of treason and spared his sentence of forfeiture of their lands in return for what he called a shameless service. He declared that each year, on the first Wednesday morning after Michaelmas Day, the local tenants from the manor would be called to assemble in the place where he discovered their plot to kill him. On this occasion each year, the Lord's Steward would kindly remind the tenants of the need to assemble. However, he would do this by whispering their names as quietly as possible.

Any tenants who failed to answer when their name was whispered would be fined double their rents for each hour they failed to respond to their name. The tenants were then required to remain assembled at that location until the cockerel crowed three times, at which point they were dismissed from the court.

Another peculiarity of this assembly was the fact that no candles were permitted. The court had to be lit by natural light. The use of ink was also forbidden, so the names of those who had answered, were written down with a piece of charcoal, in the dark.

This bizarre court continued, as a tradition, each year without fail until the late 19th century, after which it met periodically until the early 20th century.

It is believed that the tenants became so fed up with this annual tradition of waking up in the middle of the night and standing for hours in a damp room, that many instead chose to pay double rent the following morning. And as time went on, a local man was even employed to make the noise of a cockerel crowing to bring the court proceedings to a swift close.

CHAPTER SIXTEEN

OUTRAGEOUS BEHAVIOUR

S witch on the television, and most days, you can find a pro-gramme about the bizarre behaviour of the animal king-dom. Over the centuries, different generations have looked upon each other with suspicion and confusion as contemporary customs and behaviour changed. They say, *'There's nowt so queer as folk.'* This is very true, and as custodians of this planet and shepherds all creatures thereupon, we must remember that our humble domesticated pets are probably looking at us and thinking this very same thing.

In this chapter, we will examine some of our strange behaviours over the centuries for which laws have had to be passed, in some cases, to protect us from ourselves. I once knew someone who corrected facts in library books if they were wrong. Unfortunately for them, this may well have resulted in a good public whipping. If you were a woman, it was fair to say that the law didn't recognise you as owning your own body. Husbands literally owned their wives as property. Those who were married, if their husband had enough of them, they may find themself being sold off for a pint of beer at the local inn.

> *"Behaviour is the mirror in which*
> *everyone shows their image."*
> Johann Wolfgang von Goethe

Hard Labour & Whipped For Defacing Library Books

Acts of wanton damage committed for no apparent reason are sometimes called acts of vandalism. The origins of this word date back to the fourth century, when a tribe of people known as Vandals swept out of what is now southern Poland and ravaged France, Spain, North Africa and Rome, destroying many books and valuable works of art in the process.

In a sad case that pre-dates the rampage of the Vandals, there were some unfortunate mishaps at the Library of Alexandria. Historians believe that the Library of Alexandria contained around 700,000 books and scrolls. It was considered one of the greatest collections ever assembled, with some historians suggesting all the ancient world's knowledge was archived within those marble walls. The popular myth is that the library was burned in a cataclysmic pyre of papyrus, and the works were lost forever.

In reality, the library fell out of popularity, into disuse, and its funding cut and declined gradually over a few centuries ... sound familiar?

Historical records indeed show that during a civil war between Cleopatra and Ptolemy XIII in 48BC, the library or part of its collection was accidentally burned when Julius Caesar intervened and set fire to ships in the harbour. This fire spread to the library or nearby buildings and caused destruction. Whatever was left of the old Great Library is thought to have been thoroughly destroyed during Emperor Diocletian's siege of Alexandria in 297 AD.

Roll forward the clocks, and we see other mass book burnings in Nazi Germany and Austria during the 1930s. Such wanton destruction of literary works has been depicted in films and novels. In Ray Bradbury's dystopian novel 'Fahrenheit 451' books were burned in the streets by firemen operating under the instructions of a totalitarian government seeking to control public access to any 'non-conformist' publications. They do say life imitates art.

Malicious damage appears to have become a serious issue in the UK. Over the centuries, various laws have been passed to address this. In 1861 we saw the passing of the Malicious Damage Act. Whilst the Act addressed damage to all nature of property, including places of worship, buildings and animals, Section 39 specifically focused on damage to books and artwork. Section 39 stated,

"Whosoever shall unlawfully and maliciously destroy or damage any Book, Manuscript, Picture, Print, Statue, Bust, or Vase, or any other Article or Thing kept for the Purposes of Art, Science, or Literature, or as an Object of Curiosity, in any Museum, Gallery, Cabinet, Library, or other Repository ... shall be guilty of a Misdemeanor."

The penalty for being found guilty of malicious damage was imprisonment, with or without hard labour. Any males under sixteen could also face a whipping. Interestingly, it was this offence for which the playwright Joe Orton and his partner Kenneth Halliwell were found guilty and imprisoned in 1962.

Orton and Halliwell met and fell in love when they both attended RADA. In 1959, they moved into a bed-sit flat in the London borough of Islington. It was then that their latest 'collage' project had begun in earnest. Over three years, they removed illustrations from hundreds of art books shelved at their local Islington Library. They wallpapered their room with these torn-out book images. Their project also extended to creating new amusing dust jackets for other books made from the doctored scraps of artwork they had previously torn. These new alternative dust covers were quietly replaced on the library shelves for unsuspecting browsers to discover.

When their project was discovered, they were charged with 'larceny, malicious damage and wilful damage' under the Malicious Damage Act (1861). Each was sentenced to six months at Old Street Magistrates Court, London.

Orton, who became a popular playwright in 1960s London, claimed their actions were a protest against the poor choice of books available in public libraries. In 1967, he stated, "*Libraries might as well not exist; they've got endless shelves for rubbish and hardly any space for good books.*" Sadly, that same year, Halliwell bludgeoned the 34-year-old Orton to death in their home with nine hammer blows to his head. It is believed that Orton wanted to separate from Halliwell at the time. Halliwell then killed himself with an overdose.

This law was repealed when it was replaced in 1971 with the Criminal Damage Act.

Married Women Didn't Own or Control Their Own Bodies

This quaint tradition remains that when a woman gets married, she takes on her husband's surname. This was a hangover from the old 'coverture' laws when women used to get married, and their identity was effectively erased. This bizarre doctrine of coverture originated in the Middle Ages. Under these old legal practices, a husband and wife became one person upon marriage. The woman's legal rights were subsumed by her husband as he maintained complete legal, sexual and economic control over her body. Legally and commercially, the woman was the subordinate in the marriage. She was known as a *feme covert* (covered woman).

As such, a married woman no longer owned or controlled her own body and could not own any property, including the clothes on her back. She was unable to sign any legal documents, claim wages or enter into contracts and she couldn't get an education unless her husband first agreed. When it came to children, she also had minimal rights. She could not make decisions for her children without her husband's consent. The reality was that many women operated successful businesses and ran households. However, legally everything had to be in her husband's name.

Sadly, the law of coverture also meant that the husband had complete control over his wife's body, including an absolute right to sexual relations. A marriage meant implied consent, which led to many instances of marital rape, which has only been recognised as a crime in the last few decades.

This also created some unpleasant situations for husbands. Since they were legally responsible for their wives, they were usually also responsible for any crimes committed by their wives. So, a lot of the time, if the wife ran up debts, her husband would be committed to a debtor's prison until the debts were paid off. There was a very small subset of crimes known as *male in se* for which married women were held accountable. These were the more serious crimes like treason, murder and keeping a brothel.

Fortunately, coverture ended. There was no official ending to it. Instead, the doctrine slowly disappeared during the nineteenth century with the passing of several women's property Acts.

Illegal to Impute a Woman's Unchastity

Under the Slander of Women Act (1891), it was an offence to *'impute unchastity or adultery'* of any woman or girl in England, Wales or Ireland. This included words, either spoken or written.

In the interesting case of Kerr v Kennedy in 1942, it was found that implying that a woman was a lesbian was an imputation of unchastity and an offence under this Act. These were the days where Victorian thinking around the subject still prevailed. The Court had recourse to consult the dictionary to establish the correct meaning of the word 'unchaste', which, at the time, defined the word as meaning "impure" and "lasciviousness".

This law did not apply in Scotland. The Act was only repealed in England and Wales as recently as 2014, with the passing of the Defamation Act (2013).

An Offence to Sell Your Wife

In 2003, Andy Hoyle, a 35-year-old husband from Wrexham in Wales, decided to advertise his wife, Mel, for sale on the auction website eBay. In his sales pitch, he noted, "*The chassis is in excellent order for the mileage, and warranty given at extra cost."* This practice was repeated in 2016 when Simon O'Kane from Wakefield, Yorkshire, put his *"Used Wife"* Leandra up for sale on the same auction site. He wrote. *"Not new has been used but still got some good miles left in her ... Reason for selling ... feel like there HAS to someone out there that is more deserving of her [than] me (oh dear god please let there be)."* His advert listed Leandra's bodywork and paintwork as still in decent condition. He amassed 57 bids for his wife, with the highest bidder offering to pay £65,888 before eBay eventually removed the post. Whilst this was all very tongue-in-cheek and neither wife was actually sold, there have been multiple times throughout our history when husbands have sold their wives.

There are many reasons why people have sold their wives. Boredom could be one such reason. Tiring of the animosity and quarrels, another. The cost of divorce would also have been a significant factor. It is, after all, an expensive business. In December 2021, Dubai's ruler, Sheikh Mohammed bin Rashid Al Maktoum, was ordered to pay around £554million to his former wife in the UK's largest divorce settlement of its kind.

The majority of wife sales were carried out in local market squares. The husband would often parade his wife around the market square, leading her around with a halter made of rope or ribbon around her neck or waist. She would be publicly auctioned to the highest bidder. Wives were sold for varying amounts. This sometimes increased if they came with children. One of the highest amounts paid is recorded as £150. On other occasions, wives were sold for nothing more than a simple glass of ale at the local inn.

The sales weren't considered legal, but everyone turned a blind eye to them, including the judiciary of the time. It is important also to note that the sales weren't 'forcible'. By that, I mean that they depended on the wife's consent. Sales were advertised in advance of the auction through the local newspaper or on local noticeboards. In fact, in many cases, the sales were pre-arranged between seller and purchaser, and the sale in public was more of an act to convince the local community of the arrangement. Quite often, the purchaser would be a wife's lover.

Wife selling in England experienced an increase towards the late 17th century, possibly due to the high cost of divorce to end unhappy marriages. Until the passing of the Marriage Act (1753), a formal marriage before a clergyman was not a legal requirement in England and marriages didn't even need to be registered. Before that time, a marriage was a union of two people if they both agreed, provided both had reached the legal age of consent which was 12 for girls and 14 for boys. After marriage, the husband and wife became one legal entity. This is known as the law of coverture, and the wives would often become subordinate to their husbands.

Commenting on this in 1753, the prominent judge Sir William Blackstone wrote, *"the very being, or legal existence of the woman, is suspended during the marriage, or at least is con-solidated and incorporated into that of her husband: under whose wing, protection and cover, she performs everything."* At that time, married women were unable to own any property in their own name. They were themselves considered to be the property of their husbands.

There are earlier accounts of wife selling. For instance, an account exists from 1302 of a man who *"granted his wife by deed to another man."* By the early 18th century, instances of wife selling started to be reported in popular newspapers. One such report can be found in The Annual Register in August 1733. The article states, *"Three men and three women, went to the Bell Inn in Edgbaston Street, Birmingham, and made*

*the following entry in the toll book which is kept there: -
Samuel Whitehouse, of the parish of Willenhall, in the county of
Stafford, sold his wife, Mary Whitehouse, in the open market, to
Thomas Griffiths, of Birmingham. Value, one guinea. To take
her with all her faults."*

In 1740, we saw probably the most high-profile case of wife
selling, that of Henry Brydges, 2nd Duke of Chandos. He was
reported to have purchased his second wife from a local ostler
(stable hand). In another case, in 1790, a man in Ninfield, East
Sussex, sold his wife for half a pint of gin at the local village
inn. He later changed his mind and repurchased her. On 18th
July 1797, even The Times newspaper reported on wife selling.
In this case, a local butcher had *"exposed his wife to sale in
Smithfield Market, near the Ram Inn, with a halter about her
neck, and one about her waist which tied her to a railing."* The
wife's new 'owner' was a local hog driver who paid the sum of
three guineas and a crown. A year later, a wife was sold for 7
shillings and eight pots of beer in Brighton.

In January 1815, in Maidstone, Kent, local man John Osborne had made arrangements to sell his wife at the nearby market. Unfortunately, no public market was being held on that day. Records show that instead, the sale took place at *"the sign of The Coal-barge, in Earl Street"* whereby Osborne sold both his wife and child to a man named William Serjeant for the sum of £1.

In 1830, a wife was sold for just 2 shillings & 6 pence at Much Wenlock farmers' market in Shropshire. In 1855, another wife was sold in Chipping Norton in the Cotswolds for the generous amount of £25. I say 'generous' because the going rate seems to have been around 2-3 shillings. By this time, Victorian values had started to trickle through society and wife selling was seen as disrespectful. So, on this occasion, the sale didn't go according to plan. The locals had other ideas and subjected the purchaser and his new wife to three nights of rough music'. This was a form of punishment where the offenders would be subjected to irritating noises and the singing of indecent verses. On the third night, they burned an effigy of the purchaser outside his house. He reneged on his sale and offered money to her first husband to take her back. In 1865, a wife was sold for the sum of £100. Along with the sale went the two children, which cost the purchaser an additional £25 each. At the Shoulder of Mutton and Cucumber Inn in Yapton, West Sussex, in 1898, a man sold his wife for 7 shillings and 6 pence. He also insisted the buyer provide him with 1 quart of beer.

Wife selling was, thankfully, slowly becoming a dying practice. Although records indicate, that they were still occurring, albeit seldomly. In 1913, a woman gave evidence in a Leeds police court that her husband had sold her to one of his work colleagues for £1. The practice itself was illegal. You can't just sell your wife, even if she did agree. Several wife sales did result in prosecution. This increasingly became the case during the

Victorian period when attitudes towards wife selling by the general public were one of disgust. In the late 1700s, Lord Chief Justice William Murray stated that he considered wife sales to be a criminal conspiracy between three people to commit adultery. The authorities often continued to turn a blind eye, considering it too trifling a matter for the courts. In the early 1800s, at least one magistrate went on record to say that he didn't believe he had any legal power to prevent wife sales.

CHAPTER SEVENTEEN

PURITANICAL BEHAVIOUR

T hose dastardly Puritans are at it again in this chapter, with Christmas featuring heavily. It seems Christmas was banned. It wasn't an outright ban, but no-one was permitted to celebrate Christmas or any other festive period during their Puritan rule. There was to be no singing of Christmas carols, no festive family get-togethers with large meals ... even putting up decorations could land you in the village stocks.

For women attending church in Scotland, there were some very unusual practices. In an attempt to stop women from hiding the fact they were sleeping during church services, they were not permitted to let their plaids cover their faces. Preaching to congregations in the open air was also illegal.

In this chapter, we look at just how grim Christmas Day can get, especially if you have some Puritans staying as your guests. We also see how this book would likely have been banned by the Archbishop of Canterbury and burned in a public display. We would have been in good company because, for a while, The Bible was banned. At the same time, the Canterbury Tales was considered perfectly acceptable by the King.

"All religions must be tolerated ...
for every man must get to heaven in his own way."
Epictetus

Christmas is Banned!

The Puritan Parliament weren't exactly a chirpy lot. Following the bloody Civil War and the killing of King Charles I, they set about dismantling many of the freedoms they proposed to be fighting to retain. Having killed the King and alleging his oppressive rule was now over, theirs was far worse, with wide-sweeping reforms that affected everyone in England. They seemed to ban anything that provided entertainment or made people happy.

It didn't go down at all well when they introduced a law that effectively banned Christmas altogether. On 8th June 1647, they passed an ordinance called '*An Ordinance for Abolishing of Festivals*'. This ordinance enacted that all festivals and holy days were to be abolished, including Christmas, Easter and Whitsuntide. It ordered that "*the said Feast of the Nativity of Christ, Easter and Whitsuntide, and all other Festival dayes, commonly called Holy-dayes, be no longer observed as Fes-*

tivals or Holy-dayes within this Kingdome of England and Dominion of Wales."

It wasn't Christmas or any other holy day with which the Puritans took issue. Instead, they didn't like the festivities surrounding those holy days. They thought people should be praying in church, in moments of quiet contemplation, rather than rejoicing, celebrating and getting merry. They felt that Christmas had become immoral. They had already summed up their thoughts on Christmas in an earlier law, stating that they felt it should be *"a time of fasting and humiliation, for remembering the sins of those who in the past had turned the day into a feast, sinfully and wrongfully giving liberty to carnal and sensual delights."*

This piece of legislation made it a criminal offence to celebrate the feast of Christmas. There was to be no getting together with family members over Christmas lunch. Shops were forced to remain open on Christmas Day. Any Christmas or Easter decorations were banned. There was to be absolutely no partying or lavish eating. Those holy days were meant to be replaced with a day of fasting. To enforce this, Puritan soldiers patrolled the streets of London and other major cities, confiscating decorations and anything that looked like party food. On Christmas Eve, Town Criers were brought out onto the streets in force, ringing their bells and shouting *"No Christmas! No Christmas!"* as a reminder. People were not allowed to attend church on Christmas Day.

It will come as no surprise that the public didn't take too kindly to this law, and it wasn't long before riots, and general disorder broke out. On Christmas Day in 1647, a mass protest broke out around the water fountain in Cornhill, London. Angry revellers draped holly, ivy, and other Christmas decorations around the water fountain. They prevented the Mayor of London and his officials from removing the adornments. Constables were called and started to arrest the partygoers. The result was violence, utter mayhem and the death of one of the revellers in Newgate Prison.

Riots broke out elsewhere in England too. In Ipswich, a protester was killed on Christmas Day. Ironically his name was 'Christmas'. In Canterbury, massed crowds assembled to demand a Christmas Day sermon. The authorities intervened and took a heavy-handed approach to break up the congregation. One congregation member assaulted a soldier, which triggered an ensuing riot, spilling out onto the streets. They trashed the mayor's house, attacked the shops that had been ordered to remain open on Christmas Day and took control of Canterbury. They held the city for the whole Christmas period, during which they decorated doorways with holly and continued their Christmas festivities unhindered. Meanwhile, at St. Margaret's Church in Westminster, the minister Nicholas Bernard had been arrested and thrown into Fleet Street prison for attempting to preach a sermon on Christmas Day. There were other reports in the newspapers of churchgoers attending Christmas Day services armed with weapons and guarding the church doors with swords whilst the minister was in his pulpit.

After Christmas celebrations had been banned for 13 years, England had suffered enough and rejoiced with the restoration of the monarchy when King Charles II ascended the throne in 1660. The public could openly demonstrate this rejoicing with parties and mass frivolity.

You Must Fast on Christmas Day

On 24th August 1642, the Puritan Parliament passed a law ordering that the last Wednesday of every month is set aside as a day of fasting. This was '*An Ordinance for the better observation of the monthly Fast*'. The public were not happy with this. They were even more unhappy when in 1644, this mandated day of fasting fell on Christmas Day. There was an instant conflict. The majority wanted to celebrate Christmas, whereas the law had prescribed that day to be set aside for fasting.

A request was made to Parliament to waive it for that year to enable people to celebrate Christmas with their families, enjoying the festive frolics. As we know, the Puritans disagreed with festivities and frolics. As expected, Parliament refused. Instead, they published a public notice. The notice spelt out that the day would be spent fasting and in "*solemn humiliation ... in remembrance of our sins, and the sins of our forefathers.*" It reminded people that they had forgotten the memory of Christ and instead had turned to "*carnal and sensual delights.*" Just in case anyone decided not to take this public notice seriously, on 19th December 1644, they passed a further law, aptly entitled '*An Ordinance for the better observation of the monethly Fast; and more especially the next Wednesday, commonly called The Feast of the Nativity of Christ, Thorowout the Kingdome of England and Dominion of Wales*'. This law was repealed, along with most of those Acts and Ordinances made during the Inter-regnum, the instant King Charles II was restored to the throne in May 1660.

By Law, Easter Sunday Must ALWAYS Be The First Sunday After The Second Saturday in April

Easter is one of the most important festivals in the Christian calendar. It celebrates Jesus rising from the dead three days after he was crucified. Following his crucifixion on Friday, his body was laid out in a cave, with a large stone slab placed over the entrance. Roman soldiers guarded it. Three days later, on Sunday, some of Jesus's disciples and Mary Magdalene visited the cave and discovered that his body had gone. Easter Sunday is the day each year in the Christian calendar that marks Jesus's resurrection.

The problem is, unlike many of Britain's other religious holidays, Easter Sunday is not fixed. It does not fall on the same date each year. There can be over a month between the dates when it falls from year to year. It's a movable feast. Then there's the added issue that Easter is celebrated at different times between Western churches and Eastern churches. This has come about after centuries of trying to calculate the date of Easter and the Jewish Passover, to accommodate different calendars from around the world. The earliest Easter Sunday can fall is 22nd March, and the latest is 25th April. The most common date is 19 April. So far, 15 attempts have been made to set a harmonised date for Easter since the tenth century.

Not to worry, though, back in 1928, parliamentarians had the answer that had alluded everyone else for centuries. They passed an Act of Parliament to legislate the fixed date of Easter each year. This was The Easter Act (1928). It fixed Easter Sunday as the first Sunday after the second Saturday in April. So, problem solved? Well, not quite. This matter that has been pondered for centuries could hardly be resolved with the passing of an Act of Parliament. It was a valiant attempt, however.

The problem continues each year because whilst the Easter Act received Royal Assent in February 1928, the Act was passed and enacted that same year. Still, it has never been brought into effect. This is because whilst generally, most Bills come into force on the day they receive Royal Assent, some include what's known as a 'commencement clause'. This sets out the specific timing and conditions through which the Act will come into force. So, essentially, whilst there is now a law stipulating the exact date upon which Easter Sunday must fall each year, it is entirely redundant, just sitting on the statute books, waiting to be activated. The Easter Act (1928) is the most well-known example of a redundant law sitting on the statute books waiting to be activated ... for almost a century! This peculiar matter of long-standing commencement orders was debated in the House of Lords on 7th November 2013, when it was established that between 1997 and June 2010, no fewer than 147 Acts of Parliament had been passed with Sections that had never been commenced.

The Easter Act will not be going away anytime soon. The subject is still occasionally raised in Parliament. The consensus through successive governments has been that the Act will not come into force until there is an agreement upon a set date between the international Christian community. The matter was summarised succinctly in 1939 by the then Home Secretary, Samuel Hoare. He stated, "*I am afraid it is impossible to bring the Easter Act into force until there is agreement amongst the religious communities, and there appears to be no immediate prospect of such agreement.*"

The Act has never been repealed, so it is, in effect, still the law.

Singing Christmas Carols Could Get You in Trouble

The Puritans were unable to outlaw dancing. It did, after all, feature heavily in biblical scripture. They managed to outlaw what they considered to be promiscuous dancing. That is, dancing between men and women. They also tried to outlaw singing, only to find that, too, featured within the Bible: Ephesians 5:19 says, "*singing and making melody to the Lord with your heart.*"

The Puritans were unable and unwilling to ban the drinking of alcohol, so instead, they sought to ban what they considered to be the evils of drunkenness. This included acts of frivolity, games, various sports, singing ... almost anything in the open air in public, which was deemed to be not in keeping with Christian teachings.

It is well-known that Puritans disliked the celebration of Christmas. They saw any Christmas festivities, including the singing of Christmas carols, as sinful acts with no biblical justification. Christmas festivities were effectively banned by an Act of Parliament in 1644. Three years later, they abolished the feast of Christmas altogether. While singing was not itself banned, Cromwell and the Puritans sought to ban any excesses or elaborate music being played in church. They did permit the singing of psalms in church. Still, the singing of Christmas carols represented an act of celebration and the festivities of Christmas, which were all banned.

The Bible Was Banned, But The Canterbury Tales Were Allowed

In mediaeval times, the Catholic Church took it upon itself to censor publications. They maintained the '*Index Librorum Prohibitorum*' (Index of Forbidden Books), a list of books forbidden by the Roman Catholic Church. These were generally those publications considered immoral, heretic or having the potential to corrupt the Catholic faith. This list ceased to be produced in 1966. However, long before that, our own King, Henry VIII, had taken it upon himself to start censorship in England. Whatever we may think about Henry VIII and his irrational behaviour, he was nevertheless a devoutly religious man.

On 12th May 1543, the King passed the *Act for the Advancement of True Religion*. This law restricted the reading of the Bible to just a few social classes, primarily noblemen, the gentry, clerics and the wealthy. Servants, apprentices and the poor were forbidden from reading the Bible, as were women beneath the rank of the gentry. Women married to the gentry or the nobility were allowed to read the Bible but only in private. This banned at least 90% of the population of England from reading the Bible and other religious works which had been translated into English. It also claimed that *"malicious minds have, intending to subvert the true exposition of Scripture, have taken upon them, by printed ballads, rhymes...."* It forbade any plays, singing or rhymes which contradicted the interpretation of holy Scripture. Bizarrely, it did permit *"all books printed before the year 1540, entitled Statutes, Chronicles, Canterbury Tales, Chaucer's books, Gower's books, and stories of men's lives."* So, the Bible was banned, but it was considered perfectly acceptable to read The Canterbury Tales or any other works of Geoffrey Chaucer.

The Old Testament had been primarily written in Biblical Hebrew and Aramaic. The New Testament was written in Koine Greek. Over the years, the scriptures have been translated into various other languages, including Latin. Predominantly the Latin translation was used from around 300AD onwards in Europe. Despite the different other language translations, from around the ninth century onwards, Latin was considered the only authentic translation of the Bible. The first complete English translation of the Bible was finished around 1382, with additional English translations made halfway through the King Henry VIII's reign.

Henry VIII's law banning the Bible for most of England didn't last long. It was repealed by his son, King Edward VI, in 1547. Half a century later, in 1604, King James I authorised a new English translation of the Bible. Completed in 1611, it became known as the King James Bible. It remains the most famous version of all the Bible translations throughout history. It is also one of the most printed books ever. As of 2021, the Bible holds the Guinness World Record for the best-selling book, selling between 5 and 7 billion copies.

The Archbishop of Canterbury Was Able to Censor Books

On 11th July 1637, the Star Chamber, a curious court comprised of privy councillors and judges, set about to regulate the printing of all literary works in England. It was the most comprehensive attempt to regulate the printing trade since its inception. The Star Chamber issued '*A decree of the Star Chamber designed to regulate the printing of all literary works, whether ecclesiastical or secular in nature*'.

All the previous licensing provisions for the printing industry were thrown out of the window and replaced with new regulations. It required various categories of publications to be authorised by different licensors. For example, books about common law had to be licensed by the Lord Chief Justices and the Lord Chief Baron. The Earl Marshal licensed books regarding heraldry (coats of arms). Most peculiarly, all other books, including those of divinity, physic, philosophy and poetry, had to be licensed by either the Archbishop of Canterbury or the Bishop of London.

The publishers had to provide two copies of each printed work to the Archbishop of Canterbury. One copy was retained by the Archbishop, who ensured that once he had given final approval, any printed work did not deviate from the copy he had in his possession. This ensured that both the Church and the State could continue to exert significant censorship over the printing presses. Meanwhile, the Archbishop of Canterbury, already overburdened with his spiritual and pastoral duties, was undoubtedly snowed under with all the new publications to read and approve.

This decree had a short lifespan. By July 1641, amidst the turmoil between the Crown and Parliament, the Long Parliament abolished the Star Chamber.

Illegal For Women to Let Their Plaids Cover Their Faces in Church

In 1457, a sumptuary law in Scotland was being passed north of the border to restrain certain liberties. It prevented women sitting in the church from wearing plaids (a Tartan headscarf) covering their heads. This ensured that women could not fall asleep during the church service and go undiscovered. One punishment for such sleepy women was to be covered in tar. The law stated, "*na woman come to kirk nor mercat with her*

face mufflalled or covered, that she may not be kend, under
pains of escheit of the courchie [kerchief/headdress]."

This continued in Scotland over the centuries and became
quite prevalent during the seventeenth century. In 1604,
records from the Kirk Session of Glasgow noted that "*great
disorder hath been in the Kirk by women sitting with their
heads covered with plaids during sermon sleeping, therefore
ordains intimation to be made that afterword none sit with
their head covered with plaids during sermon time.*" The
church courts felt compelled to do something about this. In
1621, the same Kirk Session declared that "*no woman, married
or unmarried, come within the kirk-doors, to preaching or
prayers, with their plaids about their heads, neither lie down
in the kirk on their face in tyme of prayer, with certification
that their plaids shall be drawn up, and themselves raisit be
the beddall.*" On 17th September 1643, records from the Kirk
Session of Monifieth show that one of their court officers,
Robert Scott, was provided "*with ane pynt of tar to put upon the
women that held plaids about their heads,*" for use in church.
This continued, and on 4th March 1645, the Kirk Session of
Kinghorn recorded "*the uncomlieness of women coming to
church on the Sabbath to sermon with plaids about their heads
. . . which provocks sleeping in the time of sermone without
being espied.*" Consequently, it ordered that any woman found
in church on Sundays with a plaid over or about her head be
fined six shillings and liable to whatever other punishment the
Kirk Session felt was necessary to be inflicted for her contempt
and disobedience.

Illegal to Preach to Congregations in The Open Air

In an attempt to crack down on Nonconformists, King Charles II passed The Conventicle Act (1664). This forbade any non-Church of England religious assemblies consisting of five or more people from gathering in the open air. It only applied to those aged 16 or over and not from the same household. The penalties were quite harsh for the time. For a first offence, the offender would be forced to pay a £5 fine or suffer imprisonment for three months without bail. For a second offence, the fine was £10 or imprisonment for up to 6 months. For a third offence, the fine increased to £100 or transportation for seven years. The fines were distributed as alms to the poor of the convicted person's parish.

This led to the trial, which became so famous that it set a precedent that continues to this day. This is the trial of Penn and Meade. On 14th August 1670, Quakers William Penn and William Meade were both arrested for preaching in the open air on Gracechurch Street, London. They had attended their meeting house to find that the authorities had chained the doors so they could not preach to the amassed congregation inside their building.

The Conventicle Act was formally repealed in 1689.

It's Perfectly Legal to Drive Around With a Corpse in Your Car

According to the law, the body of a baby, child or adult may be moved anywhere within England and Wales without using a coffin or without charge or permission, as long as the Coroner's work is not obstructed. It is a myth that a fee or toll would have to be paid when conveying a dead body across boundaries, i.e. from county to county. This is not true. The only exemption is that a coroner must first consent before the deceased's body can be taken out of England and Wales.

Bizarrely, whilst certain aspects of death are heavily regulated, for example, the depth of graves and location of burial grounds (which we look at elsewhere in this book), there isn't much regulation on the conveyance of dead bodies, whether animal or human. You don't even need to place a body into a coffin. There are also no set time limits regarding the disposal of the dead. So, you literally can drive around the streets for weeks with the corpse of Aunty Ivy strapped to your roof rack or thrown into the boot. However, I suspect the local Constabulary may regularly pull you over.

CHAPTER EIGHTEEN

THE REPRESSED WELSH

We have had a love-hate relationship with all the countries within our United Kingdom at various points throughout history. One country very close to our hearts is the Welsh. From Flintshire to the Vale of Glamorgan, Wales is a proud country steeped in history and its own traditions. Interestingly, the word '*Welsh*' was an Anglo-Saxon term for '*foreigner*'. At one point, even the Scottish and Irish were considered Welsh. Nowadays, the Welsh use the term 'Cymru' as the word for Wales. This translates as '*friends*' or '*fellow countrymen*'.

It's fair to say that the English haven't always held such affection for the Welsh. This chapter looks at some of the harsh laws passed to repress any further Welsh uprisings against the Crown and the powerful English land barons. Interestingly, the Welsh were banned from owning land or speaking their language in their own country. We also address whether it is truth or a myth that Welsh people may be shot in Chester and Hereford.

"For a small country, Wales has so much to offer. You are surrounded by the most beautiful nature."
Gethin Jones

Welsh People Banned From Owning Land in Wales

Since the death of the last native Prince of Wales, Llywelyn ap Gruffydd, in 1282, the Welsh had to endure several penal laws after its conquest by King Edward I of England. They were forbidden from living in borough towns, such as Conwy and Caernarfon. They weren't allowed the same trading rights as the English ... but things were about to get considerably worse for them.

Owain Glyndŵr, a Lord from the Welsh Marches (the areas of England that border Wales), was initially loyal to the English Crown and fought alongside the English army against the Scottish in the 1380s. In 1400, he had a land dispute with Baron Grey of Ruthyn, who had seized control of some of his land. Glyndŵr appealed to Parliament and the courts, but he was ignored. This land dispute spiralled out of control, and from that moment on, the Welsh rallied behind Glyndŵr in a Welsh uprising. On 16th September 1400, Glyndŵr was proclaimed

Prince of Wales. This rebellion against English rule lasted for a further 15 years.

In 1402, the English Parliament under King Henry IV issued the Penal Laws (The Wales Act, The Wales and Welshmen Act & The Welshmen Act) against Wales to re-establish English dominance in Wales and bring an end to the Welsh rebellion. The Penal Laws stated:

- That no Englishman could be convicted by a Welshman in Wales;

- That wasters, rhymers, minstrels and vagabonds were not allowed in Wales;

- Public meetings were banned in Wales;

- Welshmen were no longer permitted to be armed & could not carry armour;

- Englishmen were forbidden from carrying any armour into Wales;

- Welshmen were not allowed to own castles, except those from the time of King Edward I;

- Welshmen were not permitted to take a senior position in public office, for example, as a Justice of the Peace, Chamberlain, Chancellor, Sheriff, Coroner, etc.

The problem is that the Penal Laws failed to suppress the uprising and had the opposite effect by fanning the flames and encouraging more Welsh people to join the rebellion. The Welsh retook much of their land and castles. When news of their gains against the English reached the Scottish and the French, they sent additional military support to bolster the Welsh uprising.

Despite this military assistance, the English had far superior numbers and greater resources. By 1409, the English had recaptured much of Wales, forcing Glyndŵr to take refuge in the sieged Harlech Castle. Glyndŵr, however, had other plans and escaped into the night, disguised as an old man. These Penal Laws were finally repealed in 1624 by King James I.

An Englishman Could Not Be Convicted by a Welshman in Wales

As a result of the Glyndŵr Rising and the land disputes between the English and the Welsh, in 1402, the English Parliament passed the Penal Laws. These were a series of laws that severely restricted the rights of the Welsh. One of the very first laws passed confidently stated,

'Englishman shall not be convict[ed] by Welshman in Wales'

This even included those who became Welsh through marriage.

Welsh People Banned From Speaking Welsh in Wales

This title may appear a little misleading, but it was technically accurate, or at least in schools and courts. Cymraeg, or Welsh as the language is known in English, has taken a battering over the centuries.

During the reign of King Henry VIII, The Laws in Wales Acts were passed in 1535 and 1542. These laws annexed Wales to the Kingdom of England, making English law enforceable in Wales and banning the use of the Welsh language in court proceedings. At the time, over 90% of the people in Wales spoke Welsh. Those who didn't speak English had issues getting work and even found that the Welsh language was suppressed in the education system.

The Welsh language remained unrecognised by the courts until the passing of the Welsh Courts Act in 1942, which allowed the Welsh language to be used in courts in Wales if the person speaking it would otherwise be at a disadvantage if they had to speak English. The Welsh Language Act (1967) further ensured that anyone in a Welsh court could be represented in Welsh.

The suppression of the Welsh language wasn't just confined to the courts. It also prevailed in schools. Children would be routinely punished in schools in Wales if they were heard speaking in Welsh. There are reported cases as far back as 1798 where Welsh-speaking children would be singled out and forced to wear a piece of wood attached to a rope around their necks.

Upon the piece of wood was inscribed the letters 'W.N.' This stood for 'Welsh Not'. Horrifically, the wearers of the Welsh Not, themselves children, were incentivised to report on other children in their class who also spoke in Welsh, after which they could duly remove the Welsh Not from their neck. It would be passed on from child to child. The last school child wearing the Welsh Not would be punished at the end of each day. This could be in the form of receiving lashings or a caning from the headmaster. Evidence indicates that the W.N. was still used in Wales as recently as the 1940s.

This practice of punishing school children with the Welsh Not was mentioned in parliament's official 1847 Reports of the Commissioners. These three-part reports understandably became the focus of national disgust from the Welsh and were nicknamed 'The Blue Books'. Saying that it wasn't a particularly complimentary enquiry into the state of education in Wales would be a gross understatement. This is a statement from The Blue Book,

"The Welsh language is a vast drawback to Wales, and a manifold barrier to the moral progress and commercial prosperity of the people. It is not easy to over-estimate its evil effects ... It dissevers the people from intercourse which would greatly advance their civilisation, and bars the access of improving knowledge to their minds."

This continued outside the education setting into the workplace. There are reports that during the 18th and 19th centuries, miners who spoke Welsh could lose their jobs. You can imagine the economic impact on an entire family and even whole villages.

In the 1960s, the Welsh Language Society began a campaign to deface or remove English-only road signs in Wales. Many of the English road signs were painted over with green paint. This eventually led to bilingual signs along the main Welsh roads.

In 2016, a new law came into force in Wales which mandated that all signs be in Welsh first, followed by the English translation. This widespread change to bilingual road signs did, at times, have some rather amusing outcomes. For example, in 2006, a bilingual pedestrian sign on the streets of Cardiff instructed pedestrians in Welsh to *"edrychwch i'r chwith"* (look left). However, the English translation stated, *"look right"*. In another case, a sign placed at the entrance to a Swansea supermarket read in Welsh, *"Nid wyf yn y swyddfa ar hyn o bryd. Anfonwch unrhyw waith i'w gyfieithu"*. The English translation being, *"I am not in the office at the moment. Send any work to be translated."* Someone had not switched off their Out of Office email reply.

When the Welsh Language Act (1993) came into force, it officially put the Welsh language on an equal footing in Wales. These laws now ensure that the Welsh language should never be treated less favourably than English. King Henry VIII's Laws in Wales Acts were finally repealed between 1993 and 1995.

The 2021 Annual Population Survey reported that 29.1% of people in Wales aged three or over were able to speak Welsh. This century has seen a rising trend for Welsh speakers.

Illegal to Be Welsh in Chester During the Hours of Darkness

A common myth states that you are entirely within your rights to shoot a Welsh person with a longbow if found after midnight in Chester. There are other variants that state they have to be found within the city walls of Chester. There is no knowing from where this myth originated. Still, it is likely to have come from a Chester City Ordinance passed on 4th September 1403 as a response to the Glyndŵr Rising. During this time, Chester was under frequent attack by the Welsh.

After the Glyndŵr Rising, the Earl of Chester (shortly to become King Henry V) sought to impose a curfew on the Welsh to reduce the likelihood of future attacks. He ordered that "*all Welsh people and Welsh sympathisers should be expelled from the city; none should enter the city before sunrise or stay after sunset on pain of decapitation.*" There's no mention of longbows or crossbows, just that the heads of Welsh transgressors would be decapitated. That law is genuine, but the reality was very different. Records show that many of the local people in Chester stood surety for Welsh men when they had been arrested under this city ordinance.

There is no indication that this city ordinance was ever repealed. Still, thankfully, modern-day homicide and offences against the person laws provide a suitable deterrence to prevent the cold-blooded murder of Welsh people within the city walls of Chester. A spokesperson for the Law Commission has previously been reported saying, "*It is illegal to shoot a Welsh or Scottish person regardless of the day, location or choice of weaponry.*"

Shooting Welsh in Hereford

Unfortunately, if you were Welsh in Mediaeval and Tudor times, your outlook would be bleak if you tried to cross the border into Hereford. As with Welsh men being found in Chester, a myth also exists surrounding a 'right' in law to shoot a Welsh man in Cathedral Close, Hereford, at any time of the day, provided it is with a longbow.

Again, there is no merit to this myth other than the fact that, like with Welsh found in Chester, it is most likely to have come from a local ordinance due to the Glyndŵr Rising. This comes with the same caveat: any attempt to murder a Welsh man by shooting them with a longbow is just that, murder.

CHAPTER NINETEEN

THE ROOT OF ALL EVIL

They say that money is the root of all evil. Once you've read this chapter, you may be inclined to agree with that statement. There have certainly been enough laws created on our statute books for money-related offences.

It's interesting to note that laws have had to be passed that leave much of the money in your wallet to be no longer legal tender. There are good reasons behind these laws, but as you'll see, there have been cases where innocent members of the public, including you, regularly break the law.

Lawmakers have not been particularly kind to those less fortunate over the centuries. Being in a state of impoverishment is a circumstance that can befall any person at any time. Luckily nowadays, we recognise that people often find themselves in a state of bankruptcy and unable to pay bills, often very innocently, through no fault of their own. This can lead to all sorts of mental health issues that place the weight of the world on an individual. People were publicly shamed for being bankrupt not so long ago, with some very unpleasant consequences.

If you ever find yourself walking across a beach or a muddy field, excitedly looking for buried treasure with your recently purchased metal detector, just be warned that many laws specifically deal with found property. You don't want to end up stealing from the Crown.

"Money does not change people, it unmasks them."
Henry Ford

In Scotland, None of The Money in Your Wallet is Legal Tender

The Bank of England is the central bank of the United Kingdom. Under Section 1(1) of the Currency and Bank Notes Act (1954), the Bank of England is the only institution authorised to issue legal tender banknotes in England and Wales. HM Treasury is responsible for defining which notes have 'legal tender' status within the United Kingdom.

According to the Bank of England, English banknotes aren't legal tender in Scotland or Northern Ireland. Likewise, Scottish bank notes aren't legal tender in England or Wales. Here's the peculiar thing, Scottish bank notes are also not even classed as legal tender in Scotland. Debit and credit cards, along with other forms of contactless payment, are now so standard. Still, surprisingly, they also aren't classed as legal tender anywhere in the United Kingdom. Neither are cheques, although I can't recall the last time I saw one.

There seems to be a trend now with people going into shops and petrol stations and handing over large denominations of commemorative coins for payment. The cashiers will often be confused by this practice and refuse to take them. The person paying with them states it's legal tender and that the cashier is legally required to accept that payment method. I'm sorry to ruin this craze. That is not the case!

So, what is meant by the term 'legal tender'?

Many people believe that if a form of payment is legal tender, then a shop has to accept it when you're paying for something. The truth is, a shop owner can choose what payment they accept or refuse. There is no obligation in law for them to accept anything at all. This applies to all bank notes, coins, cards and contactless payments. So, for example, if your local grocer decided only to accept payment in the form of cabbages and Pokémon trading cards, they're entitled to do so. However, it would probably limit their usual customer base. If you were to attempt to pay for your £4.50 burger with a £50 note, the cashier is not legally obligated to accept that from you. Nor do they have to display any signs to state that, although that would be helpful.

While many common forms of payment, such as debit cards and contactless, aren't legal tender, the reality is that it makes no difference when paying for a transaction. The truth is, the term 'Legal tender' has such a narrow technical meaning that it has no real impact on our everyday life. It relates to the offer to fully pay off a debt to someone in legal tender, after which they can not sue you for failure to repay that debt. There are stringent rules governing legal tender. For example, you would have to offer the exact amount owed because no change can be demanded.

Perhaps next time you stop at the petrol station for some fuel, see if the cashier will accept a crate of cabbages and a marrow in lieu of payment.

So, whilst Scottish bank notes are not legal tender, they are legal currency.

There is a Limit to How Many Coins You Can Legally Use

All coins minted by the Royal Mint and authorised by Royal Proclamation are legal tender in England, Scotland, Wales and Northern Ireland. The Coinage Act (1971) and the Currency Act (1983) state which denomination of coins are legal tender and to what value they may be used in a single transaction. According to these Acts, 1p and 2p coins are legal tender in the

UK only up to an amount not exceeding 20 pence if used in the same transaction. There is an exception. You can use more 1p and 2p coins if the person you're paying is happy to accept them.

In fact, there are also stipulations for 5p, 10p, 20p and 50p coins.

The maximum amounts for which coins are accepted as legal tender in the UK are as follows:

- For £2 and £1 coins: any amount

- For 50p and 20p coins: up to £10

- For 10p and 5p coins: up to £5

- For 2p and 1p coins: up to 20 pence

You may be interested to know that coins are legal tender irrespective of how they are presented ... even if they are in a block of ice or a bucket of rice pudding.

There are stories in the press of people trying to pay off parking fines with bucket loads of pennies. In 2012, a care home manager was ordered to pay a total of £1,118.62 by a judge at Colchester County Court after he tried to settle a £804 debt to his accountant by dumping five crates of mostly 1p and 2p coins in his garden. On a side note, it would have been classed as 'legal tender' and acceptable had the care home manager paid his debt using the following denominations: 774 x £1 coins; 20 x 50p coins; 50 x 20p coins; 50 x 10p coins; & 100 x 5p coins.

Illegal to Deface a Banknote But Not Illegal to Destroy It

Under Section 12 of the Currency and Banknotes Act (1928), it is an offence to deface a banknote by printing, stamping or writing any words, letters or figures on it. So, the next time you're in a restaurant and need something to write down a phone number or doodle a note, you better think twice about it.

However, whilst it is an offence to deface a banknote, it is not an offence to wilfully destroy a banknote. Quite why you would want to do that, I have no idea ... unless you're trying to hide some evidence of a bank robbery!

It's not just bank notes.

The Coinage Act of 1971 makes it an offence to destroy a metal coin that has been current in the UK since 1969 unless the Treasury granted a licence. In 2017, the Royal Mint had to issue a reminder to the general public when it became apparent that people were deliberately disassembling the new £1 coins and separating them into the two separate parts of the inner circle and outer circle and then fixing them back together, the wrong way around. These were then being sold on eBay. Understandably the Royal Mint were unhappy and issued a reminder that deliberately manipulating coins in this way was an offence under the Coinage Act (1971).

Public Shame of Bankruptcy

The Statute of Bankrupts Act (1542) was passed in the time of King Henry VIII, also known as 'An Act against such Persons as do make Bankrupt' and was one of the first pieces of legislation that covered bankruptcy in England. It treated all bankrupts as criminals who had craftily got one over on people of honest intent.

It stated, "*Whereas divers and sundry persons, craftily obtaining into their hands great substance of other men's goods, do suddenly fleet apart unknown, or keep their houses, not minding to pay or restore to any their creditors, their duties but at their own wills and pleasures consume debts and the substances obtained by credits of other men, for their own pleasure and delicate living, against all reason, equity, and good conscience.*"

Under this Act, the debtor was liable to be imprisoned.

A further bankruptcy Act was passed during Queen Elizabeth I's time in 1570, and another two Acts were passed during the time of King James I, the 1604 and 1623 Acts. The Bankruptcy Act of 1623 found that any debtor who fraudulently hid their assets from creditors in an attempt to evade repaying what they owed would be '*set upon the Pillory in some public place for the space of two hours and to have one of his or her ears nailed to the Pillory and cut off*'. The purpose of these Acts was to deeply shame those who

had become bankrupt. They afforded no recognition to those who might otherwise have found themselves bankrupt through no fault of their own or just because life had taken a wrong turn for them.

Any Discovered Treasure Belongs to The Crown

The law surrounding buried treasure has always been convoluted. Treasure trove or 'treasure that has been found' comes from the Anglo-French term *tresor trové*. It generally refers to the discovery of something of value and is classed as treasure. The idea of treasure trove comes from common law dating back to the reign of King Edward the Confessor (1042-1066). It's any discovery of gold or silver in any form, whether coin, plate or bullion, which had been hidden and now discovered, and which, at the time of discovery, no person could prove they owned it. If the person who had hidden the treasure came forward or became known later, they would again be classed as the legal owner of the treasure, and it would be returned to them or their descendants. If the rightful owner can not be discovered, it automatically belongs to the Crown. For this reason, to conceal the discovery of any treasure is classed as an offence because you would be treating it as your own property and stealing from the Crown.

To be classed as 'treasure trove', the discovered item must be made of more than 50% gold or silver. It also has to have been initially hidden by someone intending to recover it later (*animus revocandi*). Suppose the item wasn't buried or hidden *animus revocandi*. In that case, it's not classed as treasure trove and is simply something that has been lost or abandoned. That would be a case of 'finders keepers', and it would belong to the person who found it or the land owner.

There was a well-known case from 1939 at the site of two mediaeval cemeteries in Sutton Hoo, Suffolk. A wealth of Anglo-Saxon artefacts had been discovered. It was determined that they were not treasure trove because they were part of a ship burial, and there had been no intention at the burial to recover the artefacts later. However, all of this changed with the Treasure Act (1996). This Act removed the long-standing principles of treasure trove. It replaced them with new criteria for any treasure found from that point onwards. The new rules presuppose that any discovered treasure now belongs to the Crown, irrespective of how it came to be there in the first place or whether it was lost or left behind, even if there had been no intention to recover it later.

The new definition of treasure is now:

- any object at least 300 years old when found which is not a coin and at least 10% precious metal (gold or silver) by weight;

- one of at least two coins in the same find which are at least 300 years old at that time and are at least 10% precious metal by weight; or

- one of at least ten coins in the same find which are at least 300 years old at that time;

- any object at least 200 years old when found, which belongs to a class of objects of outstanding historical, archaeological or cultural importance that has been designated as treasure by the Secretary of State.

The Wicked, Pernicious and Dangerous Act of Forgery

In 1562, during Queen Elizabeth I's reign, the Forgery Act (An Act against Forgers of false Deeds and Writings) was passed. The opening of this Act described the act of forgery as a *'wicked, pernicious and dangerous practice'* and described forgers as *'such evil people.'* It required that anyone convicted of this offence of forgery would have to pay back double their costs and damages to their victim.

If that weren't enough, the forger would also *"be set upon the Pillory in some open Market Town, or other open Place, and there to have both his Ears cut off, and also his Nostrils to be slit and cut, and seared with a hot Iron, so as they may remain for a perpetual Note or Mark of his Falsehood."*

In addition, they would also have to forfeit all of their land to the Crown and spend the rest of their life in prison.

Records show that on 10th June 1731, a 70-year-old forger named Joseph Cook suffered this punishment. He was made to stand for one hour in the pillory at Charing Cross, after which he was seated in an elbow-chair. The local hangman then cut off his ears with an incision knife and held them up to the watching crowd. He then slit both his nostrils with a pair of scissors and seared them with red-hot irons. The surgeon attended to him on the pillory. He is described as having undergone this treatment 'with undaunted courage.' After this humiliating punishment, he went to the Ship Tavern at Charing Cross where he is described to have spent some time, before being carried to the King's Bench Prison, where he spent the rest of his living days.

Finders Keepers, Losers Weepers

So what do you do if you're paying for your shopping and the cashier hands over the wrong amount of change? Well, if you've been short-changed, most people would raise their concerns immediately. However, what happens when the cashier hands over more money than you're owed? Perhaps you handed them a £5, and they mistakenly thought you'd given them a £20 note. Would you say anything or go on your merry way and consider yourself lucky?

The law is quite clear about this. To do the latter and keep hold of the extra money would be wrong, not only morally but also a clear case of theft. The Theft Act (1968) states. *"A person is guilty of theft if he dishonestly appropriates property belonging to another with the intention of permanently depriving the other of it."* This law has remained essentially unchanged for almost 55 years.

If you have reasonable grounds to believe that you are not entitled to that money, and you aren't, or that the other person was mistaken in handing it to you, and you consciously decide to keep it, then according to the law, you are a thief.

The law recognises that mistakes can be made. So if you have driven home and not realised that you have accidentally accepted the extra money, it's not theft. The law requires the theft to be accompanied by *mens rea*, Latin for 'guilty mind.'

There have also been some relatively recent cases of what is known as Theft by Finding, where people find money or property that belongs to another person and treat it as their own by keeping it.

Imagine you're out shopping, and you come across what appears to be an abandoned £20 note on the floor. What do you do? Do you keep it? Do you experience that awkward moment, peering around, wondering whether it's an elaborate prank and someone is about to pounce on you? In theory, this is known as theft by finding. The law requires you to make every reasonable effort to locate the true owner before keeping it yourself. For example, if you find a bag in a shopping centre, you should look around to see whether anyone has nervously lost their bag or hand it into the building security or their lost property. The same goes for an expensive watch or a sentimental item of jewellery. And to be fair, I imagine that most people would do this. But when it comes to money, would you go to the extent of handing it in to the local police station, or would you think it's a case of 'finders keepers, losers weepers'?

Imagine walking into your local police station and suggesting to the police staff at the front counter that you found this money in a public place, you can't identify the owner, and you would like to register it as found property. Well, you'd be lucky to even get into a police station these days, considering many are now closed off to the public. You may have to contend with lengthy waiting times or wayward attitude problems if you do. Take your pick! Either way, no-one would thank you for the extra paperwork in causing them to complete a found property log.

The reality is, so long as you've taken reasonable steps to locate the owner or if you genuinely believe that the owner is untraceable, that wouldn't be dishonest and classed as theft in the eyes of the law.

If you find a 50-pence coin on the ground outside a shop, you wouldn't be expected to place a note in the shop window asking whether anyone has lost a 50p coin because it would simply be too difficult to trace the correct owner.

According to the Theft Act, any lost property will continue to belong to the owner unless it has genuinely and knowingly been abandoned by them. Just because an item of property or a small amount of cash has been found in the street doesn't mean the owner has abandoned it.

A recent case in 2017 involved a 23-year-old woman from Stoke-on-Trent who had no previous convictions. She found a £20 note on the floor of a shop. She picked up the note, failed to take any reasonable steps to trace the owner, and treated it as her own. She was found guilty of theft and received a criminal record.

CHAPTER TWENTY

THE ROYAL HOUSEHOLD

The King holds considerable power, and as we'll see, there are times when, like his ancestors from centuries ago, he still holds full executive powers. He can commit the UK armed forces to war and has the authority to prorogue Parliament. No laws can be passed without Royal Assent from the monarch. This is one of the reasons why almost 900 laws passed during the Interregnum period weren't actually laws at all.

As you can imagine, this chapter dealing with the Royal household has had its fair share of myths over the years. After all, you don't want to be hanged, drawn & quartered for affixing your postage stamps upside down. Step on the wrong side of the King, and you could be found guilty of the most heinous crime, Treason!

"I declare before you all that my whole life whether it be long or short shall be devoted to your service."
Queen Elizabeth II, 21st April 1947

The Monarch Can Prorogue Parliament

The title alone makes you think this could be about the life and times of the Stuart kings. When Parliament is prorogued, the current parliamentary session ends, and any motions that have yet to be voted on are also suspended. The only person who can prorogue Parliament is The King. This falls under The King's Royal prerogative powers. If the Prime Minister wishes to suspend Parliament, they must first obtain Royal Assent from The King. In practical terms, the monarch will never refuse the request to prorogue Parliament and acts on their Prime Minister's advice.

Since 2000, the average length of prorogation is 18 days. That is the time between the previous parliamentary session and the new session.

The term 'prorogation' originates from the 15th century, when successive governments only held sessions for brief periods. These were generally to approve Royal expenditure and taxes. Once that business had been completed, the government was prorogued by The King.

King Charles I is a prime example of one such monarch who tended to prorogue Parliament at will. Between 1625 and 1629, he dismissed Parliament three times. In 1629, he dismissed his fourth Parliament after deeming them too argumentative and hostile. He didn't reconvene Parliament for a further 11 years.

Since that time, rafts of legislation now place legal limits on the prorogation of Parliament. The Bill of Rights (1688) requires Parliament to sit *"frequently."* Parliament can also be recalled early due to exigencies, for example, when exercising powers under the Civil Contingencies Act (2004) or at the outbreak of war. On top of this legislation, there is now an established case law restriction relating to the prorogation of Parliament. In the 2019 Miller / Cherry case against the government, the Supreme Court ruled *"that a decision to prorogue Parliament (or to advise the monarch to prorogue Parliament) will be unlawful if the prorogation has the effect of frustrating or preventing, without reasonable justification, the ability of Parliament to carry out its constitutional functions as a legislature and as the body responsible for the supervision of the executive. In such a situation, the court will intervene if the effect is sufficiently serious to justify such an exceptional course."*

This judgement didn't impose a quantitative limit on Parliament's prorogation. It does make it difficult to legally justify lengthy prorogation as not affecting Parliament's constitutional functions as a legislature. This piece of case law came about after an unforeseen set of circumstances occurred in 2019, which saw the prorogation of Parliament be legally challenged

through the Supreme Court. Whilst the Sovereign's prerogative powers can not be legally challenged; it was not these
to which the Supreme Court turned its attention. It was the
counsel provided to the monarch by the then Prime Minister,
Boris Johnson. The ruling was to determine whether the Prime
Minister's advice to Her Majesty The Queen was lawful.

At the end of autumn 2019, the UK swiftly moved towards
its departure from the European Union. Unless a Brexit deal
was made before our departure from the European Union
on 31st October 2019, we were due to crash out of the EU
without a deal which would have resulted in horrific economic
consequences for the UK. On 28th August 2019, the Prime
Minister asked Her Majesty The Queen to prorogue Parliament from between 9th to 12th September. This increased the
time that parliamentarians could not vote on a Brexit deal because Parliament was also already committed to a forthcoming
three-week period of recess. This would have been the longest
period of prorogation since 1930.

The government stated the prorogation was to enable the
government to set out a new legislative agenda. There was
an outcry from parliamentarians, constitutional scholars and
even former Prime Minister Sir John Major stating that the
prorogation severely reduced the ability of parliamentarians
to prevent a no-deal Brexit. Many felt this was an attempt to
evade scrutiny of the government's Brexit plans.

Three separate legal cases were lodged with the courts, all
alleging the illegality of the prorogation. This put The Queen,
who is politically neutral, in a challenging position, as she
had correctly acted on the advice of her Prime Minister. The
High Court of Justice in London found that the issue was
non-justiciable, and they had no authority to judge the matter.
Things were different in Scotland, where a case was lodged

in the Court of Session sitting in Edinburgh. They ruled that the prorogation was unlawful, stating that it had the *"improper purpose of stymieing Parliament."*

The issue was brought before the Supreme Court, the highest court in the UK, on 17th September 2019. The former Solicitor-General Lord Garnier, responding on behalf of former Prime Minister Sir John Major argued that this prorogation was *"motivated by a desire to prevent Parliament interfering with the prime minister's policies during that period."* The shadow Attorney-General, Shami Chakrabarti, argued that if this prorogation went unchecked, Parliament would be *"deprived"* of the ability to *"perform its constitutional function."* On 24th September, the Supreme Court unanimously ruled that the prorogation was both justiciable and unlawful and therefore was null and had no effect. The Court found that the Prime Minister's advice to The Queen *'was outside the powers of the Prime Minister'.* It cited the Case of Proclamations (1610) from the time of King James I, which defined the limitations on the Royal Prerogative at that time. It ruled that the prorogation of Parliament on this occasion had the effect of frustrating Parliament's constitutional functions.

Lady Hale read the Supreme Court judgement, *"This court has already concluded that the Prime Minister's advice to Her Majesty was unlawful, void and of no effect. This means that the order in Council to which it led was also unlawful, void and of no effect and should be quashed. This means that when the Royal Commissioners walked into The House of Lords, it was as if they had walked in with a blank sheet of paper. The prorogation was also void and of no effect. Parliament has not been prorogued. This is the unanimous judgement of all eleven justices."*

Parliament was immediately recalled and continued to debate the Brexit deal.

In December 2020, the government published the Fixed-term Parliaments Act 2011 (Repeal) Bill, which sought to prohibit judicial reviews into the power to dissolve Parliament. This received Royal Assent on 24th March 2022 in the Dissolution and Calling of Parliament Act (2022).

Illegal to Affix a Stamp On An Envelope Upside Down

This next offence would appeal to someone like my father, who has a particular disdain for anyone who affixes postage stamps to envelopes in a crooked manner. He likes to place his stamps on envelopes with such precision it's as though he secretly whips out a set square to ensure the angles are perfect. I'm not sure of the reason for this peculiar affliction. Perhaps it's a touch of OCD, respect for the recipient, or fear of being 'transported to the colonies'.

There is a common belief that placing a postage stamp upside down on an envelope or package is illegal. The belief is derived from the fact that postage stamps in the UK depict an image of the current monarch. It is thought that if you were to place a stamp upside down, that would be the equivalent of putting the King's image upside down. The mind boggles when you consider that only a few years ago, one would have to lick the rear of the postage stamp before affixing it to an envelope.

This belief is founded on the premise that doing anything that would incorrectly depict His Majesty's image would be considered treason under the Treason Felony Act (1848). Section 3 of this Act makes it an offence to "*deprive or depose*" the "*style*" or "*honour*" of the Crown. The punishment for this offence was to be "*transported beyond the seas for the term of his or her natural life.*" Since penal transportation stopped in 1868, the sentence is now just to spend the rest of your life in prison.

This would be utterly bizarre if it were true, but it just isn't. The Act itself is genuine and features elsewhere in this book. However, it does not refer to postage stamps. Any consideration of affixing a stamp upside down as treasonable is certainly not within the spirit of the Act. The Royal Mail and The Law Commission have also confirmed that placing a postage stamp upside down would not be considered an offence of treason.

Treason!

'Treason' is a term that is often thrown around, although not as much as during earlier centuries. We've all most likely heard of notable people throughout history that have been tried and executed for Treason. People like Guy Fawkes, Catherine Howard (Henry VIII's fifth wife) and Sir Walter Raleigh.

The Cambridge Dictionary defines treason as '*(the crime of) showing no loyalty to your country, especially by helping its enemies or trying to defeat its government*'.

Treason is an offence. It always has been and, most likely, always will be. It is the interpretation of what constitutes an act of treason that has changed over the centuries. In law, there are two types of treason: *High Treason* and *Petty Treason*.

High treason is considered the most serious offence and is essentially a crime of disloyalty towards the Crown. This included acts like plotting the Sovereign's murder; adultery with the Sovereign's companion; levying war against the Sovereign; giving aid and comfort to the Sovereign's enemies, and taking any action to hinder the line of succession to the throne. Over the centuries, various other crimes have been categorised as high treason, including counterfeiting the realm's currency and even being a Catholic priest. Petty treason is where a crime is committed against one of the Sovereign's subjects. This would be, for example, the murder of a legal superior. It dealt with offences of the murder of a master by a servant, the murder of a husband by his wife, or the murder of a Bishop by one of his clergy. With the passing of the Offences Against the Person Act (1828), Petty Treason ceased to exist. Since then, any discussion of 'treason' has referred to High Treason.

Originally, acts of treason were defined under common law. Then it was considered that anyone performing any act that legally only the King or his appointed officers could do, was treason. In 1348, Sir John Gerberge of Royston was indicted for treason after falsely imprisoning William de Boletisford and taking his horse until he paid him £90. This definition was so wide-ranging that the powerful land barons encouraged King Edward III to pass an Act of Statute, defining limits of the offence of treason. As a result, in 1351, The Treason Act was passed.

With the passing of The Succession to the Crown Act (1707), it became treason to assert that any person not within the legitimate line of succession could legally succeed to the throne. It also became treason even to claim that the Crown or Parliament couldn't legislate to limit the line of succession. This was abolished in 1967.

The punishment for treason was death. More often than not, the mode of execution was inhumanely torturous. The statutory execution method for men in England was to be hanged, drawn and quartered. The guilty man was not even permitted to walk to their place of execution. Instead, they would be 'drawn' there by being dragged or, as was usually the case, being tied onto a hurdle and pulled by horse to their place of death. A noose would then hang him around his neck until almost dead. The rope would then be cut, allowing him to fall to the ground. He would then be stripped of his clothes. His genitals would be cut off. Whilst still alive, his abdomen would be cut open, and his intestines pulled out and burnt in front of him, after which his remaining organs would be ripped out of his body. His head would then be decapitated, and his body sliced into four quarters.

The traitor's body parts would then be boiled with salt and cumin seed to prevent putrefaction and stop the birds from pecking at the flesh. They would then be publicly displayed on a gibbet as a cautionary reminder to the local townsfolk about what happens to traitors. This remained the statutory sentence until 1814 when instead, the traitor would be hanged until dead. They would still be disembowelled, beheaded and quartered, but only after they had died. The last people to be sentenced to being hanged, drawn and quartered were the Cato Street Conspirators. They plotted to murder all the government ministers, including the Prime Minister, in 1820. Five of the conspirators were executed. Their sentences were commuted to being hanged and beheaded. The remaining five were transported to penal colonies in Australia.

Such a punishment was considered too brutal for female traitors. Instead, they were drawn and then burned alive at the stake. Catherine Murphy was the last woman to be burned for high treason in 1789. A year later, the sentence was replaced by the Treason Act (1790), after which women were hanged until dead.

The nobility was spared the torture but not the anxiety. Instead, they were beheaded in a public execution. Often, once the head was removed from the body, the executioner would hold their head up high and shout, *"Behold the head of a traitor."* This was more for theatrics than any requirement in law. Bizarrely, the sentence of beheading for treason was not removed from the statute books until 1973. The last beheading was in 1747. This was for high treason by the peer Simon Fraser, 11th Lord Lovat.

The traitor's ordeal didn't end with being tortured and executed. Once dead, they were also considered *'attainted'* (corrupted of blood). This meant they would forfeit any land, estates and property to the Crown. They also lost hereditary titles and could not pass those or any property to their heirs and successors. Treason cases required a minimum of two witnesses to prevent abuse and wrongful convictions for treason in case a monarch may wish to acquire further land and property.

Capital punishment was abolished in 1965 with the passing of the Murder (Abolition of Death Penalty) Act. Although it still remained the penalty for high treason until Section 36 of the Crime and Disorder Act (1998) changed the maximum sentence for treason to life imprisonment.

In 1916, a trial for high treason was brought against Roger Casement for attempting to obtain military aid from Germany during the First World War to help the Irish during the Easter Rising. His defence team argued that the Treason Act only applied to activities conducted on British soil. However, Casement had collaborated with the enemy whilst outside Britain. The prosecutors decided to cleverly interpret the original legislation written in Norman-French and unpunctuated. So, they decided to punctuate the text in relevant places, which allowed it to be construed so that Casement could be prosecuted. Casement wrote that he was being *"hanged on a comma."*

The last execution for treason in the UK occurred on 3rd January 1946. This was the case of William Joyce, who was tried at the Old Bailey on three counts of high treason and sentenced to death. During World War Two, he travelled to Germany and began broadcasting pro-Nazi propaganda to British radio listeners. In his nightly Germany Calling broadcast, he played the part of fictitious Lord Haw-Haw, broadcasting messages designed to undermine the British morale. In 1944, he gained the personal commendation of Adolf Hitler for his services to the German war effort. Upon his capture in May 1945, Parliament rushed through the new Treason Act (1945), which held trials for treason procedurally similar to trials for murder. This is because any previous trials for treason were conducted in an overly-elaborate procedure. Joyce appealed his conviction, stating that when he applied for a British passport in 1933, he had lied about his country of birth on his passport application and so did not owe any allegiance to Britain. His appeal was not upheld. He was executed as a traitor and hanged at Wandsworth Prison.

Treason is by no means a thing of the past. It has appeared a few times already in the 21st century. Immediately following the 9/11 terrorist attacks, the government clarified that any British citizens who fought alongside the Taliban against allied forces would be prosecuted for treason. No-one was tried for treason.

On 8th August 2005, the government was considering prosecuting several Islamic clerics for speaking in support of acts of terrorism against civilians on British soil or against British soldiers abroad. Cleric Abu Hamza al-Masri was prosecuted instead for inciting murder and convicted.

At 8.30am on Christmas Day in 2021, the Metropolitan Police arrested Jaswant Singh Chail from Southampton on the grounds of Windsor Castle and charged him with "*discharging or aiming firearms, or throwing or using any offensive matter or weapon, with intent to injure or alarm her Majesty*" under Section 2 of the Treason Act (1842). He was also charged with 'Threats to kill' under Section 16 of the Offences Against the Person Act (1861) and Possession of an offensive weapon (a crossbow) under Section 1 of the Prevention of Crime Act (1953).

In 1981, Marcus Sarjeant was imprisoned for five years under this same Section of the Treason Act. He had fired blank shots at The Queen during the Trooping the Colour parade while she was on horseback riding down The Mall in London.

At Times, The King Holds Full Executive Powers in The UK

There are certain occasions when The King will hold full executive powers, which would usually be shared with the Prime Minister. This occurs when the office of Prime Minister is vacant. This would be during the moment between the Prime Minister resigning and a new one being formally invited by The King to form a government. During this time, all executive powers are transferred to the monarch. Although, in recent times, the monarch has ensured this is of the shortest duration possible. For example, the moment between Prime Minister Boris Johnson formally resigning and Liz Truss being formally appointed lasted around one hour.

During the reign of Her late Majesty Queen Elizabeth II, this transition occurred on fifteen occasions.

Royal Assent

For any parliamentary Bill to officially become law, it must first receive Royal Assent from the monarch. Once Royal Assent has been given, the Bill becomes an Act of Parliament and enforceable in law, usually from midnight of that day.

The King doesn't actually sign the Bill himself. This hasn't happened since the sixteenth century. The monarch will instead sign what is known as Letters Patent, formally announcing that assent has been given. On other occasions, the King could sign a document called a Commission which commands his Royal Commissioners to notify the Houses of Parliament that a Bill has received his Royal Assent. This alternative method came into being with the passing of the Royal Assent by Commission Act (1541). This Act was repealed and replaced by the Royal Assent Act (1967). Although, Section 1(2) of the Act still permits the monarch to declare their Royal Assent in-person, should they so desire. Before this, the Sovereign would give their Royal Assent, in-person before Parliament. Queen Victoria was the last monarch to provide Royal Assent in-person on 12th August 1854.

Royal Assent can be given in advance of an Act of Parliament coming into force. On such occasions, responsibility is passed to the relevant minister of Parliament to set a date for the Act to come into force. In such cases, the minister will bring the Act into force by issuing what is known as a Commencement Order.

What happens if the King doesn't provide Royal Assent? Quite simply, it can't become law and is unenforceable. In previous centuries this happened a lot, especially with King Charles I, who refused to provide Royal Assent for years. He eventually dissolved Parliament altogether, not calling a new one for eleven years. Between the execution of King Charles I in 1649 and the restoration of the monarchy with King Charles II in 1660, every law passed during that 'Interregnum' period was not legally enforceable. Although that certainly didn't stop the Parliament of the day from trying to enforce them. After the restoration of the monarchy, some of the more commonsense interregnum 'laws' were assented to by the King.

In recent times, Royal Assent has never been withheld. The last monarch to do so was Queen Anne. Upon advice from her ministers, she refused to assent to the Scottish Militia Bill on 11th March 1708, fearing that such a militia might become disloyal and turn against the monarchy. Her predecessor, King William III, refused to assent to six Bills during his reign.

The King Can Send UK Armed Forces to War

These days, whilst we may see the Prime Minister in the House of Commons announcing that he is committing our armed forces to various campaigns, there's a lot more going on behind the scenes. Constitutionally, it is for the King alone, as head of our armed forces, to decide to deploy our armed forces in situations of armed conflict. This is a legal right and part of the King's prerogative power.

However, the convention has been established over recent decades. This power is used on the advice of the Privy Council, with the powers delegated to the ministers themselves. Interestingly, Parliament has no constitutional role in the declaration of war, and it is now the Prime Minister who commits our armed forces on behalf of the King. This Royal Prerogative is echoed in The King's Regulations for the Army, which state that the governance and command of our armed forces are "*vested in His Majesty The King,*" who delegates responsibility to his Secretary of State and the Defence Committee. Despite the many conflicts in which our armed forces have been committed over the last century, we have made no formal declaration of war since we declared war in Siam (now Thailand) in 1942.

Since the United Nations (UN) was established in 1945, the UN Charter prohibits the threat or use of force in international relations. This effectively makes formal declarations of war a legal quagmire. Subsequent governments have been at pains to point out that any perceived wars have not, in fact, been 'wars' in the legal or constitutional sense. The correct term is 'armed conflict' ... or if you're a Russian despot, a *"special military operation."*

The King Can Not Be Sued or Prosecuted

It is not possible to arrest or prosecute our reigning monarch for criminal proceedings, nor is it possible to sue them (in most cases). I say 'most cases' as we'll come onto that shortly. This is because the King, like all Heads of State, enjoys *Sovereign immunity* under UK law. The courts have no authority to compel the monarch to be bound by their jurisdiction because they act in the King's name and with his authority. This can be summed up with the legal maxim *'rex non potest peccare'* (The King can do no wrong). The same principle applied to the late Queen Elizabeth II, King George VI and previous monarchs. All recent monarchs have done their best to ensure their actions accord with UK law.

The principle of Sovereign immunity was last tested in court in 1911 when a scurrilous and unfounded accusation of bigamy was made against King George V by journalist Edward Mylius. The journalist was later jailed for criminal libel. The King issued proceedings against Mylius and was prepared to stand in the witness box to clear his character. The Attorney-General advised the King that giving evidence in his own court would be unconstitutional. The Lord Chief Justice also determined that the King could not be ordered to provide evidence, and the matter was therefore closed.

Much in the same way that a foreign diplomat with diplomatic immunity can not be sued or prosecuted. All that can happen is that they are made '*persona non grata*' (person not wanted) and ordered to leave the UK.

The law also prevents arrests from being made "*in the monarch's presence,*" or within the "*verges*" of a Royal palace. The normal judicial processes can not occur within a Royal residence. In addition, none of the Sovereign's personal effects can be taken under a writ of execution. Royal land can not have distress levied upon it. This means that bailiffs can not be instructed to enter a Royal residence to seize goods as security to pay a debt. Whilst all this may seem unfair to some, since the passing of The Crown Proceedings Act (1947), it has now been possible for civil actions to be brought against the Crown.

This almost brings us full circle to the original Magna Carta from 1215, with its many restraints to prevent King John from failing to adhere to the terms of the charter. This principle established that no person is above the law, not even the King. Article 61 essentially states that everyone has a duty to rebel against the King if he doesn't rule fairly and fails to respond to any complaints brought by the council of 25 barons. It enabled the barons to seize the King's properties using military force if the King violated the Magna Carta. This provision was excluded from the later versions of the Magna Carta.

In writing about the Magna Carta, former Prime Minister Sir. Winston Churchill wrote, "*Here is a law which is above the King which even he must not break. This reaffirmation of a supreme law and its expression in a general charter is the great work of Magna Carta; and this alone justifies the respect in which men have held it."*

CHAPTER TWENTY-ONE

TRANSPORT

A century ago, people were fined for travelling at speeds slower than most people now run. As bizarre as that may sound, motorists have been 'persecuted' since the early halcyon days of motoring.

Travelling can be fraught with all sorts of hidden dangers, especially if you forget to take your flagman out with you on your next drive to the local shops. From prosecutions for flashing car headlights to collisions with goats and pigeons, most drivers will be committing an offence each time they get behind the wheel of their car.

If you do insist on travelling, whatever you do, don't use someone else's sockets to charge your phone and laptop. You never know what might happen. In case you decide against travelling by car and choose a boat trip, be advised that boats in Scotland could be found guilty of homicidal acts.

> *"If you don't know where you are going,*
> *any road will get you there."*
> Lewis Carroll

All Cars Must Be Preceded by a Man on Foot Carrying a Red Flag

There are always debates about the speed limits on the UK's highways. Some people are in favour of scrapping the speed limits altogether on motorways. Others favour reducing speeds in residential areas for safety reasons. Fast cars and other vehicles only came into being in the second half of the twentieth-century. Up until then, the legislation governing powered vehicles and speed restrictions came from laws passed in the time of Queen Victoria.

The Locomotive Act (1865) enforced the first strict speed restrictions, also known as the 'Red Flag Act'. Section 4 of this Act required all locomotives and automobiles to travel at a maximum speed of 2 mph (3.2 km/h) in towns and cities or 4 mph (6.4 km/h) in the countryside. The fine for contravening this speed limit was £10. Section 3 of the Act also states that a crew of three people must accompany self-propelled vehicles and that a man carrying a red flag must walk at least 60 yards (55 metres) ahead of the vehicle.

On 28th January 1896, Walter Arnold of East Peckham, Kent, became the world's first person prosecuted for speeding. He was travelling in the Paddock Wood area of Kent when he was spotted by a police constable on a pedal cycle who furiously peddled to keep up with him. At the time, Mr. Arnold was driving in a built-up area with a 2 mph speed limit. Unfortunately for him, he was travelling at an outrageous 8 mph. The police officer charged him with four offences: using a locomotive without a horse on a public road; operating his locomotive with fewer than three people; exceeding the speed limit; and failing to clearly display his name and address on his locomotive. The constable brought Mr. Arnold before the local magistrate. He was found guilty on all four counts and fined £4 and seven shillings. The actual offence of speeding only attracted a fine of 10 shillings.

To put this into perspective, the average walking pace for a person is 2.5 to 4 mph. The record for the fastest run is held by Usain Bolt, who achieved a speed of 27.78 mph (44.72 km/h) at the 2009 World Championships in Athletics.

Walter Arnold was one of the country's earliest car dealers and was the local supplier for Benz vehicles. In his eyes, his convictions and the subsequent publicity about his 'faster than normal' car would only have brought him more commercial success. Interestingly, Mr. Arnold now posthumously holds the Guinness World Record for the first person charged with a speeding offence.

The law recognised that it was quickly becoming outdated with these new vehicles on the road, and in 1896, The Locomotives on Highways Act increased the speed limit to 14 mph. Six years later, the Motor Car Act (1903) increased the speed limit to 10 mph in towns and cities and 20 mph in the countryside. Around this time, speed traps started to be routinely intro-duced, with police constables hiding in bushes with a notepad and a stopwatch timing the speed of passing vehicles. Roll the clock forward, and in 1991, the first Gatso speed camera was introduced to the UK on the M40 motorway in West London.

You May Not Enter The Hull of The Titanic Without State Permission

The wreck of the Titanic was discovered in 1985 in international waters, approximately 350 nautical miles off the coast of Newfoundland. Just in case you are thinking of diving down to the wreck of the Titanic to retrieve the Heart of the Ocean necklace worn by Kate Winslet in the film, there are a few things to remember. Firstly, there never was a real Heart of the Ocean necklace. Secondly, you have to be a complete lunatic or a mermaid to be able to dive into the wreck of the Titanic, considering it is two and a half miles below the ocean surface. The pressure would crush you to the size of a gnat. Finally, it's important also to realise that the wreck of R.M.S. Titanic is protected by law.

Under The Protection of Wrecks (R.M.S. Titanic) Order (2003), it is an offence to enter the hull of the Titanic without prior permission from the Secretary of State.

Most of our important and historical nautical wrecks are also given protected status as war graves under the Protection of Military Remains Act (1986). In many cases, diving to the site of these wrecks is permitted. However, it is an offence to enter the wrecks, interfere with them in any way, or remove anything from them without prior permission from the Ministry of Defence.

You Must Report All Collisions With Goats But Not Cats or Pigeons

As a nation of animal lovers, this next one puzzles me. Lawmakers have given special consideration to certain types of animals under the Road Traffic Act. Still, for whatever reason, they've missed out one of the most common and popular domestic pets.

Sadly, some drivers give little consideration to other road users and instead use the British highways like their own personal Le Mans. You can walk out one day to the local shops, which is very peaceful with nothing to hear but the dulcet trills of a distant blackbird. The next minute it can be like you're stood in the middle of a Scalextric track, with cars whooshing passed at breakneck speed. It's no wonder that collisions occur daily all over the U.K. In most cases, drivers will stop briefly to exchange details. The law requires that the drivers exchange vehicle registration numbers, the names and addresses of the drivers, and the names and addresses of the vehicle owners, if different. In cases where a person is injured, the police must also be notified. The law gets quite specific regarding road traffic collisions involving animals. Section 170 of the Road Traffic Act (1988) states that in road traffic collisions where an animal is injured, it must be reported to the police. However, that section of the law defines an 'animal' as any horse, cattle, ass, mule, sheep, pig, goat, or dog. There is a notable omission ... cats! Suppose the animal injured during the collision is a cat or any other animal not included in that Section of the law above. In that case, the matter doesn't need to be reported to the police. In 2022, there are approximately 12.2 million cats kept as pets in the UK. As a dog lover, I feel it necessary to point out there are 12.5 million dogs kept as pets in the UK.

For those taking this as a carte blanche to drive around the neighbourhood intentionally looking for cats, please rest assured that other laws exist to prevent such actions.

Illegal to Cycle on Pavements

Most of us, at some point, most likely as a child, will have cycled on the pavement. You still see many people doing this today. Partly through ignorance of the law and partly through fear of being hit by passing traffic. Rule 64 of The Highway Code states that you must not cycle on the pavement. This law initially came from a time when bicycles weren't commonplace, and the term 'pavement' wasn't in use. Section 72 of the Highways Act (1835) created the offence of 'wilfully riding' on footpaths at the side of the carriageway. We can interpret this as meaning pavements.

Moving on from the Victorian era, the end of the twenti-eth-century brought us the Road Traffic Offenders Act (1988). Section 51 and Schedule 3 of this Act now provide the penalty of an on-the-spot fine with a £30 fixed penalty notice.

The Road Traffic Act (1988) created several pedal cycle of-fences. These include dangerous cycling; careless and incon-siderate cycling; and cycling under the influence of drink or drugs.

In a curious case from 2016, a gentleman from Bermondsey, South London called Charlie Alliston was charged with an offence of causing bodily harm by *wanton or furious driving.* He had been riding his bike at a speed of about 18mph, with no working front brake, when he collided with a pedestrian at a crossing in East London. Sadly, the pedestrian, a moth-er-of-two, Mrs. Kim Briggs, later died in hospital from cata-strophic head injuries sustained during the collision. Alliston was jailed for 18 months. The offence of 'wanton and furious driving' derives from Section 35 of the Offences Against the Person Act (1861). This offence was created to deter people from recklessly driving their horse carriages. It carries a max-imum penalty of two years imprisonment with the possibility of an unlimited fine.

Driving With Glass Not as Prescribed

As a young child, I was once given a lift in a car by a friend's parent. His car windscreen was obscured entirely by thick ice. You really couldn't see anything through it. It was as good as opaque. He thought it was sufficient to clear a small area of ice from the windscreen, no larger than a piece of A5 paper, using a credit card. He sat forward in his driving seat, eyes close to the windscreen and peering intensely through it like he was driving a Sherman tank.

What he was doing was not only highly dangerous to other road users but also against the law. Each winter, you can go out on the roads and see many cars being driven around with obscured windscreens. The law requires that all ice or snow be removed from the whole windscreen and not just the viewing area. It also requires that you can see out of every window in your vehicle. This law must also extend to the inside of the windscreen, to ensure it is fully demisted before setting off.

The offence is '*Using a Motor Vehicle on a Road When the Glass Was Not Maintained so as to Afford the Drivers Unobscured Vision*,' otherwise known as '*Driving with Glass not as prescribed*'. This is contrary to Regulation 30(3) of the Road Vehicles (Construction and Use) Regulations (1986), Section 42 of the Road Traffic Act (1988) and Schedule 2 to the Road Traffic Offenders Act (1988). Section 41D of the Road Traffic Act (1988) also requires a clear, unobstructed view of the road ahead before driving.

Under Section 229 of the Highway Code, it is also an offence to drive with snow piled up on your car. The rule states that drivers must "*remove all snow that might fall off into the path of other road users.*" If a police officer sees snow fall from your car while driving, you may receive three penalty points on your driving licence and a £60 fine. For safety reasons, it's clear why we need such laws, and I don't think we can criticise the lawmakers for passing a law even if it prevents just one death on the roads.

Using Mobile Phones to Pay at a Drive-Through Could Be Illegal

Imagine that you've been driving for several hours and feeling hungry. You can feel your stomach rumbling, urging you to devour some fast-food. As you drive round the bend, in the distance, you see the familiar sign of a well-known fast-food establishment and decide to drive through and avail yourself of their latest haute cuisine. You pull into the drive-through lane, put the window down, and place your order, at which point you are directed to drive to the first window to make your payment. You dutifully do so and, at that point, commit a traffic offence. This was the case until very recently when using your mobile phone to pay for goods or services at a drive-through with your car engine still running. It would technically be an offence. This dates back to mobile phone laws from 2003 which made it illegal to touch a phone or use the handset while driving.

The definition of driving is that a person is considered to be 'Driving' if they have control over the steering & propulsion of the vehicle. The vehicle doesn't need to be in motion at the time. The law is very strict about using a mobile phone while driving and with good reason due to the number of deaths and serious collisions caused on Britain's roads from driver distraction whilst using their phone. When the legislation was passed in 2003, the mobile phone was nothing more than a brick with buttons. No-one envisaged that you could conduct your entire life through that small gadget in just a few years, including making contactless payments.

According to Regulations 110(1) and (2) of the Road Vehicles (Construction and Use) (Amendment) (No 4) Regulations (2003), a person commits an offence if, whilst driving, they use a held-hand mobile telephone or a hand-held device for an interactive communication function. The penalty for breaking this law was six points on your driving licence and a £200 fine, making your fast-food takeaway similar in price to eating an hors d'oeuvre at The Ivy. Depending on the circumstances, you could also be guilty of careless driving under section 3 of the Road Traffic Act (1988).

It seems a bit harsh when you're parked in a private lane at the drive-through of a fast-food restaurant. It is, but you are, after all, technically still driving. Commonsense prevailed, and following a recent update to the law on the 25th March 2022, an exemption was added to the Road Vehicles (Construction and Use) (Amendment) (No.2) Regulations 2022. Whilst this tightened up even further, the laws surrounding the use of mobile devices, including smart watches, whilst driving, drivers may now make a contactless payment from their vehicle if it is not moving.

You Don't Own Your Vehicle Registration & It Can Be Taken Off You at Any Time

In Britain, most of us love our cars. Some even choose to name their cars. They're loved and cherished and become part of the family. For some people, their car is a status symbol, a sign of their material wealth, success or achievements.

Each car is identified with its unique identifying mark, the vehicle registration number, commonly referred to as, the number plate. Some people choose to purchase private car registrations. The most expensive private registration in the UK was sold in November 2014 for £518,480. It is '25 O'. The owner placed it on his £10 million 961 Ferrari 250 SWB.

Vehicle registration numbers are a significant way police and other road users can immediately identify a vehicle. Usually, registration numbers are allocated to vehicles when they are first registered. However, they can be transferred between vehicles at any time, provided the correct rules are followed.

Vehicle registrations have been in existence since 1904. They were first introduced in The Motor Car Act of 1903, which came into force the following year. It required that each motor vehicle carry an alphanumeric registration plate and was entered into an official vehicle register. This was so that vehicles could be easily identified and traced in the event of any accidents or contraventions of road traffic laws.

The current legislation controlling vehicle registration marks (number plates) is the Vehicle Excise and Registrations Act (1994). The Secretary of State for Transport is responsible for allocating the DVLA registration marks. All numberplates, even when assigned, always remain under the control of the Secretary of State and can be withdrawn at any time. Especially if the number plate regulations are contravened.

You're not purchasing the registration number when you purchase a car registration. You're only purchasing the entitlement to use that registration number on a vehicle. Since 2018, vehicle registration numbers have now fallen part of the vehicle MOT test. If you incorrectly display your registration number, you could be fined up to £1,000, and your vehicle will fail its MOT test.

Prosecuted For Flashing

Speed cameras seem to be everywhere, along with traffic light cameras ensuring drivers don't go through red traffic lights. Like them or loathe them, automated cameras have been around for 30 years, and police speed traps have been around for over a century. There are arguments on both sides as to whether speed cameras increase road safety. For as long as they continue to raise funds for the Treasury's consolidated fund, they won't be disappearing any time soon.

It is illegal to flash your lights, sound your horn or in any other way, warn other drivers of the presence of a police speed trap. Section 89 of the Police Act (1996) states it is an offence of *"...wilfully obstructing a constable in the execution of his duty ..."* You might think you are helping other drivers by informing them in advance. If caught, you could face a fine of up to £1,000 or even one-month imprisonment.

It's not just flashing your lights or sounding your horn that can land you in trouble for this offence. In a recent case, on 24th April 2019, a driver was reported for this offence after waving frantically at passing motorists to alert them of the presence of a mobile speed camera on the A30 near Launceston, Cornwall. Unfortunately for him, one of the drivers that he warned was a police officer in an unmarked car.

Looking at this offence of wilful obstruction a little more in-depth, the law states that to be 'wilful', the driver must know and intend their actions. In other words, it would be for the police and the Crown Prosecution Service (CPS) to prove that a driver was flashing their headlights to warn other road users of the presence of a speed camera. For the charge to be successful, the CPS must also prove that the motorists warned, were themselves speeding or likely to be speeding at that location. In other words, there has to be an actual, as opposed to potential, obstruction of the police. This was demonstrated in the 2003 case of D.P.P. v Glendinning. In this case, which went all the way to the House of Lords, the motorist Charles Glendinning was found not guilty. His original conviction had been quashed at his appeal. It was successfully argued that for any such charge to succeed, the prosecution must prove either that the motorists warned were speeding or were likely to be speeding.

By flashing your headlights to alert other road users, you can also be reported for causing undue dazzle under Regulation 27 of the Road Vehicles Lighting Regulations (1989). Rule 110 of the Highway Code states that drivers should "*Only flash your headlights to let other road users know that you are there.*"

The early speed traps consisted of three police officers working in a group. They would conceal themselves within the bushes on a straight road. The officers would be in plain clothes and position themselves at a set distance apart. One constable would signal the approach of an oncoming motorist by waving a white handkerchief. The second constable would use a stopwatch to time the motorist over that carefully measured distance. If the motorist exceeded the speed limit, the third constable wearing a uniform would step out from the bushes like a modern-day highwayman and signal the oncoming motorist to stop. They earned the nickname 'hedge-hogs'.

The well-known breakdown recovery service, the AA, was first formed in 1905 when a group formed The Motorists' Mutual Association (MMA). Their original purpose was to overcome the police oppression of early motorists using speed traps. The AA was born from this group. They formed scouts of cycling patrolmen who patrolled the main roads, warning AA members of upcoming police speed traps. AA members could be easily recognised by their membership badges affixed to their cars. The AA patrolmen would salute their members as they drove passed on the road. From 1911 onwards, it became the practice for AA patrolmen to warn oncoming drivers of a nearby police speed trap by not saluting them.

Most Drivers Commit an Offence Each Time They Get Into Their Car

The truth is that there are so many laws governing driving on the U.K.'s highways that most drivers will unknowingly commit offences each time they get behind the wheel of their car. A common offence, no doubt committed by many police officers themselves, is failing to have the correct address on a driving licence. I'm sure it is one of the most overlooked documents. When a person changes address and moves to a new house, they may forget to update their new address on their driving licence. This simple mistake can lead to fines of up to £1,000. Recent estimates show that around 1.5 million UK licence holders have out-of-date addresses.

Another common offence many drivers commit is failing to renew their photocard licence. They expire every ten years. Whilst the DVLA send out reminders; it is not an excuse to say that you haven't received a reminder. This ten years is set because a person's likeness and image presented in a photograph are likely to change over ten years and, in some cases, significantly. It doesn't mean the licence has expired; it's just the photocard.

The penalty for failing to renew your photocard driving licence is very serious. You can be charged with driving without a valid licence and even have your license revoked. The bad news is that this offence is usually charged alongside an offence of driving with no insurance, as having an expired driving licence invalidates any insurance cover. According to a 2017 Freedom of Information Request, 3,391,737 drivers had a full or provisional driving licence where the photographic licence card had expired.

Now that you've checked your driving license and exhaled a sigh of relief that your address is correct and your photocard hasn't expired, the following may be a cause for concern. By law, each time you get into your vehicle and drive off, you should be carrying with you, your driving documents. This includes your driving licence, the certificate of insurance, the MOT test certificate and the V5 vehicle registration document (log book). The offence is not committed if you drive without these documents. It is committed when a police officer asks you to produce the documents at the roadside, and you can not do so because you don't have them with you. Not having your documents with you may seem fairly innocuous, and I imagine most drivers don't carry their documents with them in the car, probably for safety reasons. However, failure to produce the documents upon request by a police officer can result in eight points on your driving licence and a fine of up to £5,000.

Sections 164 and 165 of the Road Traffic Act (1988) give a police constable the power to demand the production of these documents at the roadside. However, the law does provide a statutory defence, where no action will be taken provided they are produced within seven days. The usual practice is for the police officer to issue you with what is known as a Form HO/RT1, otherwise known as a 'producer'. This enables you to produce your documents within seven days at the police station of your choice.

In Scotland, Boats Can Be Found Guilty of Manslaughter

The common law of deodands dates back to around the eleventh-century. It was abolished by Parliament in 1846 but can still exist in some form or another in the outlying Scottish islands.

In a peculiar custom, if a fisherman has been drowned off one such Scottish island, the boats from which they fell are permanently beached. The boat is then cursed for its misdeed before being left to dry and fall to pieces in the sun. The boat is found guilty of manslaughter and must never be permitted to sail with 'innocent' boats at sea again.

ACKNOWLEDGMENTS

I would like to thank all those who so generously gave up their time to help with the production of this book and helping in translating my thoughts from paper to print.

I would also like to record my thanks and appreciation for the help and support received from the following:

(In alphabetical order)

Ms. Caitlin Williams (for Welsh translations)

Councillor Neil Darby - Mayor of Preston

The Curators of His Majesty's Historic Royal Palaces

HM Treasury, Debt and Reserves Management department

Lancaster City Council

Napthens Solicitors (Blackburn)

Mr. Nicholas Wood - Honorary Curator of
The Worshipful Society of Apothecaries of London

The Staff at The British Library, London

The Bank of England

The Librarians at The Law Society, London

His Majesty's The Royal Mint

The Rt. Hon Sir Robert Buckland KBE KC MP

Tuckers Solicitors (Manchester)

Mr. William Hunt, TD BA FCA -
former Windsor Herald, College of Arms

The Yeoman Warders of His Majesty's Royal Palace
and Fortress of the Tower of London

I would like to give a special mention to The Rt. Hon. Nigel Evans MP, Deputy Speaker (House of Commons), who helped immensely in supporting this project, as a great advocate of children's rights.

Most of all, thanks to my father, Fabian Lord, without whom this book would simply not have been written. I am deeply appreciative of his constant interest, encouragement and support in completing this book.

PERMISSIONS

Excerpts from judgements and statutes are Crown copyright defined under Section 163 of the Copyright, Designs and Patents Act (1988). Any Crown copyright material is reproduced with the permission of the Controller of The Office of Public Sector Information (OPSI) and the King's Printer for Scotland. Some quotations may be licensed under the terms of the Open Government Licence (http://www.nationalarchives.gov.uk/doc/open-government-licence/version/3).

All images used are either owned by the author or in the public domain.

NOTE ON THE TYPESET

The text of this book is set in Libre Caslon, a digital typeface of the Serif classification, designed by Pablo Impallari in 2012. Libre Caslon is a revival of the 18th-century William Caslon classic design, based on the alluring hand-lettered American Caslons typical of 1950s advertising.

ABOUT AUTHOR

Montgomery (Monty) Lord is a multi award-winning change maker, social entrepreneur and researcher dedicated to challenging injustices through the use of law. Described as an exemplar for making positive changes that impact on the community, he was named in The Independent newspaper (The Happy List 20/21) as in the top 50 inspirational people driving positive change in Britain.

Over recent years, Monty has engaged thousands of children across several countries in his ground-breaking research and was recognised with the Prime Minister's Points of Lights Award, the Diana Award, the Platinum Champion Award and the British Citizen Youth Award for services to the community & charity.

At the age of 7 years old, Monty had already released his first book and became, at the time, the UK's youngest bestselling author. He is a member of the Royal Society of Literature.

Monty maintains a keen interest in both law and history. At the age of 14, taking a semester-long distance learning course from Yale University. He developed his memory techniques (Rapid Memory Recall System®) which he later used to gain 5 Guinness World Records as a world memory champion.

In 2020, at the age of 14, he founded the national registered charity Young Active Minds. The aim is to promote education inequality & mental health awareness throughout all schools & community groups, irrespective of current attainment levels or cultural diversity of the students.

In 2021, as a world memory champion, Monty went on to become the youngest person in the UK with the most world records. He still holds that title.

Despite the constant label in the media, Monty strenuously rejects the title 'genius', claiming anyone can be a genius with some resilience and a little perseverance. He strongly believes that a good memory is not predicated on a person's intellect and that anyone can have a good memory.

An accomplished public speaker, Monty has spoken at TEDx talks events and at the age of 14, presented his 55,000-word research thesis to world leaders at the United Nations in Geneva and the All-Party Parliamentary Group on Mentoring. Monty has been involved with several published university research articles.

He has been devoting much of his free time independently over the last few years to not only helping those with mental health disorders but also raising awareness of mental health issues, saving people from suicide and depression, bringing about positive change and making life better for many others in the community. In his spare time, he creates and releases music under his music label, primarily Lo-Fi beats in support of mental health awareness.

Monty has led several campaigns, raising awareness of the United Nations Sustainable Development Goals. He formed the United Nations Association in Bolton and now chairs the group.

At the age of 16, he established Young Legal Eagles® to promote the rights, views and interests of children and young people and the Rule of Law in policies or decisions affecting their lives. Young Legal Eagles® provides legal information to children and young people, through printed and electronic media. Monty conducts the legal research, develops and publishes the guidance booklets and videos in multiple languages to benefit a wider public footprint. He took this national initiative to No.10 Downing Street with a view to integrating children's rights into the national curriculum. In December 2022, Monty spoke about children's rights as a panel speaker at Amnesty International. He later presented his findings at the United Nations in Geneva.

He created the short-documentary 'Do Children Have Rights?' With the help of a dedicated team of translators, the documentary was translated into multiple languages to help raise awareness of children's rights across all communities. The documentary was aired on Amazon Fire TV.

In his first legal case, at the age of 16, he represented 6 claimants bringing an action for breach of contract against a large national youth organisation, for multiple instances of bullying and abuse against their own staff and young cadets. He took the matter to the County Court with 85 exhibits and 317 pages of statements. The organisation decided to settle out of court, paying full damages and court fees.

As a supporter of several charities, Monty is an ambassador for both the #iWill Campaign and the British Citizen Awards and a trustee and schools engagement officer for Young Active Minds. He sat on the Diana Award judging panel and is a member of the National Anti-Bullying Youth Board. Monty sits on the committee of Amnesty UK's Children's Human Rights Network.

In recognition of his 'outstanding contribution' to volunteering, Monty was awarded the Platinum Champion Award by Her Majesty The Queen Consort and invited to the Platinum Party at Buckingham Palace.

In his free time, Monty enjoys running, swimming and Taekwon-Do, achieving black belt from an early age.

The national media has followed and widely reported upon many of Monty's various projects over the last few years, with widespread coverage on BBC & ITV News, radio and both broadsheet & tabloid newspapers.